Mastering Math

TEACHER'S EDITION

Program Consultants

Robert Abbott
Assistant Director of Special Education
Waukegan Community Unit School District No. 60
Waukegan, Illinois

Marie Davis
Principal, McCoy Elementary School
Orange County Public Schools
Orlando, Florida

Monika Spindel
Teacher of Mathematics
Austin, Texas

Suzanne H. Stevens
Specialist in Learning Disabilities
Learning Enhancement Consultant
Winston-Salem, North Carolina

STECK-VAUGHN COMPANY
A Subsidiary of National Education Corporation

Grade Level Key

Mastering Math	Math Level	Reading Level
Level A	1	1
Level B	2	2
Level C	3	2
Level D	4	3
Level E	5	3
Level F	6	4

Acknowledgments

Executive Editor
Elizabeth Strauss

Project Editor
Donna Rodgers

Design Manager
John Harrison

Product Development
Colophon Publishing Services
Cary, North Carolina

Contributing Writers
Brantley Eastman, Diane Crowley, Mary Hill, Louise Marinilli, Harriet Stevens, Susan Murphy, Helen Coleman, Ann McSweeney

Product Design
The Quarasan Group, Inc.

Illustration
Barbara Corey: pages 5, 9, 11, 14, 15, 26, 27, 30, 31, 46, 50, 51, 54, 55, 72, 73, 75, 81, 94, 95, 98, 99, 101, 105, 117, 119, 123, 128, 129, 140, 141, 145, 148, 154   Judith du Four Love: pages 2, 3, 7, 13, 24, 25, 28, 29, 32, 33, 36, 37, 48, 52, 53, 57, 58, 59, 63, 65, 77, 79, 83, 84, 85, 97, 103, 106, 107, 121, 139, 143, 147, 150, 151

Photography
© Tony Freeman/PhotoEdit: page 1
© Richard Hutchings/PhotoEdit: pages 45, 115
© Dennis MacDonald/PhotoEdit: page 137
© David Young Wolff/PhotoEdit: pages 23, 71, 93

Cover Photography
Cooke Photographics

ISBN 0-8114-3242-4

Copyright © 1994 Steck-Vaughn Company
All rights reserved. No part of the material protected by this copyright may be reproduced or utilized in any form or by any means, electronic or mechanical, including photocopying, recording, or by any information storage and retrieval system, without permission in writing from the copyright owner. Requests for permission to make copies of any part of the work should be mailed to: Copyright Permissions, Steck-Vaughn Company, P.O. Box 26015, Austin, TX 78755. Printed in the United States of America.

2 3 4 5 6 7 8 9 VP 98 97 96 95 94

Table of Contents

Teacher's Edition

◆ **About the Program** — T4
- Why Was *Mastering Math* Developed? — T4
- How Is This Program Used? — T4
- What Teaching Aids Are Included in the Teacher's Edition? — T5
- Content Charts: Levels A–F — T6

◆ **Level E Scope and Sequence** — T7

◆ **Chapter Overviews** — T8
- Chapters 1 and 2 — T8
- Chapter 3 — T9
- Chapters 4 and 5 — T10
- Chapter 6 — T11
- Chapter 7 — T12

◆ **Calculators in the Classroom** — T13

◆ **Blackline Masters Overview** — T14
- Chapter 1 Checkup — T15
- Chapter 2 Checkup — T16
- Chapter 3 Checkup — T17
- Chapter 4 Checkup — T18
- Chapter 5 Checkup — T19
- Chapter 6 Checkup — T20
- Chapter 7 Checkup — T21
- Addition Facts — T22
- Subtraction Facts — T23
- Multiplication Facts — T24
- Division Facts — T25
- Decimals: Tenths — T26
- Decimals: Hundredths — T27
- Fractions — T28
- Measuring Inches and Centimeters — T29
- Award Certificate — T30

◆ **Blackline Masters' Answer Keys** — T31

About the Program

Why Was *Mastering Math* Developed?

Mastering Math was developed for students with learning problems. These students include students assigned to special education programs, students receiving remedial instruction, and students in regular classes who are experiencing difficulty with basic math concepts and skills. Students with learning problems need a math program that helps them *master* math skills and problem-solving strategies and also shows the usefulness of these skills in everyday life. In addition, these students need a developmental program that builds on their strengths rather than on their weaknesses; a program that provides them with successful math experiences. The features incorporated into *Mastering Math* were developed to achieve these goals.

Features

- The lessons focus on the core math concepts for the grade level.
- Problem-solving lessons focus on 3 to 4 strategies for each level.
- All lessons are complete on two pages.
- A consistent lesson format is maintained throughout the series.
- Only one concept is presented in each lesson.
- The content of each book is carefully sequenced and paced to ensure mastery of all skills.
- The reading levels are one to two years below the math levels.
- The directions are clear, consistent, and easy to read.
- Color cues and bold type are used to help students identify special math vocabulary and key concepts.
- Previously presented material is reviewed frequently.

How Is This Program Used?

Mastering Math will be easy to implement in your classroom. As you look through the books, you will notice the following pages: chapter openers, two-page lessons, problem-solving lessons, chapter reviews, chapter tests, cumulative reviews, and extra practice. Each of these pages is designed to meet a specific need of students with learning problems.

Chapter Openers

Each chapter begins with a one-page *Chapter Opener*. The purpose of this page is to introduce students to the chapter content through the use of familiar situations that use mathematics.

Lessons: Computation, Money, Time, Measurement, Problem Solving

The lessons are designed to help you teach math skills effectively to your students. Each lesson is divided into four distinct sections.

The first section presents an instructional model. This carefully designed model has been developed to help you present the math skill to your students in a logical and easy-to-understand manner.

The second section, *Guided Practice,* should be used after you have presented the new skill. This section enables you to work a few problems with the students so that you may quickly assess whether they understand the new skill. If a student has difficulty with *Guided Practice,* then it is important for you to reteach the skill before moving ahead.

The third section, *Practice,* is designed for independent student use. Students should complete this section after they have demonstrated success in *Guided Practice* or have completed further instruction with you.

The last section, *Using Math,* shows how the math skill in the lesson relates to real life by means of a simple problem-solving situation. Once per chapter, the last section is called *Problem Solving* and reviews the problem-solving strategy taught in the previous chapter.

There are eight lessons in each chapter of *Mastering Math*. The first six lessons cover the core math concepts of the chapter. Lesson 7 of each chapter focuses on one aspect of money, time, or measurement, depending on the level of the book. Lesson 8 of each chapter is a problem-solving lesson. Strategies are presented in a step-by-step approach with a focus on only 3 or 4 problem-solving skills for each level. Since the concepts of money, time, measurement, and problem-solving skills are difficult for students with learning problems, *Mastering Math* uses a spiral approach to teach each skill. In other words, rather than rapidly moving from one difficult skill to the next, *Mastering Math* allows time for review, reinforcement, and mastery before moving on to the next skill. Students are given more chance for success through increased exposure over time.

Chapter Reviews

A three-page *Chapter Review* is included at the end of each chapter. The *Chapter Review* is designed to be used diagnostically. If a student has difficulty with the review exercises, you can diagnose where the problem is occurring by referring to the page numbers printed above each group of exercises. In addition, students can be directed to use these page numbers to look back in the chapter when they need help.

Extra Practice

Two pages of *Extra Practice* for each chapter are included at the back of the book. Each *Extra Practice* page provides additional practice of the skills taught in the chapter.

Chapter Tests

A two-page *Chapter Test* is included at the end of each chapter. The test is designed to assess whether students have mastered the skills presented in the chapter.

Perforated Pages

The pages in the student books are perforated. It is recommended that after a student completes a chapter, the chapter is removed from the book and sent home with the student. This will keep family members up-to-date on the skills their learner has mastered.

Cumulative Review

Each book contains two *Cumulative Reviews*. Each *Cumulative Review* is designed to review previously presented skills.

What Teaching Aids Are Included in the Teacher's Edition?

This Teacher's Edition includes a variety of teaching aids designed to make your job easier. The teaching aids include the following items.

Chapter Overviews

A brief overview is included for each chapter. Each overview provides the objective of the chapter, the new math vocabulary presented in the chapter, an activity for introducing the chapter, and some suggestions for reinforcing the skills developed in the lessons of the chapter.

Teaching Notes

Teaching notes are included at the top of each student page. The teaching notes provide a specific instructional objective for each lesson in the program. These objectives may be used to help write Individualized Education Plans (IEP's). The teaching notes also suggest activities for teaching the skills presented in each lesson.

Answer Keys

All answers are printed on your copy of each student page.

Blackline Masters

Sixteen blackline masters are included in each Teacher's Edition. The masters are designed to provide additional practice for the skills covered in this book. Steck-Vaughn Company grants you permission to duplicate enough copies for your students.

Content Charts

Levels A–F

	Level A	Level B	Level C	Level D	Level E	Level F
CHAPTER 1	Numbers through 10	Addition and subtraction facts through 10	Addition and subtraction facts through 18	Place value through ten thousands	Adding and subtracting large numbers	Adding and subtracting whole numbers
CHAPTER 2	Addition facts through 10	Place value through 999	Place value through thousands	Addition and subtraction	Multiplying 2-digit numbers	Multiplying and dividing whole numbers
CHAPTER 3	Subtraction facts through 10	Addition facts through 18	Addition and subtraction with regrouping	Multiplication facts through 9	Dividing with 1- and 2-digit divisors	Adding and subtracting decimals
CHAPTER 4	Place value through 99	Subtraction facts through 18	Multiplication facts through 5	Multiplying by 1-digit numbers	Adding and subtracting decimals	Multiplying and dividing decimals
CHAPTER 5	Addition and subtraction facts through 12	Adding and subtracting 2-digit numbers	Multiplication facts through 9	Division facts through 9	Multiplying decimals	Understanding fractions
CHAPTER 6	Adding and subtracting 2-digit numbers	Adding and subtracting 3-digit numbers	Division facts through 6	Dividing with 1-digit divisors	Dividing decimals by whole numbers	Adding and subtracting fractions
CHAPTER 7					Understanding fractions	Percents

Problem Solving Strategies	Level A	Level B	Level C	Level D	Level E	Level F
Use a picture	Chapters 1–2	Chapter 1				
Make a drawing		Chapter 2	Chapters 1–2			
Find a pattern	Chapters 3–4		Chapters 5–6			
Use a graph or table	Chapters 5–6	Chapters 3–4	Chapters 3–4	Chapters 1–2		
Choose an operation		Chapters 5–6		Chapters 5–6	Chapter 5	Chapter 7
Estimation				Chapters 3–4	Chapters 1–2	Chapters 3–4
Two-step problems					Chapters 3–4	Chapters 1–2
Identify extra information					Chapters 6–7	Chapters 5–6

Scope and Sequence

Level E

	Addition and Subtraction	Multiplication	Division	Decimals	Fractions	Measurement	Problem Solving
CHAPTER 1 pages 1–22	• Place value through hundred thousands • Adding 2- and 3-digit numbers • Adding large numbers • Subtracting 2- and 3-digit numbers • Subtracting from zeros • Rounding numbers					• Inches and feet	• Estimation
CHAPTER 2 pages 23–44		• Multiplying by 1-digit numbers • Multiplying by tens • Multiplying by 11 through 19 • Multiplying by 2-digit numbers • Multiplying 3-digit numbers				• Centimeters and meters	• Estimation
CHAPTER 3 pages 45–66			• Division with remainders • 2-digit quotients • Dividing by tens • 2-digit divisors			• Cups, pints, and quarts	• Two-step problems
CHAPTER 4 pages 71–92	• Adding decimals • Subtracting decimals			• Tenths • Hundredths • Comparing decimals • Adding decimals • Subtracting decimals		• Milliliters and liters	• Two-step problems
CHAPTER 5 pages 93–114		• Multiplying a decimal by a whole number • Multiplying tenths • Multiplying tenths and hundredths • Zeros in the product • Multiplying decimals by 10, 100, and 1,000		• Place value to thousandths • Multiplying a decimal by a whole number • Multiplying tenths • Multiplying tenths and hundredths • Zeros in the product • Multiplying decimals by 10, 100, 1,000		• Ounces and pounds	• Choose an operation
CHAPTER 6 pages 115–136			• Dividing tenths • Dividing hundredths • Zeros in the quotient • Writing zeros in the dividend • Dividing by 10, 100, 1,000	• Dividing tenths • Dividing hundredths • Regrouping whole numbers as tenths • Zeros in the quotient • Writing zeros in the dividend • Dividing by 10, 100, 1,000		• Grams and kilograms	• Identify extra information
CHAPTER 7 pages 137–158					• Parts of a whole • Fractional parts of a group • Comparing fractions • Finding equivalent fractions • Fractions in lowest terms • Mixed numbers	• Choosing measurement	• Identify extra information

Chapter Overviews

Chapter 1 Adding and Subtracting Large Numbers Pages 1–22

Chapter Objectives
Students will
- recognize place values
- change numbers from standard form to expanded form
- add and subtract 2-, 3-, 4-, and 5-digit numbers
- subtract from zeros
- round numbers
- decide whether to measure using inches or feet
- use estimation to solve addition or subtraction problems

Vocabulary and Math Symbols
digit, place-value, standard form, expanded form, regroup, round, length, height, inch, foot

Introducing the Chapter
To review place-value concepts use chalk to write an enlarged place-value chart through ten thousands on the sidewalk or pavement. Be sure to write a comma before the thousands' place on the chart. Provide large 0–9 number cards. Have five volunteers each select a number card. Then have each volunteer stand in a place on the chart. Have them hold up the number cards. Then have the remaining students read the number formed and tell the value of each digit. Vary the number of digits and let students take turns forming numbers.

Reinforcement Activities
1. Students can use population statistics to practice addition and subtraction with large numbers. Have students find the populations of two cities using an almanac or atlas. Have them use the statistics to set up an addition problem. Then have students use the same statistics to set up a subtraction problem. Continue this procedure having students use population statistics for other cities.

2. Students can reinforce their understanding of measurement with inches and feet using a tape measure. Provide a tape measure, having students take turns measuring and recording each others' height using inches, and then inches and feet. Then have students take turns measuring and recording the length of other students' arms, legs, feet, and hands.

Problem Solving
To reinforce estimating by rounding to the nearest ten, make a number line on the floor. Number 11 sheets of paper from 40 to 50 and tape them in order. Have students stand behind a designated line and toss a beanbag onto the number line. Then have students decide whether the number they landed on is nearer to 40 or 50.

Estimation
Have pairs of students make a list of 10 classroom objects—5 to be measured in inches and 5 to be measured in feet. Have them exchange their list with another pair of students. Then have students use their inch rulers from *Measuring Inches and Centimeters*, the blackline master on page T29, to measure and check their answers. Then write the following list on the chalkboard and have students estimate whether each item would be measured in inches or feet: elephant, pencil, paper clip, giraffe, kitchen table, and fly. Check the accuracy of the list.

Chapter 2 Multiplying by 2-Digit Numbers Pages 23–44

Chapter Objectives
Students will
- multiply a 2-digit number by 1- and 2-digit numbers
- multiply a 3-digit number by a 2-digit number
- decide whether to measure using centimeters and meters
- use estimation to solve multiplication problems

Vocabulary and Math Symbols
metric, centimeters, meters

Introducing the Chapter
As an introduction, discuss situations in which students might multiply larger numbers. For example, have students imagine they are making a social studies notebook which will include four maps. Tell students that you want to pass out four sheets of blank paper to each student for the maps. Explain that since you know there are 26 students in the class, you can multiply *26* by *4* to find out how many sheets of paper you will need altogether. Write the problem on the chalkboard. Remind students that they can solve this problem using multiplication facts. Discuss other situations where students might have to multiply larger numbers.

Reinforcement Activities
1. To practice multiplying 2-digit numbers by 1-digit numbers, have each student make number cards *0–9*. Have each student place his or her cards

T8

in a paper bag. To begin, each student draws three cards and uses them to make problems that have 2-digits times 1-digit. Students should write the problems on paper, and find the products. Next have students rearrange the cards to make new problems to solve. This activity can also be used to create problems with 2-digits times 2-digits and 3-digits times 2-digits.

2. To further students' understanding of the difference between centimeters and meters, distribute 2 index cards to each student. Have them write *centimeters* and *meters* on the cards. Then have each student tape the cards to something in the classroom that could be measured using either centimeters or meters.

Problem Solving

For practice in solving problems by estimation, ask students how they would estimate the number of people in the room. Have students close their eyes and guess if the number is closer to 10, 20, or 30 people in the room. Remind them that a number line can be used to show the nearest ten. Continue with other problems such as the number of books in the classroom, the number of windows in the school, and so on.

Mental Math

Use cards such as the ones shown to practice multiplying tens mentally. Give students 2 or 3 cards like the example below. Be sure to include the answer on the back of the card. Have pairs of students take turns drawing a card and completing the sentence.

$13 \times 2 = 26$ $15 \times 3 = 45$ $11 \times 7 = 77$
$13 \times 20 = ?$ $15 \times 30 = ?$ $11 \times 70 = ?$

Chapter 3 Dividing with 1- and 2-Digit Divisors
Pages 45–66

Chapter Objectives
Students will
- divide 2- and 3-digit numbers by 1- and 2-digit numbers
- divide 2- and 3-digit numbers by a multiple of 10
- convert cups, pints, and quarts
- solve two-step problems

Vocabulary and Math Symbols
remainder, divisor, dividend, capacity, cups, pints, quarts

Introducing the Chapter

To introduce students to dividing large numbers, discuss situations in which students might need to find the number of groups or the number in each group. For example, tell students that there are 150 total students in the fifth grade. Explain that you want to divide the total number of fifth graders into classes with 30 students each. Write the problem *150 ÷ 30* on the chalkboard. Tell students that the answer will tell you how many groups of 30 there will be. Then have students interview school personnel, such as the principal, lunchroom manager, counselor, nurse, etc. to find out how they use division in their jobs. Have them share this information with the group.

Reinforcement Activities

1. To reinforce the process of division provide a set of yellow number cards 0–9 and a green set 2–9. Have a volunteer draw two yellow cards and write the numbers in either order, as a 2-digit dividend on the chalkboard. Then have the volunteer draw one green card and write this number as the divisor. Have the student solve the division problem on the chalkboard while others solve it at their desks. Increase the difficulty of the problem by having students draw three yellow cards for a 3-digit dividend and then draw two green cards for a 2-digit divisor. Continue the process until everyone has had an opportunity to solve a division problem on the chalkboard.

2. For additional practice with division, have students write the digits in their phone numbers, or a friend's phone number, across the top of a sheet of paper. Tell students to use any three digits from the phone number to set up a problem. Make sure the problem has 2-digits divided by 1-digit. Then have students use any five digits from the phone number to set up a problem that has 3-digits divided by 2-digits.

3. Provide practice for using cups, pints, and quarts by having students follow the directions of a recipe to make fruit punch.

Fruit Punch
4 cups water
1 cup melted orange juice concentrate
1 pint melted lemonade concentrate
2 quarts unsweetened pineapple juice
1 cup sugar
2 quarts chilled ginger ale
2 quarts chilled carbonated water

Problem Solving

To provide practice in solving two-step problems, give pairs of students small items such as centimeter cubes (2 colors) and a paper cup. Have them use the materials to make up two-step problems such as: *Bill puts 12 red cubes and 9 green cubes in the cup. Jack takes 3 cubes away. How many cubes are left in the cup?*

Estimation

Use different-sized containers filled with water to practice estimating liquid amounts. Set up stations around the room for each size container. Have pairs of students write an estimate of the number of cups, pints, or quarts. Then have them pour the water into measuring cups to check their estimates.

Chapter 4 Adding and Subtracting Decimals
Pages 71–92

Chapter Objectives
Students will
- read and write decimals through hundredths
- compare decimals
- add and subtract decimals
- decide whether to measure using milliliters or liters
- solve two-step problems involving the addition and subtraction of decimals

Vocabulary and Math Symbols
tenth, decimal, decimal point, hundredth, <, >, liters, milliliters

Introducing the Chapter
To introduce the concept of decimals, have four girls and six boys stand in front of the class. Point out that part of the group is girls and the other part is boys. Write the decimal *0.4* on the chalkboard, explaining that this means *4* out of *10* are girls. Then write *0.6* on the chalkboard, explaining that this means *6* out of *10* are boys. Then provide examples of real-life situations which use decimals, such as money, gas pumps, stopwatches, etc.

Reinforcement Activities
1. Provide a hand calculator for each pair of students. Have one student call out a decimal. Then have the other student enter the number into the calculator. The student calling the number should check the answer on the calculator. Then have the partners switch roles.

2. Distribute two large sheets of paper to each student for *liter* and *milliliter* collages. Have students label one sheet *liter* and the other sheet *milliliter*. Have students cut out magazine pictures that show different types of containers for liquids. Then have students paste each picture on the appropriate *liter* or *milliliter* collage choosing the best way of measuring how much liquid the container will hold.

Problem Solving
Use catalogs or newspaper flyers to practice solving two-step problems involving money. Give students a spending limit of $50.00 and have them select 2 catalog items to buy. Then have students subtract the total from $50.00 to determine the amount of change. You may wish to have students use calculators for this activity.

Calculator
Have students use a calculator to multiply decimals. Write *0.04 × 0.5 = 0.02* on the chalkboard. Remind students to enter the decimal for each factor. Continue with other examples.

Chapter 5 Multiplying Decimals
Pages 93–114

Chapter Objectives
Students will
- read and write decimals through thousandths
- multiply decimals by whole numbers
- multiply two decimals
- add zeros as placeholders in products
- multiply decimals by 10, 100, and 1,000
- decide whether to measure using ounces or pounds
- choose addition, subtraction, multiplication, or division to solve problems

Vocabulary and Math Symbols
thousandths, weight, ounce, pound

Introducing the Chapter
As an introduction, discuss situations in which students might need to multiply with decimals. For example, tell students that on the way to school you stopped to buy gasoline for your car. Tell them that you bought *7.5* gallons of gas and that each gallon cost *$0.99*. Write the problem *$0.99 × 7.5* on the chalkboard, explaining that you need to multiply to solve this problem.

Reinforcement Activities
1. To practice multiplying with decimals provide a department store catalog and a set of number cards *1–9*. Allow students to locate an item in the catalog that they would like to buy. Then have students draw a number card. Have them use the number to represent how many of that item they will buy. To find the total cost, have students multiply the price of the item by the number of items. To vary this activity, provide a different set of number cards marked with the numbers *10, 100,* and *1,000*. Have students locate items in the catalog that they might buy in these larger quantities. After locating the price and drawing a number card, have students set up and solve the multiplication problems.

2. Have students follow the directions of a recipe for an assorted fruit and nut mix to provide practice using pounds and ounces.

Fruit and Nut Mix

- 3 ounces shredded coconut
- 1 pound coarsely chopped almonds
- 6 ounces sunflower seeds
- 8 ounces chopped dried apricots
- 1 pound raisins
- 2 pounds roasted peanuts

Problem Solving

To practice choosing addition, subtraction, multiplication, or division to solve a problem, write a word problem for each operation on individual index cards. Have students work in four groups (one for each operation). Give each group a card and have them decide if they can use their operation to solve it. If not, they must pass the card on to the group they think should solve the problem. Continue until each group has the correct problem.

Estimation

To have students practice rounding numbers, draw a number line on the chalkboard and label it with numbers from 10 to 20. Draw a space alien at 19, planet Earth at 20, and a spaceship at 10. Ask students if the alien is closer to Earth or the spaceship. Tell them that to be safe the alien must be closer to his spaceship than Earth. Move the alien several times, and each time ask if he is closer to the planet Earth or to his spaceship. Remind students that numbers ending in 5 round up to the next highest ten. Then ask volunteers to name the safe spaces for the alien.

Chapter 6 Dividing Decimals by Whole Numbers
Pages 115–136

Chapter Objectives
Students will
- divide tenths and hundredths by whole numbers
- regroup whole numbers as tenths in order to divide
- add zeros as placeholders in quotients
- write zeros in the dividend in order to divide
- divide by 10, 100, and 1,000
- decide whether to measure weight in grams or kilograms
- identify extra information to solve problems

Vocabulary and Math Symbols
grams, kilograms

Introducing the Chapter

Begin by discussing situations in which students might need to divide decimals. For example, tell students to imagine that they want to buy some granola bars at the grocery store. Explain that there are two brands, so students will have to choose the one that gives them the most granola for the least amount of money. Tell students that one brand has six granola bars in a box and costs $1.29. Tell them the other brand has eight granola bars in a box and costs $1.39. Write *$1.29 ÷ 6* and *$1.39 ÷ 8* on the chalkboard. Inform students that they can use division facts to find out how much each granola bar costs so that they can compare the two brands.

Reinforcement Activities

1. To practice dividing decimals, distribute department-store catalogs to students. Have each student use the catalog to locate something which comes with several items in a package, such as a box with eight cassette tapes. After locating the total price, have students set up problems to find the cost per item in the package. Then have students locate something in the catalog that is bought in packages containing 10, 100, or 1,000 items, such as a box of 100 paper clips. Have them again set up problems to find the cost per item.

2. Students can use postal rates from an almanac or a postal-rate chart to practice dividing decimals. Tell students they will be mailing an 8 ounce letter. Have students locate postal rates for first, second, and third class letters. Have students set up the three problems and divide to find the cost per ounce for the letter. Have each student make up the weight for a package to mail. Then have students divide to find the cost per pound for each package. Have students repeat the procedure making up different weights for letters and packages.

3. Have each set of paired students work together to construct a balance scale using a coat hanger, string, and two small paper cups, as indicated in the illustration.

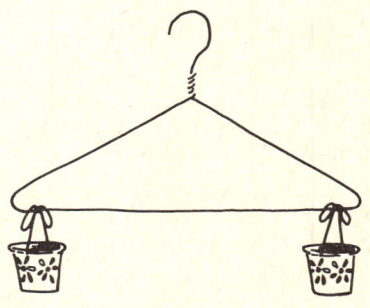

Hang each scale on a hook, doorknob, or from the ceiling by string. Tell students that a paper clip weighs about a gram. Have each pair of students locate a small object in the classroom. Have students use paper clips to find out about how many grams the object weighs. Have students locate other small objects in the classroom to weigh using their balance scale. Then tell students that one volume of an encyclopedia weighs about one kilogram. Have students name things in the classroom that they would measure using kilograms.

Problem Solving
To reinforce identifying extra information in a problem, have students work in groups of four. Write 3 facts (1 fact which is not needed to solve the problem) and the problem question on individual slips of paper. Give each group member one of the slips of paper. Have the group members share their information and decide cooperatively which information is needed to solve the problem and which fact is not needed.

Calculator
Have students work in pairs to practice the mental math skills of dividing decimals by 10, 100, and 1,000. Have one student write a decimal on a slip of paper, enter the decimal on a calculator, and divide it by 10, 100, and 1,000. Then have them show the dividend and the quotient to their partner and ask them to guess the divisor. If the guess is disputed, have students check it by multiplying on the calculator.

Chapter 7 Understanding Fractions
Pages 137–158

Chapter Objectives
Students will
- write a fraction from an illustration
- compare 2 fractions
- write equivalent fractions
- write equivalent fractions in lowest terms
- write a mixed number from an illustration
- decide the appropriate unit of measurement for an object
- identify extra information to solve problems

Vocabulary and Math Symbols
fraction, numerator, denominator, equivalent fractions, lowest terms, mixed numbers, customary measurement

Introducing the Chapter
Demonstrate what a fraction is, using four volunteers and a large sheet of paper. Explain that you want to cut the paper so that each of the four students will have an equal-sized piece. Ask how many pieces you will need, then write 4 on the chalkboard. Cut the paper into 4 *equal* pieces. After passing the pieces out, ask how many pieces "Sam" has. Return to the chalkboard to make 4 into the fraction ¼. Point out that this shows that "Sam" has one part out of the four parts that make up the whole large sheet of paper or the fraction ¼.

Reinforcement Activities
1. To give students practice with comparing and finding equivalent fractions, have students make fraction manipulatives. Distribute 7 sheets of construction paper to each student. Have them write *1* on the first sheet to denote *one whole*. Then have students cut their second sheet of paper into two equal pieces, marking each ½. Have students make thirds, fourths, and eighths. Show students how to use thirds as the model for making sixths and twelfths. Distribute 3 index cards to paired students. Have them write >, <, and = on the cards. Have partners use their manipulatives and the index cards to compare fractions. Have students record their comparisons.

2. Students can practice reducing fractions to lowest terms using recipe ingredients. Provide a list of ingredients with the fractions altered for the students to reduce.

3. Have students play a card-matching game to practice choosing between types of measurement. Divide students into groups of three. Have one student from each group cut pictures of 2 small items and 2 large items which can be measured for length from magazines or catalogs. Have them paste each picture on a large index card and write the label "length" under each picture. Have another student in each group follow the same procedure for weight. Have the third student in each group cut out pictures of 2 small, 1 medium, and 2 large items which can be measured to find capacity. Write each unit of measurement on a set of large index cards. Provide each group with a set. After shuffling all of the cards, have students spread the cards face down on a table or the floor. Have the first player turn over 2 cards. If the item pictured could be measured by the unit of measure on the other card, the student has a match. When a match is made, the student keeps the pair and gets another turn. If the cards do not match, the cards are turned back over and play resumes with the next player. The student in each group with the most pairs is the winner.

Problem Solving
To reinforce identifying the extra information in a problem, give groups of 3 students several small items such as centimeter cubes in two different colors. Have each group member list a different fact about the items. Then ask a question such as, "What fraction of the cubes are red?" Have students circle the facts that are needed and cross out the fact that is not needed.

Mental Math
To practice using mental math to write equivalent fractions, write the fraction ½ on the chalkboard. Then show students how to multiply both the numerator and the denominator by 2 to get the equivalent fraction ²⁄₄. Explain that equivalent fractions can always be made by multiplying both the numerator and the denominator by the same number. Challenge pairs of students to find as many equivalent fractions for ½ as possible within 1 minute.

Calculators in the Classroom

The National Council of Teachers of Mathematics (NCTM) recommends the integration of the calculator into the school mathematics program at all grade levels. NCTM has taken this position in response to the contrast between the extensive use of calculators in our society and the limited use of calculators in our schools. Calculators used during class, for homework assignments, and during tests will free students from tedious computations and give them additional time needed for learning problem-solving strategies and exploring numbers.

Students at every grade level need instruction in how and when to use a calculator. Calculators do not replace the need for mastery of the basic skills. On the contrary, students should know basic facts and have an understanding of the reasonableness of answers and estimation strategies before they begin using a calculator. When designing evaluations of student understanding of mathematical concepts and applications, it is important to incorporate the use of a calculator.

The National Council of Teachers of Mathematics recommends calculator use to allow students at all grade levels to:

- concentrate on the problem-solving process rather than on the calculations associated with problem solving;
- gain access to mathematics that exceed the students' level of computational skills;
- explore, develop, and reinforce concepts such as estimation, computation, approximation, and properties;
- experiment with mathematical ideas and discover patterns; and
- perform tedious computations necessary when working with real data in problem-solving situations.

Methods for Calculator Use

Calculators should not be substituted for mastering the basic facts of addition, subtraction, multiplication, and division. After students have mastered basic facts, learned estimation strategies, and developed number sense, calculators should be used to explore number concepts, to complete lengthy computations necessary for problem solving, and for self-evaluation.

Mastering Math focuses on computational skills, concepts of time, measurement, and money, and problem-solving strategies. Opportunities for calculator usage are included in Teaching Notes at each level. The following suggestions provide possible methods of implementing calculator instruction with students who have learning problems.

Students Become Familiar with the Technology

When initially exposing students to calculators, it is helpful to allow them time to explore its functions independently. Then provide students with key sequences that illustrate the functions of the calculator. Additionally, show how errors in entering data affect the outcome. Help students develop an understanding that calculators can only do what we tell them to do.

Students Explore Mathematical Concepts and Patterns

Understanding basic mathematical concepts, such as adding and subtracting 0, can be enhanced by using a calculator. Have students experiment with numbers to discover the properties. Using the constant function for skip counting helps students develop a further understanding of number patterns. Show them how to skip count by threes by simply entering 3 + ====. Accessing large numbers and using them in such computations is a confidence builder for all students, especially those with learning problems.

Students Check Their Own Work

Teaching students to use the calculator for checking as they complete independent classwork saves time, frustration, and provides them with a means of self-sufficiency. After completing three or four exercises students can check their answers to determine whether they should continue or seek more help before proceeding. Calculators can also be used to check homework answers.

Students Use Calculators in Cooperative Learning Groups

Many cooperative learning activities require students to check each others' answers. The calculator is a valuable tool for verifying accuracy in these situations.

Students Master Problem-Solving Strategies

Calculators help students focus on learning how to solve problems rather than on performing time-consuming computations. Developing thinking processes and finding alternative methods becomes the priority.

Blackline Masters Overview

The sixteen blackline masters provided for *Mastering Math, Level E* may be used in a variety of ways. The following is a list of suggestions for their use.

Chapter Checkups   T15–T21

These blacklines can be used if a student needs to review one or more of the skills covered on the *Chapter Test*.

Addition, Subtraction, Multiplication, and Division Facts   T22–T25

These blacklines may be used to review the basic facts. To encourage your students to answer the facts quickly and accurately, you may wish to set a timer and have students work the problems on one sheet until the timer rings.

Tenths and Hundredths   T26–T27

These blacklines may be used for additional practice of decimals. You may use them in two ways. Write a decimal under each picture and have students shade the picture to illustrate the decimal. Or you may wish to shade a part of each picture and have students write the decimal.

Fractions   T28

This blackline may be used for additional practice of fractions. You may use it in two ways. Write a fraction under each picture and have students shade the picture to illustrate the fraction. Or you may wish to shade a fractional part of each picture and have students write the fraction. Students needing additional practice, may find it helpful to cut out the figures and use them as manipulatives when working the lessons in Chapter 7.

Measuring Inches and Centimeters   T29

This blackline is designed to provide practice in measurement for the concepts presented in Chapters 1 and 2. Have students carefully cut out each ruler and use them to measure objects. You may wish to reproduce the rulers on heavy paper or mount the rulers on cardboard to keep them stiff.

Award Certificate   T30

The Award Certificate should be used to acknowledge student progress. Depending on the needs of your students, the Certificate may be awarded upon completion of a chapter or completion of the book. You are encouraged to use your judgment to determine when it is most appropriate to use the Certificates.

Name _____

Checkup

CHAPTER 1

◆ Complete the expanded form of each number.

1. 64,895 = 60,000 + _____ + 800 + _____ + 5

2. 352,176 = 300,000 + _____ + 2,000 + _____ + 70 + _____

◆ Write the value of each underlined digit.

3. 4 9,<u>3</u> 0 8 _____   4. <u>7</u> 0 3,9 2 5 _____

◆ Add.

| 5. 39
+85 | 6. 584
+267 | 7. 2,938
+6,735 | 8. 37,623
+12,539 |

◆ Subtract.

| 9. 83
−45 | 10. 781
−284 | 11. 4,000
−2,437 | 12. 80,000
−22,198 |

◆ Round each number to the nearest ten.

13. 43 _____   14. 165 _____

◆ Round each number to the nearest hundred.

15. 879 _____   16. 2,530 _____

◆ Ring the unit of measure you would use.

| 17. the length of a key

   inch   foot | 18. the height of the chalkboard

   inch   foot |

Mastering Math © 1994 Steck-Vaughn Co. ISBN 0-8114-3242-4

Name _____

Checkup

CHAPTER 2

◆ Multiply.

1. 97 × 6	2. 83 × 8	3. 24 × 20	4. 93 × 30	5. 13 × 70
6. 49 × 14	7. 58 × 15	8. 67 × 19	9. 46 × 42	10. 61 × 58
11. 316 × 13	12. 524 × 16	13. 275 × 34	14. 618 × 67	15. 205 × 89

◆ Ring the unit of measure you would use.

16. the length of a worm centimeter meter	17. the height of a basketball hoop centimeter meter

T16   *Mastering Math* © 1994 Steck-Vaughn Co. ISBN 0-8114-3242-4

Name _____

Checkup

CHAPTER 3

◆ Divide.

1. $4\overline{)37}$	2. $7\overline{)57}$	3. $9\overline{)95}$	4. $3\overline{)39}$
5. $6\overline{)87}$	6. $2\overline{)58}$	7. $5\overline{)327}$	8. $8\overline{)591}$
9. $30\overline{)68}$	10. $70\overline{)289}$	11. $37\overline{)80}$	12. $54\overline{)706}$

◆ Mark an X on the containers that equal the first one in the row.

13.

Mastering Math © 1994 Steck-Vaughn Co. ISBN 0-8114-3242-4

T17

Checkup

CHAPTER 4

◆ Write each decimal.

1. 9 tenths = _____
2. 6 hundredths = _____

◆ Compare the decimals. Write > or <.

3. 0.2 ____ 0.5
4. 2.8 ____ 2.4
5. 6.97 ____ 6.87

◆ Add.

6. 1.4 3 +3.2 5	7. 9.6 8 +4.2 9	8. 2 1.3 6 + 5.4 9	9. 1 3.6 5 +4 3.8 4	10. 9.4 3 +7.4 8

◆ Subtract.

11. 9.6 8 −2.4 5	12. 4.5 7 −1.9 3	13. 1 1.6 9 − 3.5 4	14. 6 7.9 3 −3 2.1 4	15. 6 3.4 9 −3 8.6 3

◆ Write zero. Then add or subtract.

16. 2.3 4 +3.6	17. 3 2.5 +1 4.2 8	18. 1 1.5 − 9.3 7	19. 4 6.8 5 −1 2.2	20. 2.8 −1.5 2

◆ Ring the unit of measure you would use.

21. eye drops in an eyedropper milliliter liter	22. water in a fish tank milliliter liter

T18

Name _____

Checkup

CHAPTER 5

◆ Write each decimal.

1. 395 thousandths = _____

2. 7 and 48 thousandths = _____

3. 2 and 6 tenths = _____

4. 31 and 79 hundredths = _____

◆ Multiply.

5. 0.6 × 8	6. 3.2 9 × 4	7. 7.3 ×0.3	8. 5.2 ×7.6
9. 1.3 8 × 4.2	10. 6.4 5 × 3.8	11. 0.1 4 × 0.3	12. 0.0 3 × 3

13. 10 × 3.7 = _____

14. 100 × 4.65 = _____

15. 1,000 × 2.198 = _____

16. 100 × 1.53 = _____

◆ Ring the word that completes each sentence.

17. A bag of sugar weighs 5 ___.   ounces   pounds

18. A box of cereal weighs 14 ___.   ounces   pounds

Mastering Math © 1994 Steck-Vaughn Co. ISBN 0-8114-3242-4

T19

Checkup

CHAPTER 6

◆ Divide.

1. $6\overline{)32.4}$	2. $9\overline{)78.3}$	3. $4\overline{)14.76}$	4. $8\overline{)20.64}$
5. $7\overline{)3.01}$	6. $3\overline{)9.018}$	7. $2\overline{)0.39}$	8. $5\overline{)7.4}$

◆ Divide. Then check your answer by multiplying.

9. $36 \div 100 =$ _____

   $100 \times$ _____ $=$ _____

10. $48.7 \div 10 =$ _____

    $10 \times$ _____ $=$ _____

◆ Ring the word that completes each sentence.

11. A bicycle weighs 12 ___.   grams   kilograms

12. A box of crackers weighs 57 ___.   grams   kilograms

Checkup

CHAPTER 7

◆ Write a fraction in each box to name the shaded part.

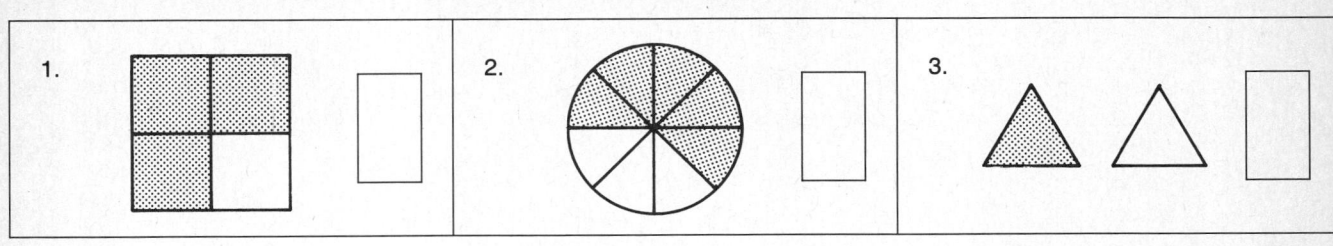

1. 2. 3.

◆ Compare the fractions. Write > or < in the box.

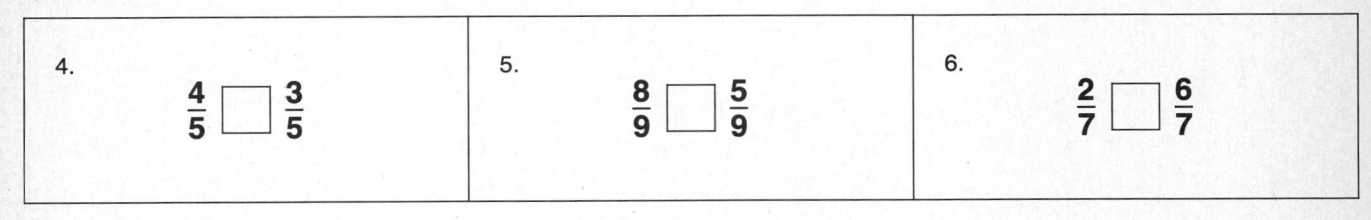

4. $\frac{4}{5} \square \frac{3}{5}$

5. $\frac{8}{9} \square \frac{5}{9}$

6. $\frac{2}{7} \square \frac{6}{7}$

◆ Write an equivalent fraction in the box.

7. $\frac{4}{6} = \frac{4 \div 2}{6 \div 2} = \square$

8. $\frac{10}{12} = \frac{10 \div 2}{12 \div 2} = \square$

9. $\frac{6}{24} = \frac{6 \div 6}{24 \div 6} = \square$

◆ Write a mixed number for each picture.

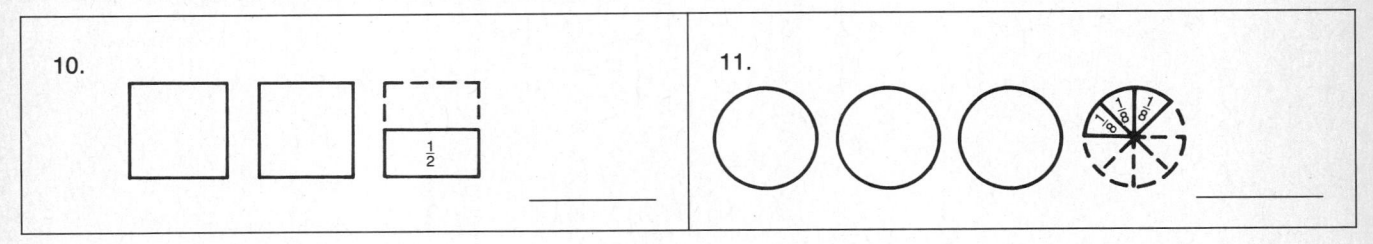

10.

11.

◆ Ring the word that completes each sentence.

12. To measure the weight of a horse use ___.   liters   kilograms

13. To measure the length of a picnic table use ___.   feet   pounds

Addition Facts

◆ Add.

1. 7 +5	2. 9 +9	3. 2 +6	4. 5 +4	5. 8 +6	6. 4 +9
7. 3 +2	8. 2 +2	9. 4 +8	10. 6 +9	11. 5 +5	12. 1 +6
13. 7 +4	14. 8 +8	15. 5 +6	16. 1 +9	17. 3 +4	18. 7 +7
19. 9 +3	20. 4 +2	21. 3 +7	22. 8 +5	23. 6 +6	24. 2 +9
25. 7 +8	26. 3 +8	27. 9 +7	28. 4 +4	29. 5 +2	30. 8 +9
31. 2 +7	32. 1 +7	33. 8 +2	34. 9 +5	35. 6 +7	36. 0 +5

Name _____

Subtraction Facts

◆ Subtract.

1. 10 − 4	2. 11 − 8	3. 14 − 5	4. 8 −7	5. 16 − 8	6. 18 − 9
7. 7 −3	8. 12 − 4	9. 8 −2	10. 10 − 5	11. 13 − 6	12. 6 −3
13. 9 −4	14. 5 −2	15. 13 − 9	16. 11 − 2	17. 7 −0	18. 14 − 8
19. 8 −4	20. 12 − 7	21. 9 −1	22. 17 − 8	23. 9 −6	24. 10 − 3
25. 2 −1	26. 14 − 7	27. 10 − 2	28. 8 −8	29. 15 − 9	30. 13 − 5
31. 6 −2	32. 16 − 7	33. 4 −2	34. 11 − 4	35. 8 −3	36. 12 − 6

Multiplication Facts

◆ Multiply.

1. 4 ×7	2. 8 ×9	3. 4 ×2	4. 6 ×8	5. 5 ×5	6. 2 ×3
7. 9 ×3	8. 6 ×6	9. 2 ×7	10. 5 ×8	11. 4 ×4	12. 7 ×9
13. 1 ×2	14. 7 ×8	15. 3 ×1	16. 9 ×9	17. 2 ×6	18. 0 ×4
19. 6 ×7	20. 3 ×8	21. 6 ×0	22. 9 ×2	23. 5 ×6	24. 7 ×7
25. 3 ×5	26. 4 ×9	27. 6 ×9	28. 8 ×8	29. 1 ×1	30. 8 ×2
31. 3 ×3	32. 0 ×5	33. 4 ×6	34. 5 ×9	35. 3 ×7	36. 2 ×2

Division Facts

◆ Divide.

1. 2)4	2. 9)63	3. 3)9	4. 5)10	5. 8)48
6. 4)4	7. 9)45	8. 6)18	9. 7)28	10. 6)30
11. 8)56	12. 5)20	13. 2)16	14. 3)6	15. 6)12
16. 3)27	17. 8)24	18. 1)8	19. 7)35	20. 9)36
21. 5)5	22. 7)49	23. 9)72	24. 4)16	25. 1)7
26. 4)12	27. 8)32	28. 7)14	29. 6)6	30. 2)18

Name _____

Decimals: Tenths

Decimals: Hundredths

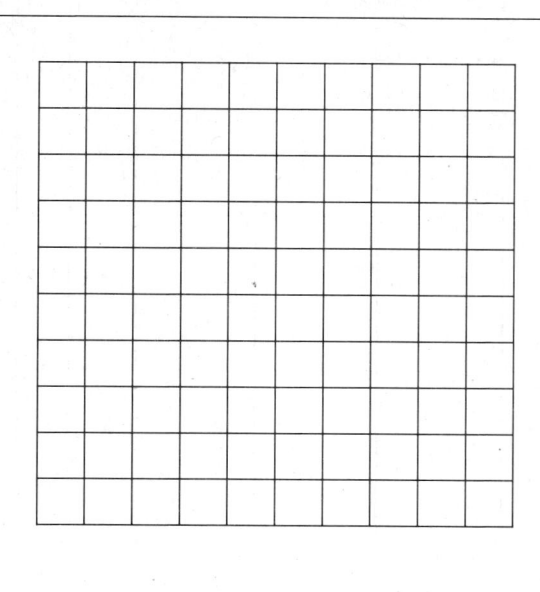

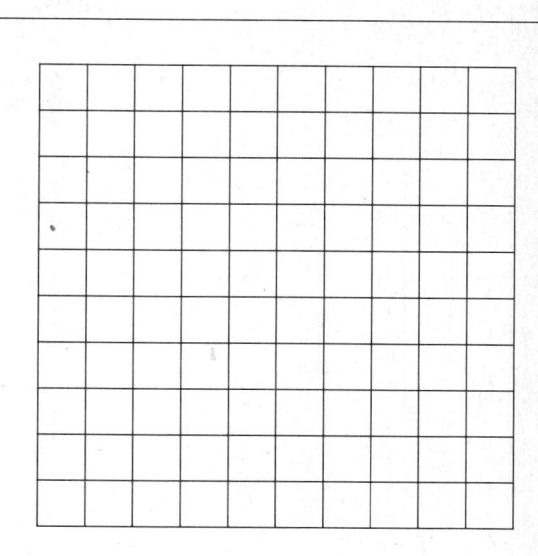

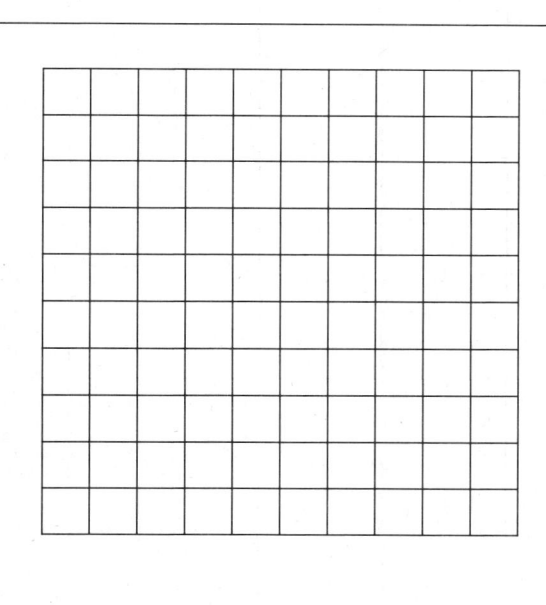

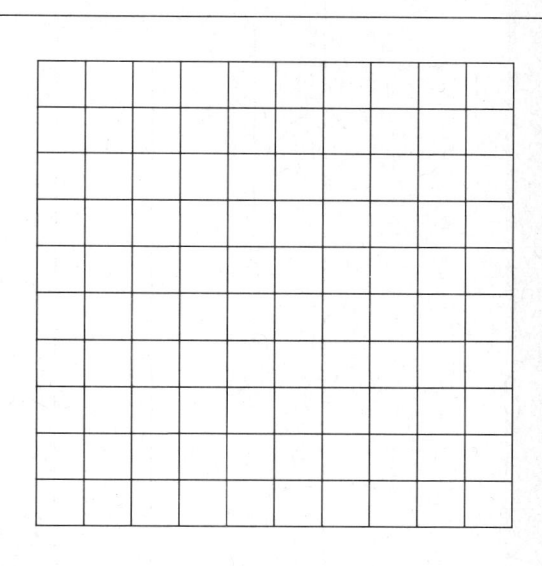

Name _____

Fractions

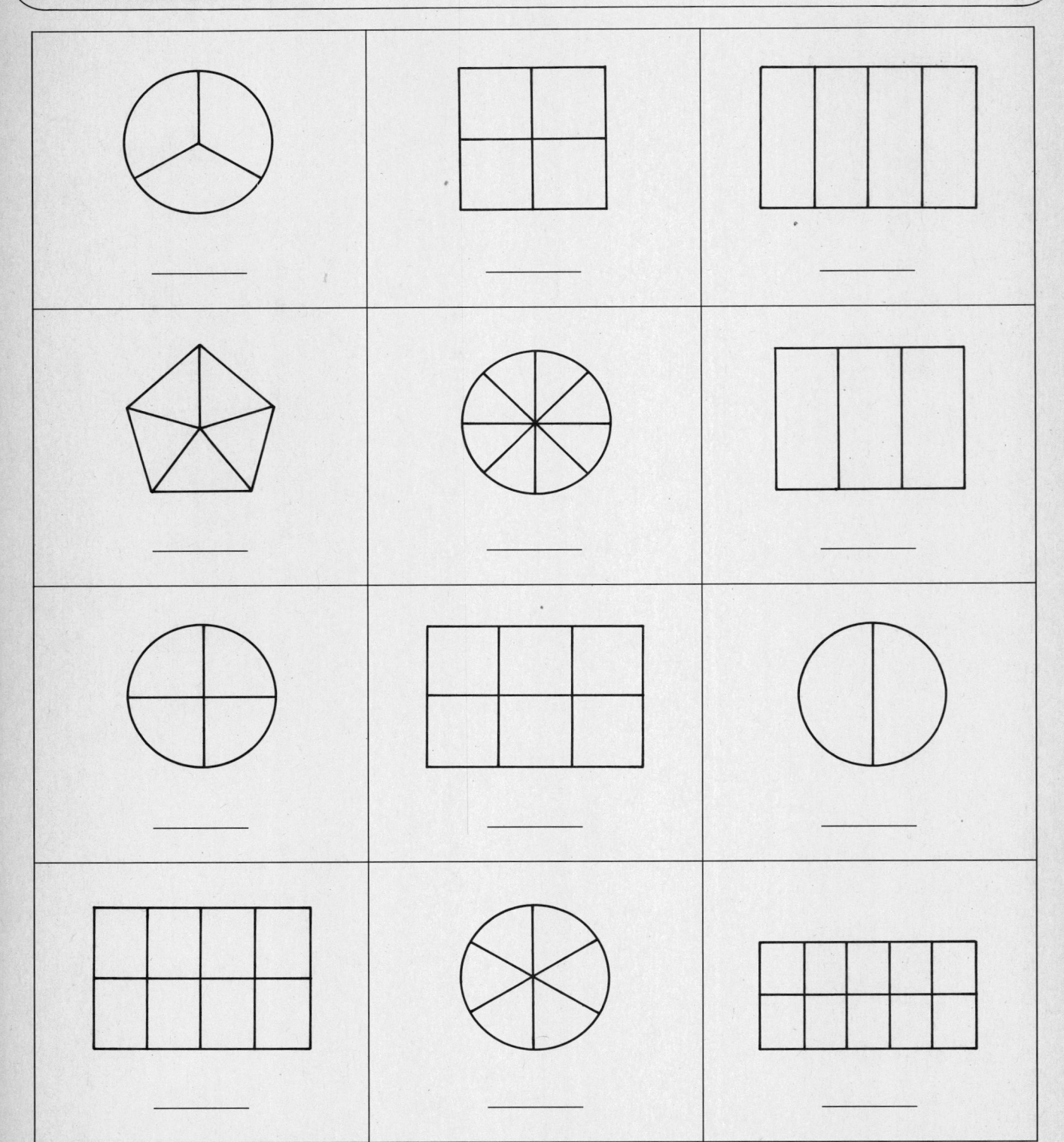

Measuring Inches and Centimeters

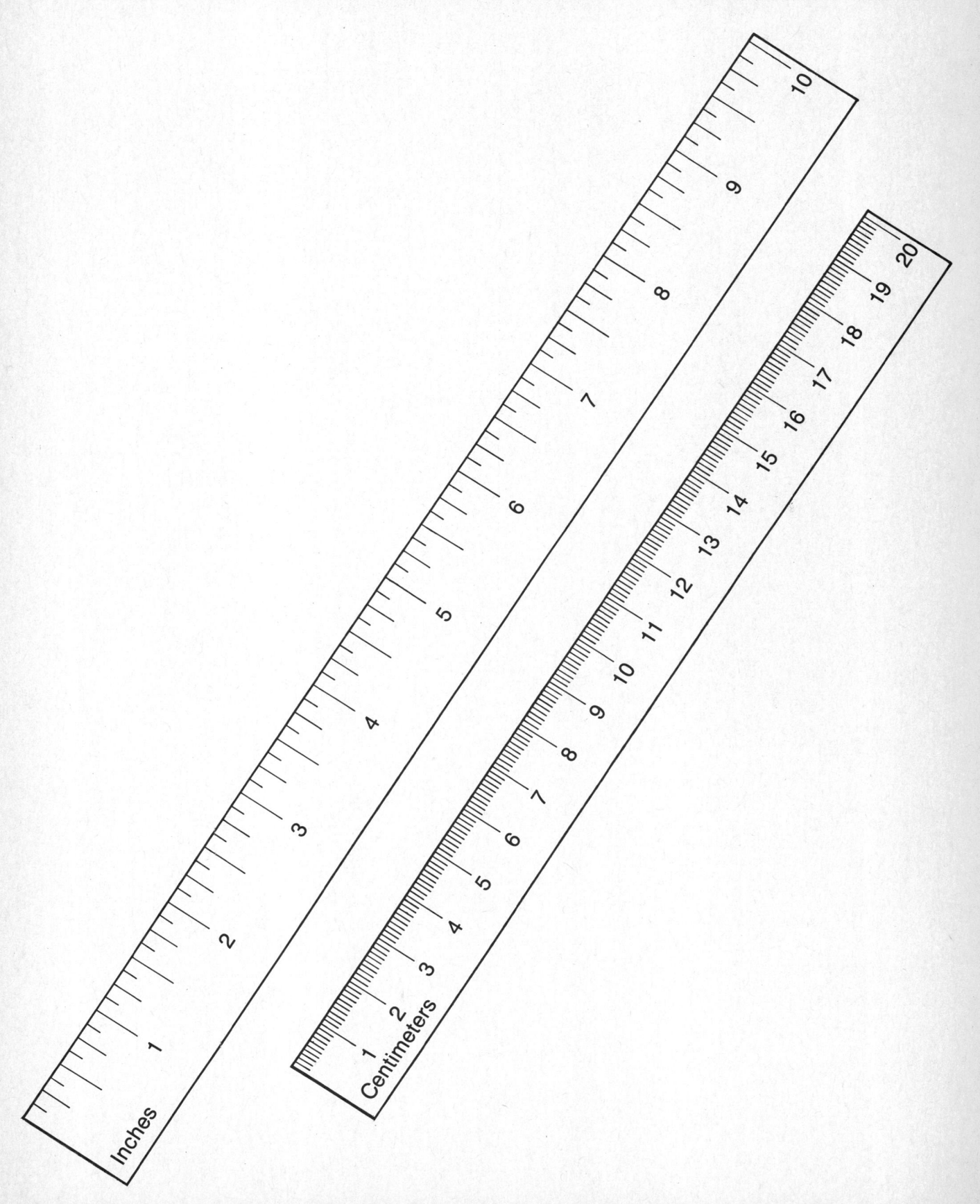

T29

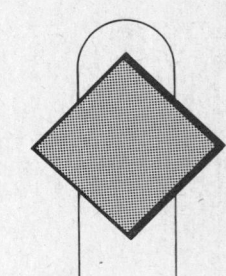

Mastering Math

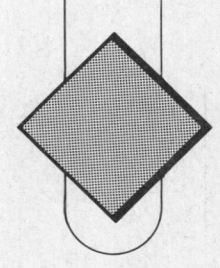

This is to certify that

_____

has successfully completed

_____

Teacher

_____

Date

Mastering Math © 1994 Steck-Vaughn Co. ISBN 0-8114-3242-4

Name _____

Checkup — CHAPTER 1

◆ Complete the expanded form of each number.

1. 64,895 = 60,000 + **4,000** + 800 + **90** + 5
2. 352,176 = 300,000 + **50,000** + 2,000 + **100** + 70 + **6**

◆ Write the value of each underlined digit.

3. 4 9,<u>3</u> 0 8   **300**
4. <u>7</u> 0 3,9 2 5   **700,000**

◆ Add.

5. 39 +85 **124**	6. 584 +267 **851**	7. 2,938 +6,735 **9,673**	8. 37,623 +12,539 **50,162**

◆ Subtract.

9. 83 −45 **38**	10. 781 −284 **497**	11. 4,000 −2,437 **1,563**	12. 80,000 −22,198 **57,802**

◆ Round each number to the nearest ten.

13. 43   **40**
14. 165   **170**

◆ Round each number to the nearest hundred.

15. 879   **900**
16. 2,530   **2,500**

◆ Ring the unit of measure you would use.

17. the length of a key — (**inch**)   foot
18. the height of the chalkboard — inch   (**foot**)

T15

Name _____

Checkup — CHAPTER 2

◆ Multiply.

1. 97 ×6 **582**	2. 83 ×8 **664**	3. 24 ×20 **480**	4. 93 ×30 **2,790**	5. 13 ×70 **910**
6. 49 ×14 **686**	7. 58 ×15 **870**	8. 67 ×19 **1,273**	9. 46 ×42 **1,932**	10. 61 ×58 **3,538**
11. 316 ×13 **4,108**	12. 524 ×16 **8,384**	13. 275 ×34 **9,350**	14. 618 ×67 **41,406**	15. 205 ×89 **18,245**

◆ Ring the unit of measure you would use.

16. the length of a worm — (**centimeter**)   meter
17. the height of a basketball hoop — centimeter   (**meter**)

T16

Name _____

Checkup — CHAPTER 3

◆ Divide.

1. 4)37 **9 R1**	2. 7)57 **8 R1**	3. 9)95 **10 R5**	4. 3)39 **13**
5. 6)87 **14 R3**	6. 2)58 **29**	7. 5)327 **65 R2**	8. 8)591 **73 R7**
9. 30)68 **2 R8**	10. 70)289 **4 R9**	11. 37)80 **2 R6**	12. 54)706 **13 R4**

◆ Mark an X on the containers that equal the first one in the row.

13. [carton] [X cup] [X cup] [bucket] [bucket]

T17

Name _____

Checkup — CHAPTER 4

◆ Write each decimal.

1. 9 tenths = **0.9**
2. 6 hundredths = **0.06**

◆ Compare the decimals. Write > or <.

3. 0.2 **<** 0.5
4. 2.8 **>** 2.4
5. 6.97 **>** 6.87

◆ Add.

6. 1.43 +3.25 **4.68**	7. 9.68 +4.29 **13.97**	8. 21.36 +5.49 **26.85**	9. 13.65 +43.84 **57.49**	10. 9.43 +7.48 **16.91**

◆ Subtract.

11. 9.68 −2.45 **7.23**	12. 4.57 −1.93 **2.64**	13. 11.69 −3.54 **8.15**	14. 67.93 −32.14 **35.79**	15. 63.49 −38.63 **24.86**

◆ Write zero. Then add or subtract.

16. 2.34 +3.6 **5.94**	17. 32.5 +14.28 **46.78**	18. 11.5 −9.37 **2.13**	19. 46.85 −12.2 **34.65**	20. 2.8 −1.52 **1.28**

◆ Ring the unit of measure you would use.

21. eye drops in an eyedropper — (**milliliter**)   liter
22. water in a fish tank — milliliter   (**liter**)

T18

T31

Name _____

Checkup — CHAPTER 5

◆ Write each decimal.

1. 395 thousandths = 0.395
2. 7 and 48 thousandths = 7.048
3. 2 and 6 tenths = 2.6
4. 31 and 79 hundredths = 31.79

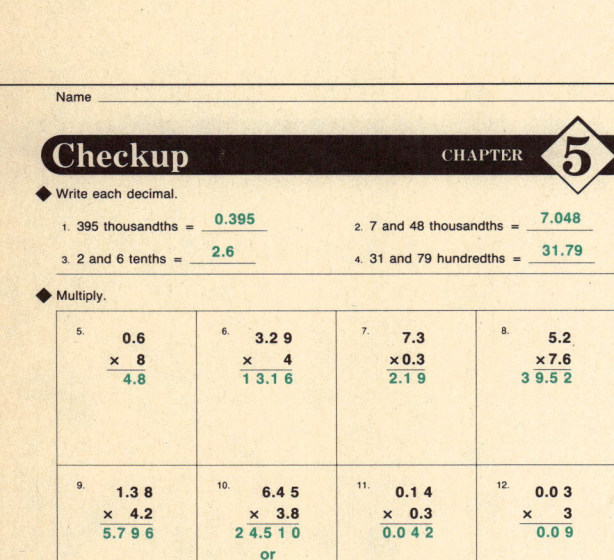

◆ Multiply.

5. 0.6 × 8 4.8	6. 3.29 × 4 13.16	7. 7.3 × 0.3 2.19	8. 5.2 × 7.6 39.52
9. 1.38 × 4.2 5.796	10. 6.45 × 3.8 24.510 or 24.51	11. 0.14 × 0.3 0.042	12. 0.03 × 3 0.09

13. 10 × 3.7 = 37
14. 100 × 4.65 = 465
15. 1,000 × 2.198 = 2,198
16. 100 × 1.53 = 153

◆ Ring the word that completes each sentence.

17. A bag of sugar weighs 5 ___.   ounces   (pounds)
18. A box of cereal weighs 14 ___. (ounces) pounds

T19

Name _____

Checkup — CHAPTER 6

◆ Divide.

1. 5.4 6)32.4	2. 8.7 9)78.3	3. 3.69 4)14.76	4. 2.58 8)20.64
5. 0.43 7)3.01	6. 3.006 3)9.018	7. 0.195 2)0.39	8. 1.48 5)7.4

◆ Divide. Then check your answer by multiplying.

9. 36 ÷ 100 = 0.36
   100 × 0.36 = 36
10. 48.7 ÷ 10 = 4.87
    10 × 4.87 = 48.7

◆ Ring the word that completes each sentence.

11. A bicycle weighs 12 ___.   grams   (kilograms)
12. A box of crackers weighs 57 ___. (grams) kilograms

T20

Name _____

Checkup — CHAPTER 7

◆ Write a fraction in each box to name the shaded part.

1. 3/4
2. 5/8
3. 1/2

◆ Compare the fractions. Write > or < in the box.

4. 4/5 > 3/5
5. 8/9 > 5/9
6. 2/7 < 6/7

◆ Write an equivalent fraction in the box.

7. 4/6 = 4÷2 / 6÷2 = 2/3
8. 10/12 = 10÷2 / 12÷2 = 5/6
9. 6/24 = 6÷6 / 24÷6 = 1/4

◆ Write a mixed number for each picture.

10. 2 1/2
11. 3 3/8

◆ Ring the word that completes each sentence.

12. To measure the weight of a horse use ___.   liters   (kilograms)
13. To measure the length of a picnic table use ___. (feet) pounds

T21

Name _____

Addition Facts

◆ Add.

1. 7 +5 12	2. 9 +9 18	3. 2 +6 8	4. 5 +4 9	5. 8 +6 14	6. 4 +9 13
7. 3 +2 5	8. 2 +2 4	9. 4 +8 12	10. 6 +9 15	11. 5 +5 10	12. 1 +6 7
13. 7 +4 11	14. 8 +8 16	15. 5 +6 11	16. 1 +9 10	17. 3 +4 7	18. 7 +7 14
19. 9 +3 12	20. 4 +2 6	21. 3 +7 10	22. 8 +5 13	23. 6 +6 12	24. 2 +9 11
25. 7 +8 15	26. 3 +8 11	27. 9 +7 16	28. 4 +4 8	29. 5 +2 7	30. 8 +9 17
31. 2 +7 9	32. 1 +7 8	33. 8 +2 10	34. 9 +5 14	35. 6 +7 13	36. 0 +5 5

T22

Name _____

Subtraction Facts

◆ Subtract.

1. 10 − 4 ___ 6	2. 11 − 8 ___ 3	3. 14 − 5 ___ 9	4. 8 − 7 ___ 1	5. 16 − 8 ___ 8	6. 18 − 9 ___ 9
7. 7 − 3 ___ 4	8. 12 − 4 ___ 8	9. 8 − 2 ___ 6	10. 10 − 5 ___ 5	11. 13 − 6 ___ 7	12. 6 − 3 ___ 3
13. 9 − 4 ___ 5	14. 5 − 2 ___ 3	15. 13 − 9 ___ 4	16. 11 − 2 ___ 9	17. 7 − 0 ___ 7	18. 14 − 8 ___ 6
19. 8 − 4 ___ 4	20. 12 − 7 ___ 5	21. 9 − 1 ___ 8	22. 17 − 8 ___ 9	23. 9 − 6 ___ 3	24. 10 − 3 ___ 7
25. 2 − 1 ___ 1	26. 14 − 7 ___ 7	27. 10 − 2 ___ 8	28. 8 − 8 ___ 0	29. 15 − 9 ___ 6	30. 13 − 5 ___ 8
31. 6 − 2 ___ 4	32. 16 − 7 ___ 9	33. 4 − 2 ___ 2	34. 11 − 4 ___ 7	35. 8 − 3 ___ 5	36. 12 − 6 ___ 6

Mastering Math © 1994 Steck-Vaughn Co. ISBN 0-8114-3242-4   T23

Name _____

Multiplication Facts

◆ Multiply.

1. 4 ×7 ___ 28	2. 8 ×9 ___ 72	3. 4 ×2 ___ 8	4. 6 ×8 ___ 48	5. 5 ×5 ___ 25	6. 2 ×3 ___ 6
7. 9 ×3 ___ 27	8. 6 ×6 ___ 36	9. 2 ×7 ___ 14	10. 5 ×8 ___ 40	11. 4 ×4 ___ 16	12. 7 ×9 ___ 63
13. 1 ×2 ___ 2	14. 7 ×8 ___ 56	15. 3 ×1 ___ 3	16. 9 ×9 ___ 81	17. 2 ×6 ___ 12	18. 0 ×4 ___ 0
19. 6 ×7 ___ 42	20. 3 ×8 ___ 24	21. 6 ×0 ___ 0	22. 9 ×2 ___ 18	23. 5 ×6 ___ 30	24. 7 ×7 ___ 49
25. 3 ×5 ___ 15	26. 4 ×9 ___ 36	27. 6 ×9 ___ 54	28. 8 ×8 ___ 64	29. 1 ×1 ___ 1	30. 8 ×2 ___ 16
31. 3 ×3 ___ 9	32. 0 ×5 ___ 0	33. 4 ×6 ___ 24	34. 5 ×9 ___ 45	35. 3 ×7 ___ 21	36. 2 ×2 ___ 4

T24   *Mastering Math* © 1994 Steck-Vaughn Co. ISBN 0-8114-3242-4

Name _____

Division Facts

◆ Divide.

1. 2 2)4	2. 7 9)63	3. 3 3)9	4. 2 5)10	5. 6 8)48
6. 1 4)4	7. 5 9)45	8. 3 6)18	9. 4 7)28	10. 5 6)30
11. 7 8)56	12. 4 5)20	13. 8 2)16	14. 2 3)6	15. 2 6)12
16. 9 3)27	17. 3 8)24	18. 8 1)8	19. 5 7)35	20. 4 9)36
21. 1 5)5	22. 7 7)49	23. 8 9)72	24. 4 4)16	25. 7 1)7
26. 3 4)12	27. 4 8)32	28. 2 7)14	29. 1 6)6	30. 9 2)18

Mastering Math © 1994 Steck-Vaughn Co. ISBN 0-8114-3242-4   T25

Table of Contents

- **Chapter 1: Adding and Subtracting Large Numbers** — 1
  - Problem Solving: Estimation — 16
- **Chapter 2: Multiplying by 1- and 2-Digit Numbers** — 23
  - Problem Solving: Estimation — 38
- **Chapter 3: Dividing with 1- and 2-Digit Divisors** — 45
  - Problem Solving: Two-Step Problems — 60
- **Cumulative Review: Chapters 1–3** — 67
- **Chapter 4: Adding and Subtracting Decimals** — 71
  - Problem Solving: Two-Step Problems — 86
- **Chapter 5: Multiplying Decimals** — 93
  - Problem Solving: Choose an Operation — 108
- **Chapter 6: Dividing Decimals by Whole Numbers** — 115
  - Problem Solving: Identify Extra Information — 130
- **Chapter 7: Understanding Fractions** — 137
  - Problem Solving: Identify Extra Information — 152
- **Cumulative Review: Chapters 4–7** — 159
- **Extra Practice:**
  - Chapter 1 — 165
  - Chapter 2 — 166
  - Chapter 3 — 168
  - Chapter 4 — 169
  - Chapter 5 — 171
  - Chapter 6 — 172
  - Chapter 7 — 173

Acknowledgments

Executive Editor
Elizabeth Strauss

Project Editor
Donna Rodgers

Design Manager
John Harrison

Product Development
Colophon Publishing Services
Cary, North Carolina

Contributing Writers
Brantley Eastman, Diane Crowley, Mary Hill, Louise Marinilli, Harriet Stevens, Susan Murphy, Helen Coleman, Ann McSweeney

Product Design
The Quarasan Group, Inc.

Illustration
Barbara Corey: pages 5, 9, 11, 14, 15, 26, 27, 30, 31, 46, 50, 51, 54, 55, 72, 73, 75, 81, 94, 95, 98, 99, 101, 105, 117, 119, 123, 128, 129, 140, 141, 145, 148, 154
Judith du Four Love: pages 2, 3, 7, 13, 24, 25, 28, 29, 32, 33, 36, 37, 48, 52, 53, 57, 58, 59, 63, 65, 77, 79, 83, 84, 85, 97, 103, 106, 107, 121, 139, 143, 147, 150, 151

Photography
© Tony Freeman/PhotoEdit: page 1
© Richard Hutchings/PhotoEdit: pages 45, 115
© Dennis MacDonald/PhotoEdit: page 137
© David Young Wolff/PhotoEdit: pages 23, 71, 93

Cover Photography
Cooke Photographics

ISBN 0-8114-3241-6

Copyright © 1994 Steck-Vaughn Company
All rights reserved. No part of the material protected by this copyright may be reproduced or utilized in any form or by any means, electronic or mechanical, including photocopying, recording, or by any information storage and retrieval system, without permission in writing from the copyright owner. Requests for permission to make copies of any part of the work should be mailed to: Copyright Permissions, Steck-Vaughn Company, P.O. Box 26015, Austin, TX 78755. Printed in the United States of America.

2 3 4 5 6 7 8 9 VP 98 97 96 95 94

Name _____

CHAPTER 1

Review place value with students by asking them if 14,000 or 41,000 is greater. Discuss the photograph with students. Read aloud the sentences and questions on the page and have students discuss their answers. Have students subtract the numbers given and find out how many more people went to the theme park on Saturday than on Tuesday. Tell students that in this chapter they will be adding and subtracting large numbers like these.

Adding and Subtracting Large Numbers

On Tuesday, 14,708 people went to the theme park to ride the rides and to watch the shows. On Saturday 40,165 people went to the theme park. Do you think it would be better to go on a Tuesday or on a Saturday? Why?

Objective: Students will write the values of given digits through hundred thousands.
Instructional Model: Direct students' attention to the number 386,527 in the place-value chart, stressing the use of the comma. Discuss each digit in terms of its place in the chart and its value in that particular position. Explain that the values of all the digits in a number in expanded form, when added together equal the number in standard form. Draw a place-value chart on the chalkboard similar to the one on page 2. Rearrange the digits in *386,527* to form other 6-digit numbers such as *785,623; 573,268;* and *658,237.* Ask volunteers to write these numbers in the place-value chart; have students state the place and value of the individual digits in each. Then choose a digit, such as the

1

Place Value Through Hundred Thousands

A **digit** can have different values. The value of a digit depends on its place in a number. You can use a **place-value** chart to find the value of a digit.

hundred thousands	ten thousands	thousands	hundreds	tens	ones
3	8	6 ,	5	2	7

↑
comma

Digit	Place	Value		
3	hundred thousands	300 thousands	or	300,000
8	ten thousands	80 thousands	or	80,000
6	thousands	6 thousands	or	6,000
5	hundreds	5 hundreds	or	500
2	tens	2 tens	or	20
7	ones	7 ones	or	7

386,527 = 300,000 + 80,000 + 6,000 + 500 + 20 + 7
standard form   expanded form

Guided Practice

◆ Complete the expanded form of each number.

1. 95,874 = 90,000 + __5,000__ + 800 + 70 + __4__

2. 178,346 = 100,000 + __70,000__ + 8,000 + 300 + __40__ + 6

◆ Write the value of each underlined digit.

3. 6 <u>6</u>,4 9 2   __6,000__

4. <u>7</u> 2 8,0 6 3   __700,000__

2

6, and have students compare its position and value in the different numbers.
Guided Practice: Work through the exercises with students. Point out to students that all the digits in a number, except zero, have a corresponding value in the expanded form of the number.
Practice: Tell students to complete these exercises independently. Check all answers. Have students correct their errors by writing the numbers in standard form in a place-value chart, to help them see the value of each digit.
Using Math: Have students complete this section independently. As a group activity, collect interesting facts involving numbers through hundred thousands from various reference sources.

Practice

◆ Complete the expanded form of each number.

1. 17,632 = 10,000 + __7,000__ + 600 + __30__ + 2
2. 48,950 = 40,000 + 8,000 + __900__ + __50__
3. 63,747 = __60,000__ + 3,000 + __700__ + 40 + __7__
4. 259,620 = 200,000 + __50,000__ + __9,000__ + 600 + 20
5. 644,813 = __600,000__ + 40,000 + __4,000__ + 800 + __10__ + 3
6. 527,500 = 500,000 + __20,000__ + 7,000 + __500__

◆ Write the value of each underlined digit.

7. <u>3</u> 8,5 2 1   __30,000__
8. 4 <u>9</u>,4 0 0   __9,000__
9. 1 2,7 <u>9</u> 4   __90__
10. 5 0,6 <u>3</u> 3   __30__
11. 4 5,<u>8</u> 2 0   __800__
12. 7 1,5 5 <u>6</u>   __6__
13. 1 <u>9</u> 1,7 4 5   __90,000__
14. <u>8</u> 6 2,9 4 0   __800,000__
15. 3 5 0,<u>2</u> 0 1   __200__
16. 2 2 <u>6</u>,5 0 0   __6,000__
17. <u>4</u> 7 7,3 3 3   __400,000__
18. 6 9 8,9 <u>2</u> 5   __20__

Using Math

◆ There are 372,634 people who live in Miami, Florida. Write the number of people who live in Miami in the place-value chart.

hundred thousands	ten thousands	thousands	hundreds	tens	ones
3	7	2 ,	6	3	4

How many hundred thousands are in the number 372,634?

There are __3__ hundred thousands in 372,634.

3

Objective: Students will add two 2- and 3-digit numbers.
Instructional Model: Use flash cards to review the basic addition facts through 18. Then present students with a problem such as, "Pete scored 683 points in his first computer game and 572 points in his second game. How many points did he score in all?" Ask students how they could find the answer. Select a volunteer to solve the problem on the chalkboard. Remind students that the numbers we add are called *addends*. Remind students that sometimes you need to regroup to add. Discuss the steps for adding 3-digit numbers.
Guided Practice: Work through the problems with

2

Adding 2- and 3-Digit Numbers

When you add numbers with more than one digit, start by adding the ones. Next, add the tens.

```
  28
+ 51
----
  79
```

Sometimes you need to **regroup** to add.

Step 1 Add the ones.
```
  683
+ 572
-----
    5
```

Step 2 Add the tens.
```
   1
  683
+ 572
-----
   55
```
Regroup 15 tens as 1 hundred 5 tens.

Step 3 Add the hundreds.
```
   1
  683
+ 572
-----
1,255
```
Regroup 12 hundreds as 1 thousand 2 hundreds.

Guided Practice

◆ Add.

1. ¹64 + 29 = 93	2. 35 + 17 = 52	3. 480 + 362 = 842	4. 839 + 476 = 1,315	5. 543 + 68 = 611
6. 198 + 12 = 210	7. 201 + 49 = 250	8. 333 + 628 = 961	9. 639 + 721 = 1,360	10. 905 + 198 = 1,103

students. Check to see that students place the digits correctly when regrouping. Students may wish to draw vertical lines to separate the places in the problems. Remind students that only sums of 10 or more have to be regrouped.
Practice: Spot check students' work as they complete the problems independently. After reviewing the answers, have students put selected examples on the chalkboard. Ask them to explain where and how they regrouped.
Using Math: Set up the problem and work through the addition as a group activity. Have students use store advertisements to make up their own problems about purchasing items.

Practice

◆ Add.

1. 58 +21 **79**	2. 19 +34 **53**	3. 68 +29 **97**	4. 75 +98 **173**	5. 26 +95 **121**
6. 86 +64 **150**	7. 59 +72 **131**	8. 205 +193 **398**	9. 158 +346 **504**	10. 593 +247 **840**
11. 581 +290 **871**	12. 279 +186 **465**	13. 487 +612 **1,099**	14. 936 +847 **1,783**	15. 654 +721 **1,375**
16. 792 +568 **1,360**	17. 155 + 43 **198**	18. 374 + 62 **436**	19. 547 + 93 **640**	20. 836 + 25 **861**

Using Math

◆ Bob and his mother bought airplane tickets. Bob's ticket cost $125. His mother's ticket cost $176. How much did both tickets cost?

Both tickets cost ___**$301**___.

Work here.

Objective: Students will add two 4- and 5-digit numbers.
Instructional Model: Review addition facts with the blackline master, *Addition Facts,* on page T22, stressing speed and accuracy. Then ask students how they would solve a problem such as "24,395 fans attended an afternoon performance of a rock concert. 68,403 fans attended the same concert at night. How many fans attended the two performances?" Select a volunteer to write the problem on the chalkboard. Point out that the use of the comma helps align the digits properly. Work through the "rock concert" problem with students, emphasizing that we always start with the ones' column and work toward the left. Question students about where and how to regroup. Remind students that in addition *sum* means *answer.* Discuss the steps for

3

Adding Large Numbers

To add large numbers, start by adding the ones. Regroup when needed.

Step 1 Add the ones.

```
  24,395
+ 68,403
────────
       8
```

Step 2 Add the tens.

```
  24,395
+ 68,403
────────
      98
```

Step 3 Add the hundreds.

```
  24,395
+ 68,403
────────
     798
```

Step 4 Add the thousands.

```
     1
  24,395
+ 68,403
────────
   2,798
```

Regroup 12 thousands as 1 ten thousand 2 thousands.

Step 5 Add the ten thousands.

```
     1
  24,395
+ 68,403
────────
  92,798
```

Guided Practice

◆ Add.

1.
```
  1 1
  3,492
+ 1,857
───────
  5,349
```

2.
```
  5,608
+ 6,429
───────
 12,037
```

3.
```
 74,537
+38,087
───────
112,624
```

4.
```
 27,506
+  4,891
───────
 32,397
```

5.
```
  1,987
+ 1,031
───────
  3,018
```

6.
```
 33,144
+  6,138
───────
 39,282
```

7.
```
 52,934
+  2,591
───────
 55,525
```

8.
```
 31,844
+45,933
───────
 77,777
```

6

adding 5-digit numbers.
Guided Practice: Work through the problems with students, stressing correct regrouping and careful computation. If necessary, help students focus on adding one column at a time by having them cover up the other columns.
Practice: Have students complete the problems on their own. Evaluate students' errors to determine if more drill on basic facts or more regrouping practice is needed. It may help students to work the problems on a piece of lined paper turned so the holes are at the top. This will help them keep the digits aligned.
Using Math: Have students complete the problem by themselves. For further practice vary the number of people.
Blackline Master: *Addition Facts,* page T22.
Practice Book E: Pages 1–2.

Practice

◆ Add.

1. 6,907 + 1,243 = 8,150	2. 5,496 + 4,238 = 9,734	3. 1,642 + 3,785 = 5,427	4. 7,392 + 6,578 = 13,970
5. 4,165 + 9,847 = 14,012	6. 3,657 + 8,989 = 12,646	7. 25,213 + 42,654 = 67,867	8. 15,637 + 23,441 = 39,078
9. 37,869 + 42,320 = 80,189	10. 13,674 + 20,579 = 34,253	11. 48,279 + 23,651 = 71,930	12. 29,782 + 35,687 = 65,469
13. 31,768 + 75,489 = 107,257	14. 56,025 + 68,794 = 124,819	15. 73,628 + 8,251 = 81,879	16. 23,745 + 14,965 = 38,710

Using Math

◆ In June, 65,698 people went to Fantasy Park. In July, 62,137 people went to the park. How many people went to the park in June and July?

Work here.

In June and July ___127,835___ people went to the park.

7

Objective: Students will subtract two 2- and 3-digit numbers.

Instructional Model: Use flash cards to review the basic subtraction facts. Then present students with a problem such as, "Sue has a collection of 623 stamps. 489 stamps are from foreign countries, the rest from the United States. How many stamps are from the United States?" Ask students how they could find the answer. Select a volunteer to write the problem on the chalkboard. Remind students that you need to regroup in subtraction when the top number is smaller than the bottom number. Work through the "stamp" problem with students step-by-step, each time asking students where and how they would regroup. Discuss the steps for subtracting a 3-digit number. Explain the pro-

4

Subtracting 2- and 3-Digit Numbers

When you subtract, start by subtracting the ones. Sometimes you will need to regroup.

```
  623
 -489
```

Step 1

```
  1 13
  6 2 3
 -4 8 9
        4
```

Subtract the ones.
Can you subtract 9 ones from 3 ones?
No. Go to the tens.
Regroup 2 tens 3 ones as 1 ten 13 ones.
Now subtract the ones.

Step 2

```
     11
   5 1 13
   6 2 3
  -4 8 9
       3 4
```

Subtract the tens.
Can you subtract 8 tens from 1 ten?
No. Go to the hundreds.
Regroup 6 hundreds 1 ten as 5 hundreds 11 tens.
Now subtract the tens.

Step 3 Subtract the hundreds.

```
     11
   5 1 13
   6 2 3
  -4 8 9
   1 3 4
```

You can check your answer by adding.

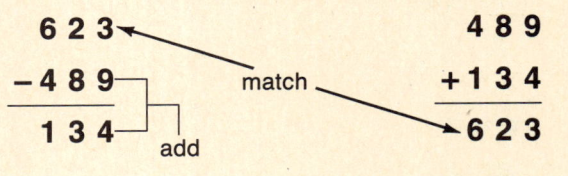

```
  6 2 3              4 8 9
 -4 8 9    match    +1 3 4
  1 3 4              6 2 3
      add
```

Guided Practice

◆ Subtract.

1.  ```
     5 16
     6 6
    -3 9
     2 7
    ```

2.  ```
     7 1
    -5 2
     1 9
    ```

3.  ```
     8 9 2
    -6 7 5
     2 1 7
    ```

4.  ```
     5 3 1
    -4 6 8
        6 3
    ```

5.  ```
     9 6 1
    -   8 5
     8 7 6
    ```

8
    ```

cedure for checking answers.
Guided Practice: Work through the problems with students. Check to see that students regroup correctly.
Practice: Spot check students' work for correct regrouping as they complete the problems independently. Go over problems 1–10, then have students check their answers for 11–20 by adding.
Using Math: Review the concept of subtracting to find the difference before students solve the problem on their own. Substitute a football player's weight on Earth (276 lbs.) and on the moon (49 lbs.) for further practice.

Practice

◆ Subtract.

1. 96 − 53 = 43	2. 27 − 19 = 8	3. 85 − 29 = 56	4. 66 − 47 = 19	5. 74 − 37 = 37
6. 89 − 41 = 48	7. 95 − 28 = 67	8. 587 − 316 = 271	9. 829 − 293 = 536	10. 749 − 365 = 384
11. 428 − 267 = 161	12. 641 − 237 = 404	13. 833 − 514 = 319	14. 542 − 256 = 286	15. 790 − 135 = 655
16. 934 − 759 = 175	17. 387 − 94 = 293	18. 599 − 71 = 528	19. 448 − 59 = 389	20. 273 − 29 = 244

Using Math

◆ A motorcycle weighs 894 pounds on Earth. The same motorcycle weighs 149 pounds on the moon. What is the difference in the weight of the motorcycle on Earth and on the moon?

The difference is __745__ pounds.

Work here.

9

Objective: Students will subtract 3-, 4- and 5-digit numbers from numbers with zeros.

Instructional Model: Review subtraction facts with the blackline master, *Subtraction Facts*, on page T23, stressing speed and accuracy. Then present students with the following problem: "Anchorage is about 4,000 miles from Montreal. Portland is about 2,793 miles from Montreal. How much closer to Montreal is Portland?" Write the problem on the chalkboard, noting that the use of the comma helps align the digits properly. Explain to students that subtracting from zeros can be tricky because sometimes we need to regroup several times before we can subtract. Begin with the ones and point out that it is necessary to go to the thousands because there are no tens or hundreds to regroup. Explain that after the thousands are regrouped, students must then regroup the hundreds and the tens so that there

5

Subtracting from Zeros

When you subtract from numbers with zeros, you may have to regroup to more than one place. Before you can subtract the ones, you must regroup. To regroup 4,000, begin with the thousands.

$$\begin{array}{r} 4,000 \\ -2,793 \\ \hline \end{array}$$

Step 1 Regroup the thousands. 4 thousands = 3 thousands 10 hundreds $$\begin{array}{r} \overset{3\ 10}{4{,}000} \\ -2{,}793 \\ \hline \end{array}$$	**Step 2** Regroup the hundreds. 10 hundreds = 9 hundreds 10 tens $$\begin{array}{r} \overset{\ \ 9}{\overset{3\ 10\ 10}{4{,}000}} \\ -2{,}793 \\ \hline \end{array}$$
Step 3 Regroup the tens. 10 tens = 9 tens 10 ones $$\begin{array}{r} \overset{\ \ 9\ \ 9}{\overset{3\ 10\ 10\ 10}{4{,}000}} \\ -2{,}793 \\ \hline \end{array}$$	**Step 4** Now you can subtract. Remember to start with the ones. $$\begin{array}{r} \overset{\ \ 9\ \ 9}{\overset{3\ 10\ 10\ 10}{4{,}000}} \\ -2{,}793 \\ \hline 1{,}207 \end{array}$$

Guided Practice

◆ Subtract.

1. $\overset{\ \ 9\ \ 9}{\overset{6\ 10\ 10\ 15}{7{,}005}}$ $-3{,}859$ $\overline{3{,}146}$	2. 600 -139 $\overline{461}$	3. $30{,}000$ $-19{,}468$ $\overline{10{,}532}$	4. $49{,}006$ $-\ \ 9{,}878$ $\overline{39{,}128}$
5. $1{,}001$ $-\ \ 233$ $\overline{768}$	6. $9{,}000$ $-1{,}825$ $\overline{7{,}175}$	7. $70{,}000$ $-36{,}667$ $\overline{33{,}333}$	8. $19{,}000$ $-\ \ 4{,}887$ $\overline{14{,}113}$

will be enough ones to subtract from. Demonstrate the mechanics of crossing out the appropriate digits in the proper order and correct renaming. Have students subtract one column at a time to find the difference. Remind students that in subtraction *difference* means *answer*. Discuss the steps for subtracting from zeros.

Guided Practice: Work through the problems with students, discussing the mechanics of regrouping.

Practice: Spot check students' work for correct regrouping as they complete the problems independently.

Using Math: Have students solve the problem independently. Have them make up similar subtraction problems.

Blackline Master: *Subtraction Facts*, page T23.

Practice Book E: Pages 3–6.

Practice

◆ Subtract.

1. 600 −218 **382**	2. 900 −333 **567**	3. 800 −176 **624**	4. 700 −594 **106**
5. 6,004 −2,587 **3,417**	6. 9,005 −1,037 **7,968**	7. 4,000 −1,957 **2,043**	8. 4,000 −3,422 **578**
9. 7,000 −3,014 **3,986**	10. 17,000 −10,338 **6,662**	11. 90,900 −83,456 **7,444**	12. 28,002 −14,773 **13,229**
13. 80,075 −43,280 **36,795**	14. 32,000 − 7,926 **24,074**	15. 23,000 − 6,746 **16,254**	16. 42,000 −36,394 **5,606**

Using Math

◆ A company opened a bank account with $26,000. In one week the company took $14,966 out of the bank. How much money does the company have left?

The company has ___**$11,034**___ left.

Work here.

11

Objective: Students will round numbers to the nearest ten, hundred, or thousand.
Instructional Model: Begin the lesson by asking students various questions which have approximate answers, for example, "How many records or tapes do you own?" or "How many students go to our school?" Explain to students that it is not always necessary to know the exact number. Point out that most of their answers were probably rounded numbers, preceded by the word *about*. Direct students' attention to the Instructional Model. As you discuss the steps for rounding, it may be helpful to have students trace over the underlined and circled digits in the example.
Guided Practice: Work through the problems with students, referring to the 3 steps as needed. For students

6

Rounding Numbers

You **round** numbers to find out about how many.

Round 363 to the nearest ten.

Is 363 nearer to 360 or to 370?

360 361 362 363 364 365 366 367 368 369 370

363 is nearer to 360.

Follow these steps to help you round numbers.

Step 1	Underline the place you are rounding to.	3 6 3
Step 2	Circle the next digit to the right.	3 6 ③
Step 3	If the circled digit is **less than 5**, round down. If the circled digit is **5 or more**, round up.	3 6 0

Round 1,538 to each given place.

Nearest Ten	**Nearest Hundred**	**Nearest Thousand**
1,5 3 ⑧ round up 1,5 4 0 (ten)	1,5 ③ 8 round down 1,5 0 0 (hundred)	1,⑤ 3 8 round up 2,0 0 0 (thousand)

Guided Practice

◆ Round each number to the nearest ten.

1. 75 ___80___   2. 858 ___860___   3. 4,922 ___4,920___

◆ Round each number to the nearest hundred.

4. 310 ___300___   5. 884 ___900___   6. 6,721 ___6,700___

◆ Round each number to the nearest thousand.

7. 1,840 ___2000___   8. 5,430 ___5,000___   9. 12,536 ___13,000___

having difficulty, it may be helpful to provide 2 possible choices for each answer. Point out that the answer will have as many zeros as the number they are rounding to (nearest ten = 1 zero, etc.).

Practice: Have students complete the problems independently, one section at a time. Check to see that each section is completed correctly before proceeding to the next one. A place value chart might be helpful to those students having difficulty.

Using Math: Have students solve the problem independently.

Practice Book E: Pages 7–8.

Practice

◆ Round each number to the nearest ten.

1. 22 __20__
2. 55 __60__
3. 388 __390__
4. 912 __910__
5. 506 __510__
6. 1,843 __1,840__

◆ Round each number to the nearest hundred.

7. 740 __700__
8. 458 __500__
9. 943 __900__
10. 3,929 __3,900__
11. 6,522 __6,500__
12. 78,378 __78,400__
13. 99,406 __99,400__
14. 55,720 __55,700__

◆ Round each number to the nearest thousand.

15. 4,800 __5,000__
16. 8,622 __9,000__
17. 1,756 __2,000__
18. 20,998 __21,000__
19. 36,510 __37,000__
20. 52,100 __52,000__

Using Math

◆ The city has a parade every year. One year 13,758 people walked in the parade. And 3,826 people rode on cars, floats, and fire engines.

About how many people walked in the parade?

(Round to the nearest hundred.) __13,800__

About how many people rode in the parade?

(Round to the nearest hundred.) __3,800__

Objective: Students will decide whether an object is measured in inches or feet.

Instructional Model: Write the words *measurement* and *length* on the chalkboard and discuss how they are related. Ask students if they can name any units of length (inch, foot, yard, mile, etc.). To show the importance of using units of the same size to measure objects, have students trace the outline of their right foot on oaktag and cut it out. Instruct students to measure various objects in the classroom such as the floor or the chalkboard, and to record their lengths in numbers of "feet." When the measurements are complete, have students compare their findings to discover that their answers are different. Point out that a better way to approach the task would be if everyone had a "foot" of the same size. Read the *Instructional Model* with students. Distribute copies of the inch ruler from the *Measuring Inches and Cen-*

7

Inches and Feet

The distance from one end of an object to the other end is its **length** or **height**. You measure how long an object is to find its length. You measure how tall an object is to find its height.

An **inch** and a **foot** are units of measurement used to tell length or height. Inches are used to measure short objects. Feet are used to measure long objects or distances.

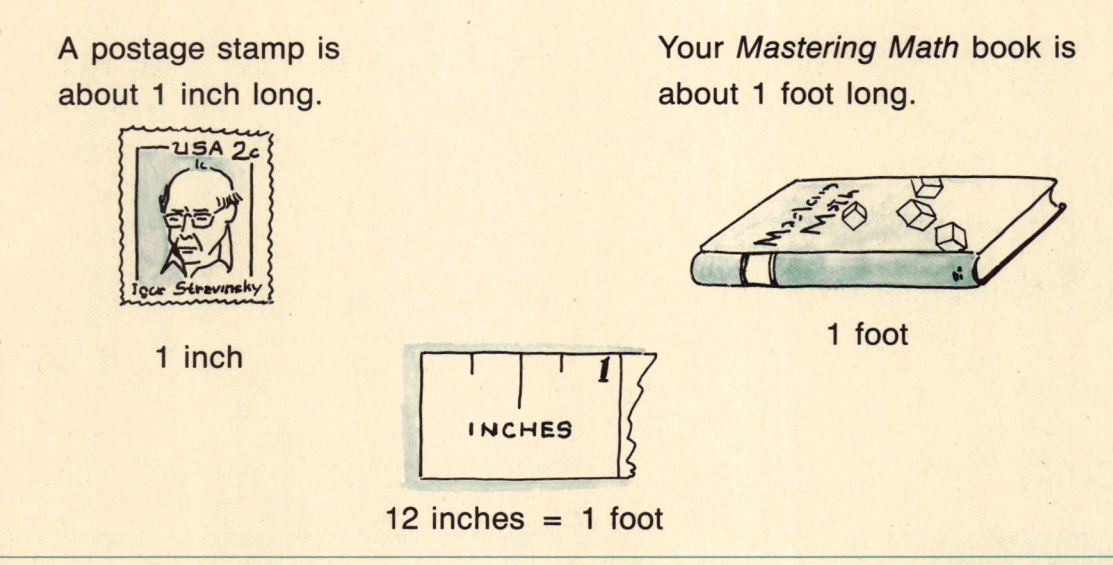

A postage stamp is about 1 inch long.

1 inch

Your *Mastering Math* book is about 1 foot long.

1 foot

12 inches = 1 foot

Guided Practice

◆ Ring the unit of measure you would use.

1. the height of a friend inch (foot)	2. the length of a toothbrush (inch) foot
3. the length of a photograph (inch) foot	4. the height of a door inch (foot)

timeters blackline master on page T29. Have students measure objects in inches or feet. Have students compare their answers to find that their measurements are alike.
Guided Practice: Work the exercises with students. Remind them that long objects are measured in feet and short objects are measured in inches.
Practice: Have students complete the exercises independently.
Using Math: Discuss the problem with students. Explain why "inches" is a more logical answer. Provide students with practice measuring objects in inches and feet as you proceed through the next chapter.
Blackline Master: *Measuring Inches and Centimeters,* page T29.

Practice

◆ Ring the unit of measure you would use.

1. the length of a rug inch　　(foot)	2. the length of a paper clip (inch)　　foot
3. the length of an ink pen (inch)　　foot	4. the length of a swimming pool inch　　(foot)
5. the length of a car inch　　(foot)	6. the height of a cup (inch)　　foot
7. the length of a feather (inch)　　foot	8. the length of a street inch　　(foot)
9. the height of a cat (inch)　　foot	10. the length of a jump rope inch　　(foot)
11. the length of a pair of scissors (inch)　　foot	12. the height of a flagpole inch　　(foot)

Using Math

◆ Laura painted a picture for her dad. It is going to be his Father's Day gift. Laura wants to frame the painting before she gives it to him. Laura needs to measure the painting to get the right-size frame. Should Laura measure the painting in inches or feet?

She should measure the painting in ___**inches**___.

Objective: Students will estimate to solve addition and subtraction problems by rounding to the nearest hundred.
Instructional Model: Review rounding numbers with students. Draw a number line on the chalkboard and number it from 430 to 440. Indicate the number 433 on the number line and ask students if 433 is nearer to 430 or 440. Explain to students that rounding to the nearest hundred is similar to the way you round to the nearest ten. Read the instructional model and the steps with students to show them how to round to the nearest hundred. Ask students to explain why 387 was rounded up and 221 was rounded down. Explain to students that when the number in the tens place is 5, you round up to the next highest hundred.

Problem Solving 8

Estimation

Mark drove 387 miles on Monday.

He drove 221 miles on Tuesday.

About how many miles in all did Mark drive?

> The word **about** means an exact answer is not needed. You can estimate the answer.

Round each number to the nearest hundred.

Step 1 Underline the place you are rounding to.

$\underline{3}$ 8 7

$\underline{2}$ 2 1

Step 2 Circle the next digit to the right.

$\underline{3}$ ⑧ 7

$\underline{2}$ ② 1

Step 3 If the circled digit is less than 5, round down.

If the circled digit is 5 or more, round up.

$\underline{3}$87 ⟶ 400 round up

+ $\underline{2}$21 ⟶ + 200 round down

Mark drove about 600 miles.

Guided Practice

◆ Round to the nearest hundred.

Estimate to solve.

1. Kay is reading a 372-page book. She has read 126 pages. About how many pages does Kay have left to read?	372 ⟶ 400 − 126 ⟶ −100 about 300 pages
2. Alicia hit a golf ball 288 yards. Leo hit a golf ball 214 yards. About how much farther did Alicia hit the golf ball than Leo?	288 ⟶ 300 − 214 ⟶ − 200 about 100 yards

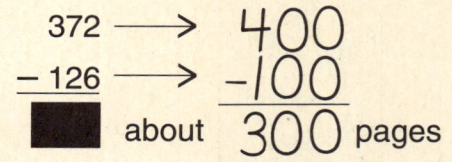

Guided Practice: Work through the problems in *Guided Practice* with students, referring to the three steps on the page as needed. Point out to students that the answers will be in hundreds. Then review answers with students.
Practice: Read the directions and the first problem to students. Encourage students to complete the problems independently by rounding to the nearest hundred. Review answers with the students when they complete the problems on the page.
Practice Book E: Page 7–8.

Practice

◆ Round to the nearest hundred.
Estimate to solve.

1. Food Mart has 226 workers at one store.
   They have 178 workers at the other store.
   About how many workers in all
   does Food Mart have?

   226 → 200
   + 178 → + 200
   about **400** workers

2. There are 312 seats on the train.
   There are 228 people seated in the train.
   About how many empty seats
   are there on that train?

   312 → 300
   − 228 → − 200
   about **100** seats

3. Luis has saved 598 pennies.
   Carl has saved 215 pennies.
   About how many more pennies
   does Luis have than Carl?

   598 → 600
   − 215 → − 200
   about **400** pennies

4. Seafood Plus needed 424 chairs
   for the main dining room.
   They need 188 chairs for another room.
   About how many chairs in all did they need?

   424 → 400
   + 188 → + 200
   about **600** chairs

5. Sam has a 205-page book.
   He has read 97 pages.
   About how many pages of the book
   has Sam not read yet?

   205 → 200
   − 97 → − 100
   about **100** pages

6. Ernie has 375 polished rocks in his rock collection.
   Karen has 284 polished rocks.
   About how many rocks in all do they have?

   375 → 400
   + 284 → + 300
   about **700** rocks

Review

◆ Complete the expanded form of each number. pages 2–3

1. 42,863 = 40,000 + **2,000** + 800 + **60** + 3

2. 18,790 = **10,000** + 8,000 + 700 + **90**

3. 655,315 = 600,000 + **50,000** + 5,000 + 300 + **10** + 5

4. 964,200 = **900,000** + **60,000** + 4,000 + 200

◆ Write the value of each underlined digit. pages 2–3

5. <u>2</u>6,393 **20,000**

6. 8<u>1</u>,752 **1,000**

7. 748,<u>5</u>46 **500**

8. <u>3</u>90,480 **300,000**

◆ Add.

pages 4–5

9.   43
   +19
   ——
    62

10.   76
    +27
    ——
    103

11.   194
    +558
    ——
    752

12.   491
    +718
    ——
   1,209

pages 6–7

13. 4,589
    +2,656
    ——
    7,245

14. 9,635
    +3,108
    ——
   12,743

15. 23,637
    +30,287
    ——
    53,924

16. 17,659
    +85,608
    ——
   103,267

◆ Subtract.

pages 8–9

17.   62
    −19
    ——
     43

18.   92
    −34
    ——
     58

19.   957
    −468
    ——
    489

20.   831
    −255
    ——
    576

CHAPTER 1

◆ Subtract. pages 10–11

| 21. 8,009
   −5,824
   ───
    2,185 | 22.   300
   −172
   ───
    128 | 23. 50,007
   −33,423
   ─────
    16,584 | 24. 76,000
   − 9,562
   ─────
    66,438 |

◆ Round each number to the nearest ten. pages 12–13

25. 83 ___80___ 26. 18 ___20___

27. 145 ___150___ 28. 789 ___790___

◆ Round each number to the nearest hundred. pages 12–13

29. 107 ___100___ 30. 875 ___900___

31. 7,439 ___7,400___ 32. 48,552 ___48,600___

◆ Round each number to the nearest thousand. pages 12–13

33. 3,540 ___4,000___ 34. 5,299 ___5,000___

35. 91,328 ___91,000___ 36. 40,790 ___41,000___

◆ Ring the unit of measure you would use. pages 14–15

| 37. the length of a pencil
    (inch)   foot | 38. the height of a basketball net
    inch   (foot) |
| 39. the length of a newborn baby
    (inch)   foot | 40. the length of a bowling alley
    inch   (foot) |

Review

CHAPTER 1

♦ Round to the nearest hundred.
Estimate to solve. pages 16–17

41. Hotel America has 384 rooms.
    136 rooms are empty.
    About how many rooms are in use?

    $384 \longrightarrow 400$
    $-136 \longrightarrow -100$
    about **300** rooms

42. The auditorium has 575 seats.
    There are 428 students sitting in the auditorium.
    About how many seats are empty?

    $575 \longrightarrow 600$
    $-428 \longrightarrow -400$
    about **200** seats

43. Jessie drove 405 miles on Saturday.
    She drove 362 miles on Sunday.
    About how many miles in all did she drive?

    $405 \longrightarrow 400$
    $+362 \longrightarrow +400$
    about **800** miles

44. There were 245 pup tents in Parker Campground. There are 123 dome tents. About how many tents in all were at the campgrounds?

    $245 \longrightarrow 200$
    $+123 \longrightarrow +100$
    about **300** tents

45. Mr. Granowski sold 479 hot dogs in June. He sold 399 hot dogs in July. About how many hot dogs in all did Mr. Granowski sell?

    $479 \longrightarrow 500$
    $+399 \longrightarrow +400$
    about **900** hot dogs

46. Paula needed to sell 823 boxes of cookies to get a radio. She already sold 667 boxes of cookies. About how many more boxes of cookies did Paula need to sell?

    $823 \longrightarrow 800$
    $-667 \longrightarrow -700$
    about **100** cookies

Test — CHAPTER 1

Complete the expanded form of each number. pages 2–3

1. 73,458 = 70,000 + **3,000** + 400 + **50** + 8
2. 149,362 = 100,000 + **40,000** + 9,000 + **300** + 60 + **2**

Write the value of each underlined digit.

3. 17,<u>6</u>42 **600**
4. <u>4</u>3,951 **40,000**

Add. pages 4–7

5.	6.	7.	8.
78 +64 **142**	256 +479 **735**	5,356 +3,736 **9,092**	28,542 +17,539 **46,081**

Subtract. pages 8–11

9.	10.	11.	12.
56 −27 **29**	734 −388 **346**	6,000 −3,294 **2,706**	30,000 −15,672 **14,328**

Round each number to the nearest ten. pages 12–13

13. 25 **30**
14. 451 **450**

Round each number to the nearest thousand.

15. 5,830 **6,000**
16. 24,370 **24,000**

Ring the unit of measure you would use. pages 14–15

17. the height of a diving board	18. the length of one finger
inch (**foot**)	(**inch**) foot

21

Test

CHAPTER 1

◆ Round to the nearest hundred.
Estimate to solve.

19. Northside School has 598 students.
Southside School has 316 students.
About how many students are in both schools?

$$\begin{array}{r}598\\+316\end{array} \longrightarrow \begin{array}{r}600\\+300\end{array}$$
about **900** students

20. Tim has 659 tickets to sell for a school play. He sells 225 tickets. About how many more tickets must Tim sell?

$$\begin{array}{r}659\\-225\end{array} \longrightarrow \begin{array}{r}700\\-200\end{array}$$
about **500** tickets

21. Laura has driven 372 miles from home. She must drive 249 more miles to get to St. Louis. About how far is it from Laura's house to St. Louis?

$$\begin{array}{r}372\\+249\end{array} \longrightarrow \begin{array}{r}400\\+200\end{array}$$
about **600** miles

22. Marco has a book that has 481 pages. He has read 117 pages. About how many more pages does Marco have to read in his book?

$$\begin{array}{r}481\\-117\end{array} \longrightarrow \begin{array}{r}500\\-100\end{array}$$
about **400** pages

23. There are 263 seats on a train. The conductor counted 185 passengers on the train. About how many empty seats are on the train?

$$\begin{array}{r}263\\-185\end{array} \longrightarrow \begin{array}{r}300\\-200\end{array}$$
about **100** seats

24. Ann's Flower Shop ordered 297 roses on Wednesday. They ordered 174 roses on Friday. About how many roses did Ann's Flower Shop order both days?

$$\begin{array}{r}297\\+174\end{array} \longrightarrow \begin{array}{r}300\\+200\end{array}$$
about **500** roses

Before testing be sure students can read all the directions on the page. You can use the page references, printed only in the Teacher's Edition, to diagnose where students need help.

Name _____

CHAPTER 2

Discuss the photograph with students. Read aloud the sentences on the page. Have students discuss the questions and explore how the answers might be different if the girls must pay tax on video rentals. Discuss how multiplying can help the girls know how much money they will need. Have students make up other multiplication problems about the photograph. Then tell students that in this chapter they will learn more about multiplication.

Multiplying by 1- and 2-Digit Numbers

Kim and her friends took $12.00 to the video store. The videos cost $3.00 each to rent. Can the girls rent all 4 of the videos they are holding now? Do they have enough money with them to rent more than 4 videos?

23

Objective: Students will multiply a 2-digit number by a 1-digit number.
Instructional Model: Review multiplication facts with the blackline master, *Multiplication Facts,* on page T24. Read the problem in the Instructional Model with students. Remind students that they multiply to find the answer because the number of students on each bus is the same. Write the problem in a place-value chart (through 100's) on the chalkboard. Discuss the steps with students, beginning with the ones. Remind students that they need to regroup when any individual product is 10 or more. Stress the correct placement of digits in the product and in regrouping. Review the terms *factors* and *product.*
Guided Practice: Work through the problems with

1

Multiplying by 1-Digit Numbers

Each school bus carries 43 students to the soccer game. How many students are on 4 buses?

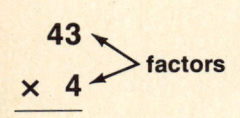

```
  43  ⟶
×  4  ⟶ factors
```

Multiply 43 by 4 to find the answer.

Step 1 Multiply the ones.

```
    1
   43
 ×  4
 ————
    2
```

4 × 3 ones = 12 ones
Regroup 12 ones as 1 ten 2 ones.
Write 2 in the ones' place.
Write 1 in the tens' column.

Step 2 Multiply the tens.

```
    1
   43
 ×  4
 ————
  172  ← product
```

4 × 4 tens = 16 tens
16 tens + 1 ten = 17 tens
17 tens = 1 hundred 7 tens
Write 7 in the tens' place.
Write 1 in the hundreds' place.
There are 172 students on 4 buses.

Guided Practice

◆ Multiply.

1.	2.	3.	4.	5.
¹53	43	36	20	78
× 4	× 2	× 3	× 9	× 7
212	86	108	180	546

students, reminding them to write the digits in the proper place when regrouping.
Practice: Have students complete the problems independently, stressing careful computation and correct regrouping. Evaluate student errors to determine where additional instruction is needed. Students who have difficulty keeping digits in the correct column should work the problems on lined paper turned so the holes are at the top.
Problem Solving: Work *Problem Solving* as a group. Remind students that looking at the digit in the tens place will tell them whether to round up or down to the nearest hundred. Have students answer the question independently. Then review answers with them.
Blackline Master: *Multiplication Facts*, page T24.

Practice

◆ Multiply.

1. 14 × 2 = 28	2. 22 × 6 = 132	3. 42 × 3 = 126	4. 46 × 7 = 322	5. 89 × 5 = 445
6. 21 × 9 = 189	7. 96 × 8 = 768	8. 73 × 4 = 292	9. 40 × 3 = 120	10. 56 × 6 = 336
11. 93 × 2 = 186	12. 68 × 9 = 612	13. 72 × 4 = 288	14. 67 × 8 = 536	15. 36 × 4 = 144
16. 53 × 7 = 371	17. 81 × 9 = 729	18. 48 × 6 = 288	19. 75 × 3 = 225	20. 26 × 8 = 208

Problem Solving

◆ Round to the nearest hundred.
Estimate to solve.

Chu read a book with 382 pages.
He read another book with 330 pages.
How many pages in all did Chu read?

382 → 400
+ 330 → + 300
about 700 pages

25

Objective: Students will multiply a 2-digit number by tens.
Instructional Model: Write the problem *4 × 23* on the chalkboard. Next, write the problem *40 × 23* on the chalkboard, and explain that when you multiply a 2-digit number by another 2-digit number, first you multiply the top factor by the ones of the bottom factor, then you multiply by the tens. Ask students for the product of *0 × 23*. Point out that because any number times *0* equals *0*, a zero is written in the ones' place. Writing a zero in this place shows that you have multiplied by *0 ones*. Explain that the next step is to multiply by the tens, and work through each step. Point out that the digit *2* (of the product *12 tens*) is written in the tens' place because you are multiplying by tens. Work other examples on the chalkboard in related groups, such

Multiplying by Tens

Multiply 23 by 40.

Step 1 Multiply 23 by 0 ones.

```
   23
 × 40
    0
```

0 × 23 = 0
Write 0 in the ones' place.

Step 2 Multiply 23 by 4 tens.

```
    1
   23
 × 40
  920
```

4 × 3 = 12
Write 2 in the tens' place.
Write 1 in the tens' column.
4 × 2 = 8, 8 + 1 = 9
Write 9 in the hundreds' place.

Guided Practice

◆ Multiply.

1. 46 × 20 = 920	2. 53 × 10 = 530	3. 28 × 30 = 840	4. 30 × 60 = 1,800	5. 67 × 70 = 4,690
6. 46 × 10 = 460	7. 34 × 10 = 340	8. 53 × 40 = 2,120	9. 15 × 50 = 750	10. 19 × 80 = 1,520

as *1 × 13* and *10 × 13*, so students will see that when multiplying by tens only a zero is written in the ones' place. Direct students to the steps in the lesson, reviewing the multiplication process.

Guided Practice: Work through the problems with students, reminding them to write a *0* in the ones' place. Point out the need for 2 zeros in the product of #4.

Practice: Have students complete the problems independently. Review all answers at the chalkboard.

Using Math: Have students solve the problem independently. For further practice, substitute "The baseball park has 20 rows of bleachers with 58 seats in each row. How many seats are there in the bleachers?" (1,160)

Practice

◆ Multiply.

1. 42 × 10 = 420	2. 35 × 20 = 700	3. 41 × 30 = 1,230	4. 56 × 40 = 2,240	5. 31 × 10 = 310
6. 63 × 30 = 1,890	7. 37 × 50 = 1,850	8. 54 × 70 = 3,780	9. 28 × 10 = 280	10. 49 × 20 = 980
11. 33 × 30 = 990	12. 64 × 40 = 2,560	13. 90 × 10 = 900	14. 67 × 50 = 3,350	15. 15 × 40 = 600
16. 90 × 60 = 5,400	17. 18 × 10 = 180	18. 25 × 60 = 1,500	19. 74 × 20 = 1,480	20. 59 × 70 = 4,130

Using Math

◆ The Willowbrook Bowling Center has 22 bowling lanes. Each lane has 10 pins. How many bowling pins are there in all?

There are ___220___ bowling pins in all.

Work here.

Objective: Students will multiply a 2-digit number by a factor from 11 through 19.

Instructional Model: Write *10 × 62* on the chalkboard and review multiplying by *10*. Next, write *15 × 62* on the chalkboard. Show students that *15 = 5 + 10*. Point out that when multiplying by *15* the problem can be rewritten as two multiplication problems (*5 × 62* and *10 × 62*). Remind students that the first step in multiplying by a 2-digit number is to multiply by the ones. Write and work the problem *5 × 62*. Remind students that the next step is to multiply by the tens. Work the problem *62 × 10*. Point out that since *5 + 10 = 15*, the product of *15 × 62* is found by adding the two products *310* and *620*. Direct students to the steps in the lesson, reviewing the multiplication and

3

Multiplying by 11 Through 19

Three steps are needed to multiply 62 by 15.

Step 1 Multiply 62 by 5 ones.

```
   1
   62
 ×  5
  310    5 × 62 = 310
```

Step 2 Multiply 62 by 1 ten.

```
   1
   62
 × 15
  310
  620   ← 10 × 62 = 620
```
Remember to write the 0 in the ones' place.

Step 3 Add.

```
   1
   62
 × 15
  310
 +620
  930
```

Guided Practice

◆ Multiply.

1. 26 × 12 = 52 + 260 = 312	2. 32 × 14 = 448	3. 52 × 11 = 572	4. 83 × 15 = 1,245	5. 45 × 18 = 810
6. 37 × 13 = 481	7. 44 × 16 = 704	8. 58 × 17 = 986	9. 61 × 19 = 1,159	10. 79 × 11 = 869

addition process. Stress remembering to write the *0* in the ones' place when multiplying by the tens.
Guided Practice: Work through the problems with students. To help students multiply the digits in the correct sequence, they may wish to first cover the tens' digit in the multiplier, then the ones' as they solve each problem.
Practice: Spot check students' work for the correct alignment of digits as they complete the problems independently. Review the partial products as well as the answers to help students determine if their errors were in multiplying or adding.
Using Math: Have volunteers work the problem on the chalkboard while others solve it on their own. Have students create and illustrate their own sports problems.

Practice

◆ Multiply.

1. 65 × 11 = 715	2. 39 × 14 = 546	3. 52 × 12 = 624	4. 27 × 13 = 351	5. 33 × 18 = 594
6. 84 × 15 = 1,260	7. 63 × 16 = 1,008	8. 92 × 12 = 1,104	9. 87 × 17 = 1,479	10. 44 × 13 = 572
11. 23 × 18 = 414	12. 66 × 19 = 1,254	13. 48 × 14 = 672	14. 73 × 17 = 1,241	15. 21 × 15 = 315

Using Math

◆ Bob runs in the marathon every year. He prepares by running 16 miles every week. How many miles does he run in 25 weeks?

Bob runs ___400___ miles in 25 weeks.

Work here.

Objective: Students will multiply a 2-digit number by a 2-digit number.
Instructional Model: Write the problem 42 × 68 on the chalkboard. Explain each step of the multiplication process as volunteers do the computation on the chalkboard. In Step 1, cover up the 4 so that students can focus on multiplying 2 ones × 68, emphasizing proper regrouping. In Step 2, remind students to cross out the regrouped 1 to avoid confusion when regrouping the second time. Cover up the 2 so that students can focus on 4 tens × 68. Stress putting the 0 in the ones' place. In Step 3, point out the importance of aligning the digits properly in order to add the products.

4

Multiplying by 2-Digit Numbers

Multiply 68 by 42.

Step 1 Multiply 68 by 2 ones.

```
   1
   6 8
 × 4 2
 ─────
 1 3 6
```

Step 2 Multiply 68 by 4 tens.

```
   3
   1̸
   6 8
 × 4 2
 ─────
 1 3 6
 2 7 2 0
```

Step 3 Add.

```
   3
   1̸
   6 8
 × 4 2
 ─────
   1 3 6
 +2 7 2 0
 ───────
 2,8 5 6
```

Guided Practice

◆ Multiply.

1. 3̸ 8 × 24 ──── 152 +760 ──── 912	2. 62 ×35 ──── 2,170	3. 45 ×32 ──── 1,440	4. 29 ×63 ──── 1,827	5. 41 ×87 ──── 3,567
6. 52 ×35 ──── 1,820	7. 67 ×42 ──── 2,814	8. 74 ×51 ──── 3,774	9. 37 ×73 ──── 2,701	10. 83 ×21 ──── 1,743

Guided Practice: Work through the problems with students. If needed, students may cover up the digit in the bottom factor not being used to help them multiply the digits in the correct sequence.

Practice: Have students complete the problems in the first row independently. Check for errors in basic facts, regrouping, placement of the 0, and alignment of digits. Then have students complete the remaining problems. Review all answers.

Using Math: Have students complete the problem independently. For further practice, vary the crop and the number of rows planted.

Practice Book E: Pages 9–10.

Practice

◆ Multiply.

1. 23 × 25 = **575**	2. 92 × 44 = **4,048**	3. 48 × 81 = **3,888**	4. 36 × 57 = **2,052**	5. 63 × 26 = **1,638**
6. 40 × 58 = **2,320**	7. 66 × 35 = **2,310**	8. 89 × 24 = **2,136**	9. 75 × 43 = **3,225**	10. 97 × 48 = **4,656**
11. 86 × 52 = **4,472**	12. 21 × 48 = **1,008**	13. 67 × 94 = **6,298**	14. 73 × 82 = **5,986**	15. 51 × 71 = **3,621**

Using Math

◆ There are 35 rows in the cornfield. Each row has 24 stalks of corn. How many stalks of corn are there in the field?

Work here.

There are ___**840**___ stalks of corn.

Objective: Students will multiply a 3-digit number by a number between 11 and 19.
Instructional Model: Write the problem *17 × 320* on the chalkboard. Explain to students that this problem is a combination of the two types of problems they have just done.

Have students explain each step of the multiplication process as volunteers do the computation on the chalkboard. Be sure to explain the need for 2 zeros in the second partial product.
Guided Practice: Work through the problems with

5

Multiplying 3-Digit Numbers

Multiply 320 by 17.

Step 1 Multiply 320 by 7 ones.

```
    1
  3 2 0
×   1 7
-------
  2 2 4 0
```

Step 2 Multiply 320 by 1 ten.

```
    1
  3 2 0
×   1 7
-------
  2 2 4 0
  3 2 0 0
```

Step 3 Add.

```
    1
  3 2 0
×   1 7
-------
  2 2 4 0
+ 3 2 0 0
-------
  5,4 4 0
```

Guided Practice

◆ Multiply.

1. $\begin{array}{r}12\\137\\\times13\\\hline 411\\+1370\\\hline 1,781\end{array}$	2. $\begin{array}{r}245\\\times15\\\hline 3,675\end{array}$	3. $\begin{array}{r}159\\\times11\\\hline 1,749\end{array}$	4. $\begin{array}{r}487\\\times16\\\hline 7,792\end{array}$	5. $\begin{array}{r}827\\\times19\\\hline 15,713\end{array}$
6. $\begin{array}{r}332\\\times14\\\hline 4,648\end{array}$	7. $\begin{array}{r}365\\\times12\\\hline 4,380\end{array}$	8. $\begin{array}{r}596\\\times18\\\hline 10,728\end{array}$	9. $\begin{array}{r}543\\\times17\\\hline 9,231\end{array}$	10. $\begin{array}{r}616\\\times13\\\hline 8,008\end{array}$

students emphasizing the regrouping process and the correct placement of the 0.
Practice: Spot check students' work for the correct second partial product and proper alignment of digits as they complete the problems independently. After reviewing all answers, have students put selected problems on the chalkboard and explain them.
Using Math: Have students work in pairs to solve the problem.

Practice

◆ Multiply.

1. 276 × 13 3,588	2. 482 × 11 5,302	3. 573 × 12 6,876	4. 842 × 14 11,788	5. 398 × 16 6,368
6. 646 × 18 11,628	7. 219 × 15 3,285	8. 697 × 12 8,364	9. 893 × 17 15,181	10. 159 × 19 3,021
11. 258 × 11 2,838	12. 371 × 15 5,565	13. 816 × 16 13,056	14. 945 × 12 11,340	15. 725 × 15 10,875

Using Math

◆ The Lincoln Theater has 368 seats. The play is given 16 times each month. How many people can see the play each month if the theater is full every time?

Work here.

___5,888___ people can see the play each month.

33

Objective: Students will multiply a 3-digit number by a 2-digit number.
Instructional Model: Review the 3 steps in the Instructional Model with students. Provide several problems of this type on the chalkboard. Have students explain each step of the multiplication process as volunteers work the problems on the chalkboard. Emphasize the importance of accurate computation, correct regrouping, the placement of 0 in the ones' place, and the correct alignment of digits.
Guided Practice: Work through the problems with

◆ 6

Multiplying 3-Digit Numbers

Multiply 592 by 86.

Step 1 Multiply 592 by 6 ones.

```
   5 1
   5 9 2
 ×    8 6
  3 5 5 2
```

Step 2 Multiply 592 by 8 tens.

```
   7 1
   5̸ 1̸
   5 9 2
 ×    8 6
   3 5 5 2
 4 7 3 6 0
```

Step 3 Add.

```
   7 1
   8̸ 1̸
   5 9 2
 ×    8 6
   3 5 5 2
+4 7 3 6 0
 5 0,9 1 2
```

Guided Practice

◆ Multiply.

1. 235 × 25 = 1175 + 4700 = **5,875**	2. 313 × 37 = **11,581**	3. 468 × 42 = **19,656**	4. 639 × 47 = **30,033**	5. 726 × 93 = **67,518**
6. 547 × 26 = **14,222**	7. 271 × 36 = **9,756**	8. 102 × 58 = **5,916**	9. 824 × 81 = **66,744**	10. 328 × 75 = **24,600**

34

students.
Practice: Have students complete the problems in the first row independently. Review the partial products as well as the answers to evaluate where students may need additional help. Continue this procedure for the next two rows.

Using Math: Have volunteers work the problem on the chalkboard while the others solve it on their own. For further practice, vary the number of milk cartons and days.
Practice Book E: Pages 11–14.

Practice

◆ Multiply.

1. 163 × 27 = 4,401	2. 422 × 78 = 32,916	3. 731 × 46 = 33,626	4. 250 × 35 = 8,750	5. 584 × 11 = 6,424
6. 806 × 67 = 54,002	7. 399 × 52 = 20,748	8. 647 × 47 = 30,409	9. 919 × 96 = 88,224	10. 723 × 84 = 60,732
11. 535 × 60 = 32,100	12. 281 × 72 = 20,232	13. 143 × 59 = 8,437	14. 428 × 33 = 14,124	15. 867 × 24 = 20,808

Using Math

◆ Mrs. Troy orders milk for the school cafeteria. She needs 284 cartons for each day. How many cartons of milk should she order for 85 days?

Work here.

She should order __24,140__ cartons of milk.

Objective: Students decide whether an object is measured in centimeters or meters.
Instructional Model: Review inches and feet as two units used to measure length. Explain that length and height can also be measured in *metric* units. Read the Instructional Model with students. Distribute copies of the centimeter ruler from the blackline master, *Measuring Inches and Centimeters,* on page T29. Also provide meter sticks for students. Show students that 100 centimeters = 1 meter by looking at the centimeters marked off on a meter stick. Have students measure objects in centimeters or meters.

7

Centimeters and Meters

You learned that length and height can be measured in inches and feet. Now you will learn another way to measure length and height. In this lesson you will learn about **metric** measurement. **Centimeters** are used to measure short things. **Meters** are used to measure longer things.

A crayon is about 7 centimeters long.

A door is about 2 meters tall.

100 centimeters = 1 meter

Guided Practice

◆ Ring the unit of measure you would use.

1. the length of a tennis court centimeter (meter)	2. the length of a sheet of paper (centimeter) meter
3. the length of a pencil (centimeter) meter	4. the length of your classroom centimeter (meter)
5. the height of the ceiling centimeter (meter)	6. the length of a grasshopper (centimeter) meter

Guided Practice: Work the exercises with students. Remind them that long objects are measured in meters and short objects are measured in centimeters.
Practice: Have students complete the exercises independently.
Using Math: Discuss the problem with students. Explain why "meters" is a more logical answer. Provide students with practice measuring objects in centimeters and meters as you proceed through the next chapter.
Blackline Master: *Measuring Inches and Centimeters,* page T29.

Practice

◆ Ring the unit of measure you would use.

1. the length of a firetruck centimeter (meter)	2. the length of a lizard (centimeter) meter
3. the length of a school hallway centimeter (meter)	4. the height of a sparrow (centimeter) meter
5. the height of a giraffe centimeter (meter)	6. the height of a flagpole centimeter (meter)
7. the length of one finger (centimeter) meter	8. the length of your shoe (centimeter) meter
9. the length of a caterpillar (centimeter) meter	10. the length of a soccer field centimeter (meter)

Using Math

◆ Lamont's father is a truck driver. His new truck is an 18-wheeler. Lamont wants to tell his friends about the truck. He knows they will want to know how big it is. So Lamont decides to measure the truck's length. But he doesn't know whether to measure the length in centimeters or meters. Which should Lamont use?

Lamont should measure the length of the truck in ____**meters**____.

Objective: Students will estimate to solve multiplication problems by rounding to the nearest hundred.
Instructional Model: Review rounding numbers with students. Draw a number line on the chalkboard and number it by tens from 600 to 700. Write the number 678 and review the steps for rounding a number to the nearest hundred. Ask volunteers to complete the steps by underlining the digit in the hundreds' place, circling the digit to the right, and deciding whether to round up or down. Then read through the instructional model with students. Make sure they can find the nearest hundred and use that information to solve the problem given. Remind students that numbers less than 10 do not need to be rounded.
Guided Practice: Work through *Guided Practice* with

Problem Solving 8

Estimation

Ms. Morales is printing 3 play tickets for every student.

There are 484 students.

About how many tickets will Ms. Morales print?

> The word **about** means an exact answer is not needed.
> You can estimate the answer.

Round to the nearest hundred.

Step 1	Underline the place you are rounding to.	4̲ 8 4
Step 2	Circle the next digit to the right.	4̲ ⑧ 4
Step 3	If the circled digit is less than 5, round down.	
	If the circled digit is 5 or more, round up.	

$$\begin{array}{r} 4\underline{8}4 \\ \times\ 3 \end{array} \longrightarrow \begin{array}{r} 500 \\ \times\ 3 \end{array} \text{ round up}$$

Do not round numbers less than 10.

Ms. Morales will print about 1,500 tickets.

Guided Practice

◆ Round to the nearest hundred.
Estimate to solve.

1. Bill has 210 customers on his paper route.
   He delivers papers 5 days each week.
   About how many papers does Bill deliver each week?

   $$\begin{array}{r} 210 \\ \times\ 5 \end{array} \longrightarrow \begin{array}{r} 200 \\ \times\ \ \ 5 \end{array}$$ about 1,000 papers

2. Maria runs 4 miles every day.
   There are 365 days in a year.
   About how many miles does Maria run in a year?

   $$\begin{array}{r} 365 \\ \times\ 4 \end{array} \longrightarrow \begin{array}{r} 400 \\ \times\ \ \ 4 \end{array}$$ about 1,600 miles

the students, referring to the three steps as needed. Remind students that answers will be in hundreds. Ask students to explain how they found the answers. Review their answers with them.
Practice: Read the first problem with students and make sure they understand how to round 682 to the nearest hundred. Encourage students to complete the problems independently. Then review their answers with them.
Practice Book E: Pages 13–14.

Practice

◆ Round to the nearest hundred.
Estimate to solve.

1. The Grand Theater seats 682 people.
   All seats were filled for a show
   that ran 7 nights.
   About how many people saw the show?

   682 → 700
   × 7 → × 7
   about **4,900** people

2. Circle City Movie House seats 314 people.
   All seats were filled for 3 shows
   on Saturday. About how many people
   saw the show Saturday?

   314 → 300
   × 3 → × 3
   about **900** people

3. 531 people visit the zoo
   each day during the summer.
   The zoo is open 6 days a week. About how
   many people visit the zoo each week?

   531 → 500
   × 6 → × 6
   about **3,000** people

4. At the fair, 822 people went through
   each gate every day. There are 4 gates.
   About how many people
   went to the fair each day?

   822 → 800
   × 4 → × 4
   about **3,200** people

5. Erika sleeps 8 hours every night.
   There are 365 days in one year.
   About how many hours
   does Erika sleep in one year?

   365 → 400
   × 8 → × 8
   about **3,200** hours

6. Lorenzo does 101 sit-ups every day.
   There are 7 days in one week. About how
   many sit-ups does Lorenzo do in one week?

   101 → 100
   × 7 → × 7
   about **700** sit-ups

Review

◆ Multiply.

pages 24–25

1. 17 × 5 = 85
2. 36 × 8 = 288
3. 72 × 6 = 432
4. 45 × 7 = 315
5. 64 × 5 = 320

pages 26–27

6. 27 × 10 = 270
7. 56 × 20 = 1,120
8. 73 × 30 = 2,190
9. 41 × 40 = 1,640
10. 53 × 50 = 2,650

pages 28–29

11. 42 × 12 = 504
12. 81 × 16 = 1,296
13. 57 × 14 = 798
14. 69 × 18 = 1,242
15. 37 × 13 = 481

pages 30–31

16. 28 × 22 = 616
17. 76 × 31 = 2,356
18. 84 × 62 = 5,208
19. 59 × 43 = 2,537
20. 74 × 51 = 3,774

page numbers to diagnose where their difficulties are occurring. By looking back at the pages, you can identify the skills that have not been mastered. It is important that you reteach these skills to students before allowing them to move ahead. After you have diagnosed student deficiencies and have retaught those skills, have students complete the *Extra Practice* for Chapter 2 on page 166.

CHAPTER 2

◆ Multiply.

pages 32-33 21. 313 × 11 —— 3,443	22. 472 × 13 —— 6,136	23. 262 × 12 —— 3,144	24. 189 × 15 —— 2,835	25. 332 × 14 —— 4,648
pages 34-35 26. 333 × 24 —— 7,992	27. 419 × 42 —— 17,598	28. 515 × 63 —— 32,445	29. 729 × 38 —— 27,702	30. 547 × 26 —— 14,222

◆ Ring the unit of measure you would use.   pages 36–37

31. the length of a rubber band (centimeter) meter	32. the height of a ladder centimeter (meter)
33. the length of a racetrack centimeter (meter)	34. the length of a shoestring (centimeter) meter
35. the length of a worm (centimeter) meter	36. the length of a volleyball net centimeter (meter)

41

Review

CHAPTER 2

◆ Round to the nearest hundred.
Estimate to solve. pages 38–39

37. Gail sold 127 drinks at the concession stand each hour. She worked 3 hours. About how many drinks did Gail sell?

$\begin{array}{r}127\\\times\ 3\\\hline\end{array}$ ⟶ $\begin{array}{r}100\\\times\ 3\\\hline\end{array}$
about **300** drinks

38. Alice flew 723 miles to visit her grandmother. Alice made this trip 4 times last year. About how many miles did Alice fly last year?

$\begin{array}{r}723\\\times\ 4\\\hline\end{array}$ ⟶ $\begin{array}{r}700\\\times\ 4\\\hline\end{array}$
about **2,800** miles

39. A music book has 235 pages. Bill makes 6 copies of the book. About how many pages did Bill copy?

$\begin{array}{r}235\\\times\ 6\\\hline\end{array}$ ⟶ $\begin{array}{r}200\\\times\ 6\\\hline\end{array}$
about **1,200** pages

40. Chan's class needs 468 bows to decorate the auditorium. Each bow takes 3 yards of ribbon. About how much ribbon in all does Chan need?

$\begin{array}{r}468\\\times\ 3\\\hline\end{array}$ ⟶ $\begin{array}{r}500\\\times\ 3\\\hline\end{array}$
about **1,500** yards

41. There are 511 cookies in a case of cookies. Mrs. Cruz ordered 8 cases of cookies. About how many cookies did Mrs. Cruz order?

$\begin{array}{r}511\\\times\ 8\\\hline\end{array}$ ⟶ $\begin{array}{r}500\\\times\ 8\\\hline\end{array}$
about **4,000** cookies

42. There are 324 seats in the movie theater. The theater shows a movie 5 times in one day. About how many people can see the movie in one day?

$\begin{array}{r}324\\\times\ 5\\\hline\end{array}$ ⟶ $\begin{array}{r}300\\\times\ 5\\\hline\end{array}$
about **1,500** people

Chapter Test: Before testing be sure students can read all the directions on the page. It may be necessary to divide the test into sections that can be completed at different times. You may find that providing a marker helps them keep their place. You can use the page references, printed only in the Teacher's Edition, to diagnose where students need help. It is important to reteach skills that have not been mastered before proceeding to the next chapter. After reteaching the skills students did not master on the *Chapter Test,* have students complete Chapter 2 Checkup, the blackline master on page T16.

Blackline Master: *Chapter 2 Checkup,* page T16.

Test   CHAPTER 2

◆ Multiply.

pages 24–27				
1. 43 × 7 = **301**	2. 68 × 5 = **340**	3. 36 × 10 = **360**	4. 82 × 40 = **3,280**	5. 15 × 50 = **750**

pages 28–31				
6. 46 × 13 = **598**	7. 79 × 18 = **1,422**	8. 44 × 16 = **704**	9. 24 × 23 = **552**	10. 63 × 35 = **2,205**

pages 32–35				
11. 245 × 12 = **2,940**	12. 463 × 15 = **6,945**	13. 271 × 25 = **6,775**	14. 567 × 48 = **27,216**	15. 102 × 58 = **5,916**

◆ Ring the unit of measure you would use.   pages 36–37

16. the height of a telephone pole

   centimeter   (meter)

17. the height of a blade of grass

   (centimeter)   meter

43

Test

CHAPTER 2

◆ Round to the nearest hundred.
Estimate to solve. pages 38–39

18. A hospital has 241 nurses on staff for each work shift. There are 3 shifts each day. About how many nurses work in one day?

   241 → 200
   × 3 → × 3
   about **600** nurses

19. A train has 563 seats. The train makes 8 trips each day. About how many people can ride the train each day?

   563 → 600
   × 8 → × 8
   about **4,800** people

20. There are 387 pencils in a box. There are 5 boxes of pencils on a shelf. About how many pencils are on the shelf?

   387 → 400
   × 5 → × 5
   about **2,000** pencils

21. Jaime sold 659 candy bars. He earned 3 points for each candy bar he sold. About how many points did Jaime earn?

   659 → 700
   × 3 → × 3
   about **2,100** points

22. 217 people shop in Galaxy Food Store each day. The store is open 7 days a week. About how many people shop at the store each week?

   217 → 200
   × 7 → × 7
   about **1,400** people

23. Mrs. Baker needs to sew 150 robes for the school chorus. Each robe takes 2 yards of fabric. About how many yards of fabric in all does Mrs. Baker need?

   150 → 200
   × 2 → × 2
   about **400** yards

Name _____

CHAPTER 3

Discuss the photograph with students. Read aloud the sentences on the page. Help students use multiplication, division, and logic to answer the question. You may wish to have students draw 30 dancers, circle groups of 3, and tell the number of groups they found in 30. Have students make up other examples of situations that involve multiplication and division. Explain to students that they will learn more about division in this chapter.

Dividing with 1- and 2-Digit Divisors

Tamara's dance troup had a talent show in the city park. There were 3 dancers in each group. There were 30 dancers in the show, and everyone danced only once. Could Tamara's group have been the twelfth group to perform?

45

Objective: Students will divide a 2-digit number by a 1-digit number, writing a remainder with the quotient.
Instructional Model: Review division facts with the blackline master, *Division Facts,* on page T25. Then ask students how they would divide 12 paper clips into groups of 3. Select a volunteer to solve the problem using paperclips. Next, direct students' attention to the illustration at the top of the page as you read the text aloud. In Step 1, have students count aloud by threes to find the closest multiple that is less than 13. Emphasize the placement of the quotient *4* over *3*. In Step 2, stress the importance of aligning the digits properly under the dividend when multiplying. In Step 3, point out that the remainder must always be less than the divisor. Show students how to check their answers by multiplying the quotient by the

1

Division with Remainders

When you divide a group of 13 paper clips into groups of 3, there is 1 paper clip left over. The amount left over is called the **remainder**.

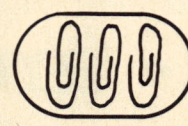

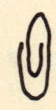

← 4 groups of 3 →   1 left over

Step 1 **Divide** 13 by 3.	Step 2 **Multiply** 4 by 3.	Step 3 **Subtract** 12 from 13.
3)13 There are 4 groups of 3 in 13. 4 3)13	4 × 3 = 12 Write the 12 under the 13. 4 3)13 12	13 − 12 = 1 4 3)13 −12 1

The remainder is written with the quotient.
The **divisor** is 3. The **dividend** is 13.

    4 R1
3)13   or   13 ÷ 3 = 4 R1
−12
  1

Guided Practice

◆ Divide.

| 1.   5 R1
     4)21
     −20
       1 | 2.   6 R1
     3)19 | 3.   6 R1
     2)13 | 4.   9 R1
     6)55 |

divisor, then adding the remainder to obtain the dividend. Review the terms *quotient, remainder, divisor,* and *dividend.*
Guided Practice: Work through the problems with students, reminding them of the correct sequence of steps. Students may wish to draw vertical lines to help them align the digits properly in the quotient and when multiplying.

Practice: Have students complete the problems independently. Spot check students' work for correct alignment of the digits and make sure the remainders are less than the divisor.
Using Math: Set up and solve the problem as a group activity.
Blackline Master: *Division Facts,* page T25.

Practice

◆ Divide.

1. 8)33̄ **4 R1**	2. 2)15̄ **7 R1**	3. 9)55̄ **6 R1**	4. 6)25̄ **4 R1**
5. 8)49̄ **6 R1**	6. 3)28̄ **9 R1**	7. 6)13̄ **2 R1**	8. 2)17̄ **8 R1**
9. 5)26̄ **5 R1**	10. 4)29̄ **7 R1**	11. 9)46̄ **5 R1**	12. 7)43̄ **6 R1**

Using Math

◆ John wants to give away his 50 baseball cards to 7 friends.
He wants to give each friend the same number of cards.
How many cards should he give to each friend?

John should give ___**7**___ cards to each friend.

How many cards will he have left?

He will have ___**1**___ card left.

Work here.

47

Objective: Students will divide 2-digit numbers by 1-digit numbers.

Instructional Model: Write the problem 8)83 on the chalkboard. Discuss the division steps as you work through the problem with students. In Step 1, explain that we write the *1* in the tens' place because we are dividing *8 tens* by 8. Stress the proper placement of the *8* when multiplying *8* by *1 ten*. In Step 2, explain that we bring down the *3 ones* to begin the division process again. Stress the correct placement of the *0* when multiplying *8* by *0 ones*. Have students check the remainder to be sure it is less than the divisor. Finally, review the procedure for checking division.

2

2-Digit Quotients

Divide 83 by 8.   8)83

Step 1 Divide the tens.

Divide 8 ÷ 8
   Write 1 in the tens' place.
Multiply 1 × 8
Subtract 8 − 8

```
   1
8)83
  -8
   0
```

Step 2 Divide the ones.

Bring down the 3 ones.
Divide 3 ÷ 8
   Can you divide 3 by 8? No.
   Write 0 in the ones' place.
Multiply 0 × 8
Subtract 3 − 0
   Write the remainder
   with the quotient.

```
   10 R3
8)83
  -8↓
   03
   -0
    3
```

Guided Practice

◆ Divide.

1.
```
   20 R1
3)61
  -6
   01
   -0
    1
```

2.
```
   11
4)44
```

3.
```
   10 R5
9)95
```

4.
```
   22 R1
4)89
```

48

Guided Practice: Work through the problems with students. Stress the correct alignment of digits in the quotient and when multiplying.

Practice: Tell students that not all problems have remainders. Spot check students' work for correct alignment of digits and for two digits in the quotient as they complete the problems independently. After reviewing the answers, have students put selected problems on the chalkboard and show the steps used to complete them.

Using Math: Have volunteers work the problem on the chalkboard while the others solve it on their own. Vary the cost and number of payments for further practice.

Practice

◆ Divide.

1. 10 R1 4)41	2. 11 R3 6)69	3. 10 R2 5)52	4. 22 3)66
5. 11 R2 7)79	6. 10 R6 9)96	7. 22 R2 3)68	8. 12 2)24
9. 10 R7 8)87	10. 42 R1 2)85	11. 20 R3 4)83	12. 34 R1 2)69

Using Math

◆ Sam had an accident. His baseball broke a window. It will cost $68 to fix. If he makes one payment a month for 6 months, how much will each payment be?

Each payment will be ___$11___.

How much will he have left to pay?

He will have ___$2___ left to pay.

Work here.

49

Objective: Students will divide 2-digit numbers by 1-digit numbers.

Instructional Model: Write the problem 3)77 on the chalkboard. Remind students that we first divide the tens. Introduce *compare* as a way to check the first division. Point out that there is a remainder "left over" from dividing the tens. Explain that we *compare* to be sure this remainder is less than the divisor. Since 1 < 3, we may continue with Step 2. Explain that if the remainder is larger than the divisor, we must use a larger number in the quotient. In Step 2, remind students that we bring down the 7 *ones*. Point out that the new dividend is *17*. Stress the correct placement of the digits as you complete the problem on the

3

2-Digit Quotients

Divide 77 by 3.   3)77

Step 1 Divide the tens.	Step 2 Divide the ones.
Divide 7 ÷ 3 **Multiply** 2 × 3 **Subtract** 7 − 6 **Compare** Is 1 less than 3? Yes. Go on to Step 2.	**Bring down** the 7. **Divide** 17 ÷ 3 **Multiply** 5 × 3 **Subtract** 17 − 15 Write the remainder with the quotient.

$$\begin{array}{r} 2 \\ 3\overline{)77} \\ -6 \\ \hline 1 \end{array} \qquad \begin{array}{r} 25\ R2 \\ 3\overline{)77} \\ -6 \\ \hline 17 \\ -15 \\ \hline 2 \end{array}$$

Guided Practice

◆ Divide.

1. $\begin{array}{r} 23\ R1 \\ 4\overline{)93} \\ -8 \\ \hline 13 \\ -12 \\ \hline 1 \end{array}$	2. **15 R4** 6)94	3. **39** 2)78	4. **12 R2** 5)62
5. **12 R3** 8)99	6. **14** 4)56	7. **12 R1** 7)85	8. **26** 3)78

chalkboard. Review the procedure for checking division problems.
Guided Practice: Work through the problems with students. Remind them to compare the remainder with the divisor after dividing the tens and to bring down the ones to form a new dividend.
Practice: Have students complete the problems independently, stressing careful computation and proper alignment of digits. Evaluate student errors to determine whether additional instruction is needed.
Using Math: Tell students to solve the problem independently. Have students create their own division problems to exchange with a partner to solve and check.

Practice

◆ Divide.

1. 4)62 **15 R2**	2. 3)89 **29 R2**	3. 5)88 **17 R3**	4. 7)98 **14**
5. 8)99 **12 R3**	6. 6)95 **15 R5**	7. 5)83 **16 R3**	8. 2)38 **19**
9. 6)79 **13 R1**	10. 4)98 **24 R2**	11. 3)80 **26 R2**	12. 2)91 **45 R1**

Using Math

◆ Lynn bought 4 stamps. She paid the clerk with 90¢. She received 2¢ change. How much did each stamp cost?

Work here.

Each stamp cost __**22**__ ¢.

51

Objective: Students will divide 3-digit numbers by 1-digit numbers.

Instructional Model: Write the number *265* in a place-value chart on the chalkboard. Remind students that since *1 hundred = 10 tens,* we can think of *2 hundreds 6 tens* as *26 tens.* Continue this exercise practicing regrouping with other 3-digit numbers. Direct students' attention to the problem 3)179 on the page. Explain to students that because we cannot divide *1* by *3,* we think of *1 hundred 7 tens* as *17 tens.* Review Step 1. Point out that the *5* is written in the tens' place because we divide *17 tens* by *3.* Remind students that we compare the remainder with the divisor after dividing the tens. Since *2 < 3,* we can proceed to Step 2. Stress the correct alignment of the

4

2-Digit Quotients

Divide 179 by 3.   3)179   Can you divide 1 by 3? No.
Think   179 = 1 hundred 7 tens 9 ones
         1 hundred 7 tens = 17 tens
         Can you divide 17 tens by 3? Yes.

Step 1 Divide the tens.

Divide 17 tens by 3.
Remember to write the 5 over the 7. This is the tens' place.
Multiply 5 × 3
Subtract 17 − 15
Compare Is 2 less than 3? Yes. Go on to Step 2.

```
   5
3)179
 -15
   2
```

Step 2 Divide the ones.

Bring down the 9.
Divide 29 ÷ 3
Multiply 9 × 3
Subtract 29 − 27
Write the remainder with the quotient.

```
  59 R2
3)179
 -15
   29
  -27
    2
```

Guided Practice

◆ Divide.

1.
```
   55 R3
7)388
 -35
   38
  -35
    3
```

2.
```
  68 R2
6)410
```

3.
```
   63
9)567
```

4.
```
  59 R6
8)478
```

52

digits as a volunteer works the problem on the chalkboard.
Guided Practice: Work through the problems with students, stressing the correct placement of the first digit in the quotient. Remind students to compare the remainder with the divisor after dividing the tens and ones.
Practice: Remind students that not all the problems have remainders. Spot check students' work as they complete the problems independently.
Using Math: Have students solve the problem by themselves. Substitute $135 \div 3 = 45$ with $185 \div 5 = 37$ and $168 \div 6 = 28$ for further practice.
Practice Book E: Pages 15–16.

Practice

◆ Divide.

1. 35 R2 6)212	2. 42 R2 3)128	3. 29 R6 8)238	4. 67 R3 7)472
5. 48 R3 9)435	6. 83 R1 2)167	7. 66 R3 6)399	8. 79 5)395
9. 64 R3 9)579	10. 81 R7 8)655	11. 56 R3 7)395	12. 84 R3 4)339

Using Math

◆ Hank has 135 shells. He divided them evenly and put them in 3 jars. How many shells did he put in each jar?

He put __45__ shells in each jar.

Work here.

53

Objective: Students will divide 2- and 3-digit numbers by a multiple of 10.
Instructional Model: Write the problem 10)47 on the chalkboard. Explain that with divisors of 10 or more, students must estimate to find the quotient. Ask students if they can divide 4 by 10; then 47 by 10. Remind students that because 47 = 4 tens 7 ones and 10 = 1 ten, they can divide 4 by 1 to estimate the number of groups of 10 in 47.

Emphasize that the 4 is written over the ones' place because students are dividing 47 ones by 10 ones. Remind students to compare the remainder with the divisor. Explain that if the remainder is larger than the divisor, then the estimate was too low. Have students practice dividing other 2-digit numbers by 10. Then write the problem 20)138 on the chalkboard. First ask students where to place the digit in the quotient. Have students estimate the answer by dividing

5

Dividing by Tens

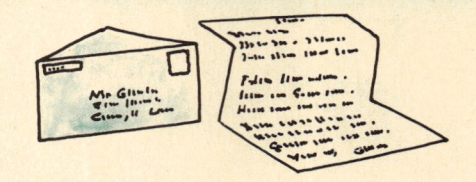

Divide 138 by 20.   20)138
  Can you divide 1 by 20? No.
  Can you divide 13 by 20? No.
  Can you divide 138 by 20?
  Think 138 = **13** tens 8 ones
         20 = **2** tens
         13 ÷ 2

Now divide.   6 R18
Divide 138 ÷ 20   20)138
  Write the 6 over the 8.   − 120
  This is the ones' place.   18
Multiply 6 × 20
Subtract 138 − 120
Compare Is 18 less than 20? Yes.
  Write the remainder with the quotient.

Guided Practice

◆ Divide.

1. 3 R6 30)96 −90 6	2. 2 40)80	3. 8 R8 70)568	4. 5 R27 50)277
5. 2 R2 20)42	6. 3 R5 10)35	7. 9 R15 80)735	8. 4 60)240

54

13 by 2. Remind students to place the *6* over the ones' place because they are dividing *138 ones* by *20 ones.* Stress the importance of comparing the remainder to the divisor in order to confirm the estimate.
Guided Practice: Work through the problems with students, emphasizing the estimating process. Make sure students place the digit in the quotient correctly. Remind students to compare the remainder with the divisor.

Practice: Spot check students' work as they complete the problems independently. Have students check each other's work by multiplying and adding.
Problem Solving: Work *Problem Solving* as a group. Remind students that numbers less than 10 do not need to be rounded. You may want students to work in pairs or small groups. Then review answer with students.

Practice

◆ Divide.

1. $10\overline{)90}$ = 9	2. $40\overline{)85}$ = 2 R5	3. $30\overline{)63}$ = 2 R3	4. $20\overline{)88}$ = 4 R8
5. $50\overline{)59}$ = 1 R9	6. $10\overline{)23}$ = 2 R3	7. $60\overline{)245}$ = 4 R5	8. $70\overline{)560}$ = 8
9. $30\overline{)251}$ = 8 R11	10. $80\overline{)415}$ = 5 R15	11. $90\overline{)630}$ = 7	12. $80\overline{)329}$ = 4 R9

Problem Solving

◆ Round to the nearest hundred. Estimate to solve.

The bus company has 257 buses. Each bus makes 8 trips a day. About how many trips in all do the buses make each day?

$$257 \rightarrow 300$$
$$\times\ 8\ \rightarrow\ \times\ 8$$

about **2,400** trips

55

Objective: Students will divide 2- and 3-digit numbers by rounding the 2-digit divisor to the nearest ten.
Instructional Model: Review rounding by drawing a number line on the chalkboard. Present various numbers to round to the nearest ten. Explain to students that rounding the divisor to the nearest ten will help them find the first digit of the quotient more easily. Write the problem 18)84 on the chalkboard. Point out that if 18 is rounded up to 20, the basic fact, 8 ÷ 2, can be used. Stress that the quotient 4 is written over the 4 in the dividend because 84 ones are being divided by 20 ones. Point out that although the divisor is rounded to 20, the actual divisor, 18, is used in the multiplication step. Complete the problem, showing the quotient as 4 R12. Next, write the problem from the text,

6

2-Digit Divisors

To divide by a 2-digit divisor, first **round the divisor up or down to the nearest ten**. This helps you find the quotient easier.

Divide 841 by 18.   18)841
To divide 841 by 18, first round 18 up to 20.
Can you divide 8 by 20? No.
Can you divide 84 by 20? Yes.
Now divide.

Step 1 Divide the tens.		Step 2 Divide the ones.	
Divide 84 ÷ 18	4 18)841 −72 12	**Bring down** the 1. **Divide** 121 ÷ 18	46 R13 18)841 −72 121 −108 13
Think 84 ÷ 20		Think 121 ÷ 20	
Try 4.		Try 6.	
Write the 4 over the 4.			
Multiply 4 × 18		**Multiply** 6 × 18	
Subtract 84 − 72		**Subtract** 121 − 108	
Compare Is 12 less than 18? Yes.		**Compare** Is 13 less than 18? Yes.	
Go on to Step 2.		Write the remainder with the quotient.	

Guided Practice

◆ Divide.

1. 2 R3 31)65 −62 3	2. 3 R10 29)97	3. 25 R16 28)716	4. 15 R5 52)785

18)841, on the chalkboard. Begin by rounding 18 up to 20, and continue working through the steps. Select a volunteer to check the division problem by multiplying and adding.

Guided Practice: *Numbers in this lesson have been controlled to avoid over- or under-estimating the quotient when rounding.* Work through the problems with students. Help students round the divisor and estimate correctly. Students having difficulty in the multiplication step with regrouping should use separate paper to do the computation.

Practice: Have students complete the problems independently.

Using Math: Before students solve the problem, explain that an additional bus will be needed if there is a remainder.

Practice Book E: Pages 17–18.

Practice

◆ Divide.

1. 21)86 **4 R2**	2. 42)91 **2 R7**	3. 27)63 **2 R9**	4. 23)92 **4**
5. 19)75 **3 R18**	6. 36)85 **2 R13**	7. 72)792 **11**	8. 23)969 **42 R3**
9. 32)425 **13 R9**	10. 42)891 **21 R9**	11. 17)421 **24 R13**	12. 19)653 **34 R7**

Using Math

◆ Union Hill School's basketball team is in the play-offs. There are 496 people who want to go to the game. A bus holds 44 people. How many buses are needed to take all the people to the game?

Work here.

___12___ buses are needed.

57

Objective: Students will show equivalencies between cups, pints, and quarts.
Instructional Model: Explain to students that we can measure liquids. Ask students to suggest activities in which they would need to measure liquids, for example, baking a cake, making lemonade. Show students a one-cup measure, one-pint measure, and one-quart measure. Have them pour water from one container to another to discover equivalents. Read with students the text on the page. Review the new vocabulary words **capacity, cup, pint,** and **quart.**

7

Cups, Pints, and Quarts

Capacity tells how much a container holds. Liquid capacity is measured using **cups**, **pints**, or **quarts**.

1 cup

1 pint = 2 cups

1 quart = 2 pints = 4 cups

Guided Practice

◆ Mark an X on the containers that equal the first one in the row.

1.	1 quart	✗ pint ✗ pint pint pint
2.	1 pint	✗ cup ✗ cup cup cup cup
3.	4 cups	✗ pint ✗ pint pint pint
4.	1 quart	✗ cup ✗ cup ✗ cup ✗ cup

58

Guided Practice: Work the exercises with students. Check each answer by having students measure liquids with the cup, pint, and quart measures.

Practice: Have students complete the exercises independently.

Using Math: Have students work the problem independently. To help students become proficient in measurement using cups, pints, and quarts, provide additional experiences in measuring liquids as you proceed through the next chapter.

Practice

◆ Mark an X on the containers that equal the first one in the row.

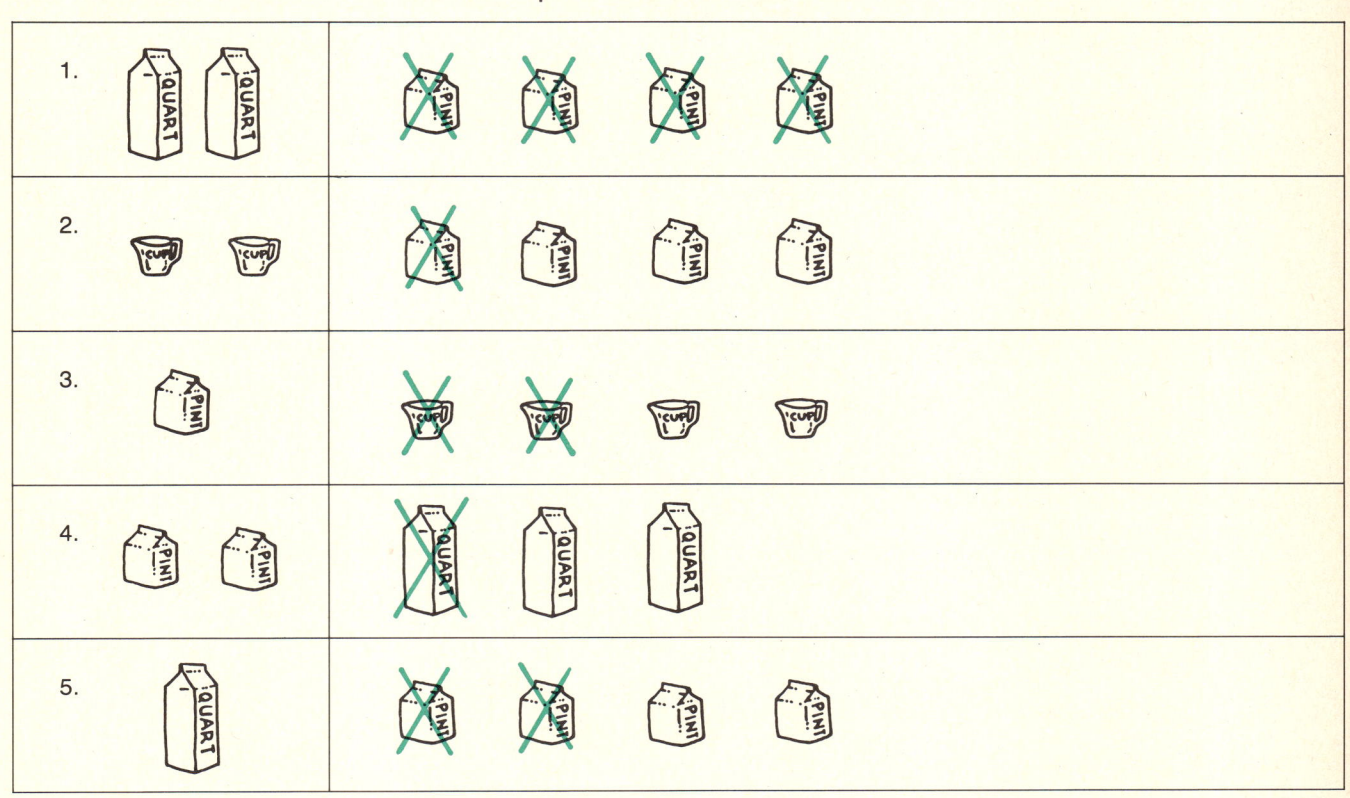

Using Math

◆ Ernie wants to cook some noodles. The directions say to boil the noodles in 1 quart of water. Ernie has a big pan and a 1-cup measure. How many times does he need to fill the cup to equal 1 quart?

He needs to fill the cup __4__ times.

59

Objective: Students will solve two-step problems involving addition and subtraction.

Instructional Model: Ask the students to imagine they are going on a jet trip from Los Angeles to Atlanta. Tell them that 151 people board the jet in Los Angeles. The jet stops in Dallas, after 108 people get off and 217 get on. As the jet flies on to Atlanta, how many people are on it?

Write the word problem on the chalkboard and ask students to identify what they need to know first, the number of people on the plane when 108 get off. Write 151 - 108 on the board and ask students to solve that part. Then explain to students that the answer to this will help them finish the problem. Write 43 + 217 on the board and have students solve. Explain to students that this two-step prob-

Problem Solving 8

Two-Step Problems

Andy had 24 baseball cards. He got 32 more cards.

Then Andy gave 6 baseball cards to a friend.

How many baseball cards did Andy have left?

> This is a two-step problem.
> You will use more than one operation to solve it.

Step 1 Read the problem to find what you need first. Solve for that part.

Andy had 24 baseball cards.
He got 32 more cards.

```
  24
+ 32
----
  56   baseball cards
```

Step 2 Read the problem to find the next fact. Use the answer from Step 1 to solve.

Then Andy gave 6 baseball cards to a friend.

```
  56
-  6
----
  50   baseball cards
```

Guided Practice

◆ Use two steps to solve.

	Step 1	Step 2
1. Luke had 65 tapes. He got 12 more tapes. Then he gave away 3 tapes. How many tapes did Luke have left?	65 + 12 ---- 77	77 - 3 ---- 74 tapes
2. Nichole had 28 comic books. She gave 11 comic books to Fran. Then Nichole got 14 new comic books. How many comic books does Nichole have now?	28 - 11 ---- 17	17 + 14 ---- 31 comic books

lem is the type of problem that an airline reservationist must use every day in order to make sure that everyone can get a seat on the jet to where they want to go.
Guided Practice: Direct students to the first model. Read the problem together and make sure students can set up the problems they need to solve. Have students complete the other problem in *Guided Practice*. Then review their answers with them.

Practice: Read the directions and the first problem to the students. Encourage students to complete the problems independently. For students needing more guidance, help them set up the problems until they can do this independently. Review answers with the students when they complete all the problems.
Practice Book E: Pages 19–20.

Practice

◆ Use two steps to solve.

		Step 1	Step 2
1.	Ms. Garza baked 36 cookies. Her son ate 6 of the cookies. Then Ms. Garza baked 48 more cookies. How many cookies does she have now?	36 − 6 ――― 30	30 + 48 ――― 78 cookies
2.	Su had 64 cans of apple juice and 32 cans of grape juice. She sold 18 cans of juice. How many cans of juice does Su have left?	64 + 32 ――― 96	96 − 18 ――― 78 cans of juice
3.	Rob had 19 video game tokens. He got 25 more tokens. Then Rob used 10 tokens. How many video game tokens does Rob have left?	19 + 25 ――― 44	44 − 10 ――― 34 tokens
4.	Jesse flew on a jet that had 16 seats in first class and 212 seats in coach class. There were 197 passengers seated in the plane. How many empty seats were there?	16 + 212 ――― 228	228 − 197 ――― 31 empty seats
5.	There are 23 students in Mr. Wong's class and 20 students in Mr. Shimizu's class. The classes went on a field trip together, but 4 students did not go. How many students went on the trip?	23 + 20 ――― 43	43 − 4 ――― 39 students

Review

◆ Divide.

pages 46–47

1. 5)21̄ **4 R1**
2. 6)55̄ **9 R1**
3. 9)64̄ **7 R1**
4. 8)41̄ **5 R1**

pages 48–49

5. 4)85̄ **21 R1**
6. 3)95̄ **31 R2**
7. 8)84̄ **10 R4**
8. 2)47̄ **23 R1**

pages 50–51

9. 8)97̄ **12 R1**
10. 2)93̄ **46 R1**
11. 6)84̄ **14**
12. 3)88̄ **29 R1**

pages 52–53

13. 3)137̄ **45 R2**
14. 4)168̄ **42**
15. 5)339̄ **67 R4**
16. 7)614̄ **87 R5**

62

page numbers to diagnose where their difficulties are occurring. By looking back at the pages, you can identify the skills that have not been mastered. It is important that you reteach these skills to students before allowing them to move ahead. After you have diagnosed student deficiencies and have retaught those skills, have students complete the *Extra Practice* for Chapter 3 on page 168.

CHAPTER 3

◆ Divide.

pages 54–55

17. $20\overline{)80}$ = **4**

18. $30\overline{)92}$ = **3 R2**

19. $40\overline{)362}$ = **9 R2**

20. $70\overline{)211}$ = **3 R1**

pages 56–57

21. $23\overline{)96}$ = **4 R4**

22. $18\overline{)63}$ = **3 R9**

23. $12\overline{)36}$ = **3**

24. $31\overline{)78}$ = **2 R16**

25. $31\overline{)779}$ = **25 R4**

26. $42\overline{)548}$ = **13 R2**

27. $71\overline{)852}$ = **12**

28. $17\overline{)423}$ = **24 R15**

◆ Mark an X on the containers that equal the first one in the row.   pages 58–59

29. 2 cups | ✗ pint, pint, pint, pint

30. 2 pints | ✗ quart, quart, quart, quart

63

Review

CHAPTER 3

◆ Use two steps to solve.
pages 60–61

	Step 1	Step 2
31. Isaac caught 18 fish. He threw 5 fish back into the water. He caught 11 more fish. How many fish did he have then?	18 − 5 --- 13	13 + 11 --- 24 fish
32. There were 32 students on a playground. 28 more students come out to the playground. Later, 8 students left. How many students were on the playground then?	32 + 28 --- 60	60 − 8 --- 52 students
33. There were 176 cars in a parking lot. 48 cars left the parking lot at 2:00. 61 more cars left the parking lot at 5:00. How many cars were still in the parking lot?	176 − 48 --- 128	128 − 61 --- 67 cars
34. Jill put 78 oranges in a basket. She put 69 oranges in another basket. She put 83 oranges in a third basket. How many oranges in all does Jill have?	78 + 69 --- 147	147 + 83 --- 230 oranges
35. Jay has 211 rocks in his rock collection. Beth has 138 rocks in her rock collection. Beth got 27 more rocks. How many rocks do they have altogether?	211 + 138 --- 349	349 + 27 --- 376 rocks

Chapter Test: Before testing be sure students can read all the directions on the page. It may be necessary to divide the test into sections that can be completed at different times. You may find that providing a marker helps them keep their place. You can use the page references, printed only in the Teacher's Edition, to diagnose where students need help. It is important to reteach skills that have not been mastered before proceeding to the next chapter. After reteaching the skills students did not master on the *Chapter Test*, have students complete *Chapter 3 Checkup*, the blackline master on page T17.

Blackline Master: *Chapter 3 Checkup*, page T17.

Test   CHAPTER 3

◆ Divide.

pages 46–49

1. 2)15̄ **7 R1**
2. 6)25̄ **4 R1**
3. 3)61̄ **20 R1**
4. 2)82̄ **41**

pages 50–53

5. 2)73̄ **36 R1**
6. 6)78̄ **13**
7. 4)209̄ **52 R1**
8. 5)448̄ **89 R3**

pages 54–57

9. 20)62̄ **3 R2**
10. 40)321̄ **8 R1**
11. 28)92̄ **3 R8**
12. 62)870̄ **14 R2**

◆ Mark an X on the containers that equal the first one in the row.   pages 58–59

13. [pint] | [cup] ✗ [cup] ✗ [cup] [cup]

65

Test

CHAPTER 3

◆ Use two steps to solve.
pages 60–61

	Step 1	Step 2	
14. There were 182 people seated in a train. 74 more people got on and sat down. The train has 350 seats. How many seats are empty?	182 + 74 ――― 256	350 − 256 ――― 94	seats
15. There are 84 people in the grocery store. 18 people leave the store. 22 more people leave the store. How many people are left in the store?	84 − 18 ――― 66	66 − 22 ――― 44	people
16. Janet baked 234 muffins. She sent 120 muffins to the school bake sale. Her family ate 17 muffins. How many muffins does Janet have left?	234 −120 ――― 114	114 − 17 ――― 97	muffins
17. Bernie and Hillary worked on a puzzle that had 500 pieces. Bernie put 154 pieces in place. Hillary put 96 pieces in place. How many pieces were not in place then?	154 + 96 ――― 250	500 − 250 ――― 250	pieces
18. On Friday morning, a car dealer had 39 cars on the lot. She sold 5 cars. She received a shipment of 12 new cars. How many cars were on the lot then?	39 − 5 ――― 34	34 + 12 ――― 46	cars

Cumulative Review: When students periodically review new skills, they are more likely to remember them. Therefore, this *Cumulative Review* is designed to help students retain the skills they learned in Chapters 1–3. Page references have been printed on the student pages so students may look back when they need help. Most students will perform best if allowed to complete the *Cumulative Review* over several days. Before students begin, tell them that the exercises on these pages will help them remember the math they learned in Chapters 1–3. Be sure students can read all the directions. Then have them work independently.

Cumulative Review — CHAPTER 1

◆ Write the value of each underlined digit.   pages 2–3

1. 3̲3,495   **30,000**
2. 938,7̲31   **700**

◆ Add.   pages 4–7

3. 27 + 15 = **42**	4. 64 + 29 = **93**	5. 183 + 485 = **668**	6. 419 + 616 = **1,035**
7. 3,509 + 2,364 = **5,873**	8. 8,536 + 3,281 = **11,817**	9. 24,916 + 32,827 = **57,743**	10. 14,361 + 62,509 = **76,870**

◆ Subtract.   pages 8–11

11. 64 − 18 = **46**	12. 91 − 36 = **55**	13. 875 − 486 = **389**	14. 942 − 367 = **575**
15. 8,006 − 4,725 = **3,281**	16. 400 − 281 = **119**	17. 40,006 − 35,321 = **4,685**	18. 87,000 − 7,946 = **79,054**

◆ Round each number to the nearest hundred.   pages 12–13

19. 109   **100**
20. 37,531   **37,500**

◆ Ring the unit of measure you would use.   pages 14–15

21. the length of a truck inch (**foot**)	22. the height of a puppy (**inch**) foot

67

CHAPTER 2

◆ Multiply.

pages 24–27				
1. 16 × 4 = **64**	2. 38 × 6 = **228**	3. 85 × 4 = **340**	4. 28 × 10 = **280**	5. 65 × 10 = **650**

pages 28–31				
6. 53 × 13 = **689**	7. 72 × 18 = **1,296**	8. 63 × 12 = **756**	9. 29 × 24 = **696**	10. 82 × 57 = **4,674**

pages 32–35				
11. 326 × 12 = **3,912**	12. 568 × 13 = **7,384**	13. 271 × 15 = **4,065**	14. 242 × 25 = **6,050**	15. 658 × 53 = **34,874**

◆ Ring the unit of measure you would use. pages 36–37

16. the length of a telephone
   (centimeter)   meter

17. the height of a bus
   centimeter   **(meter)**

68

CHAPTER 3

◆ Divide.

pages 46–49			
1. **5 R2** 4)22	2. **9 R3** 6)57	3. **21 R2** 3)65	4. **42 R1** 2)85
pages 50–53			
5. **13 R1** 6)79	6. **27 R2** 4)110	7. **43 R2** 3)131	8. **85 R4** 6)514
pages 54–57			
9. **3** 20)60	10. **8 R5** 40)325	11. **4 R3** 18)75	12. **21 R4** 16)340

◆ Mark an X on the containers that equal the first one in the row.   pages 58–59

13.
14.

69

CHAPTERS 1–3

◆ Round to the nearest hundred.
Estimate to solve. pages 16–17

1. There were 470 music students at jazz night. Of those students, 311 were in the chorus. About how many music students were not in the chorus?	470 ⟶ 500 − 311 ⟶ − 300 ■ about **200** students	

◆ Round to the nearest hundred.
Estimate to solve. pages 38–39

2. There are 234 windows on each floor of a building. There are 3 floors. About how many windows are in the building?	234 ⟶ 200 × 3 ⟶ × 3 ■ about **600** windows

◆ Use two steps to solve. pages 60–61

	Step 1	Step 2
3. There were 17 people waiting in line at a restaurant. The hostess sat 8 people. 13 more people got in line. How many people were waiting in line then?	17 − 8 **9**	9 + 13 **22** people
4. Carla baked 36 cupcakes. She baked 39 more cupcakes. She sent 45 cupcakes to school with her son. How many cupcakes does Carla have left?	36 + 39 **75**	75 − 45 **30** cupcakes
5. Barry drove 15 miles to the grocery store. He drove 9 more miles to the gas station. Then, he drove 7 more miles to the park. How many miles in all did Barry drive?	15 + 9 **24**	24 + 7 **31** miles

Name _____

CHAPTER 4

Discuss the photograph with students. Read aloud the sentences on the page. Write the two amounts of money on the chalkboard. Help students subtract the numbers to find out how much change Rick received. Ask them why Rick would want to know if he got the correct change. Point out the decimal point in each number. Explain to students that they will learn the values of decimals and how to add and subtract decimals in this chapter.

Adding and Subtracting Decimals

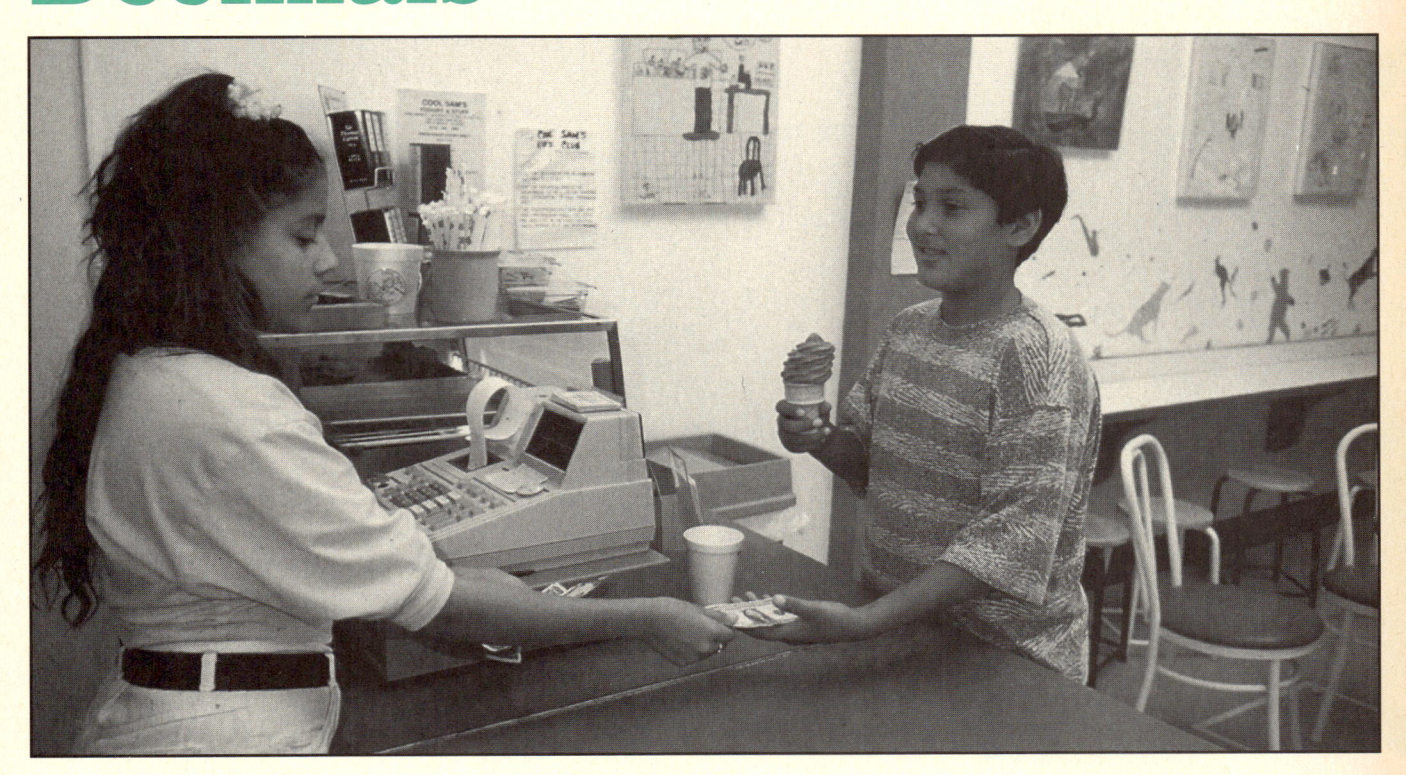

Rick bought a frozen yogurt cone for $1.29. He gave the store clerk $5.00. To find how much change to give Rick, did the clerk add or subtract? How do you know?

71

Objective: Students will read and write decimals to tenths.
Instructional Model: Draw on the chalkboard an illustration similar to the one at the top of the page. Shade one tenth of the figure. Explain that the figure is divided into ten sections and *one tenth* is shaded. Write the word *ten* on the board and add *th* with colored chalk. Have students read *tenth*. Draw a place-value chart divided into *ones* and *tenths* on the chalkboard. Be sure to include a decimal point. Write *0.1* in the chart and point out that *0* written before the decimal point means *no ones*. Repeat the procedure for 0.2 through 0.9, shading various sections of the figure and writing the equivalent decimal in the place-value chart. Read through the text on the page with students. Direct their attention to the illustration of *1.3* and explain how to read and write the decimal.

1

Tenths

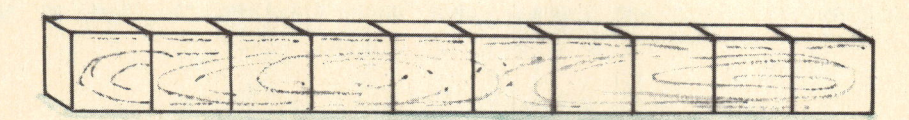

The board is divided into 10 equal parts. Each part is 1 **tenth** of the board. There are 10 tenths in the whole board.

You can name a part of a whole with a **decimal**. A decimal has a **decimal point**. When a decimal is less than 1, there is a zero before the decimal point.

Here is how to write tenths in decimal form.

1 tenth = 0.1   5 tenths = 0.5   10 tenths = 1.0 or 1 whole

You can also name wholes and parts of a whole as a decimal.

1 and 0.3 = 1.3 = 1 and 3 tenths
↑
decimal point

Read the decimal point as **and** in a number greater than 1.

1   and   0.3   = 1.3

Guided Practice

◆ Write each decimal.

1. 2 tenths = __0.2__

2. 3 tenths = __0.3__

3. 4 tenths = __0.4__

4. 8 tenths = __0.8__

5. 2 and 9 tenths = __2.9__

6. 12 and 8 tenths = __12.8__

7. 1 and 6 tenths = __1.6__

8. 3 and 4 tenths = __3.4__

Guided Practice: Work through the problems with students, stressing the correct use of the decimal point. Remind students to write 0 before the decimal point in decimals less than 1. Students may wish to use place-value charts if needed.
Practice: Have students complete the problems independently.

Using Math: Discuss and solve the problem as a group activity. For further practice, vary the number of boards.
Blackline Master: Reinforce the skills in this lesson with *Tenths* on page T26. Write decimals under some of the pictures and have students shade each picture to illustrate the decimal. Then shade a part of each remaining picture and have students write the decimal.

Practice

◆ Write each decimal.

1. 7 tenths = __0.7__
2. 5 tenths = __0.5__
3. 9 tenths = __0.9__
4. 6 tenths = __0.6__
5. 1 tenth = __0.1__
6. 3 tenths = __0.3__
7. 2 tenths = __0.2__
8. 4 tenths = __0.4__
9. 4 and 5 tenths = __4.5__
10. 2 and 3 tenths = __2.3__
11. 17 and 6 tenths = __17.6__
12. 1 and 8 tenths = __1.8__
13. 10 tenths = __1.0__
14. 25 and 4 tenths = __25.4__
15. 9 and 9 tenths = __9.9__
16. 3 and 6 tenths = __3.6__
17. 14 and 1 tenth = __14.1__
18. 8 and 7 tenths = __8.7__
19. 32 and 8 tenths = __32.8__
20. 10 and 2 tenths = __10.2__

Using Math

◆ Michael is building a tool shed. The back side of the shed needs 10 boards. Michael has put up 6 of the 10 boards. What part of the back side of the shed has Michael completed? Write the number as a decimal.

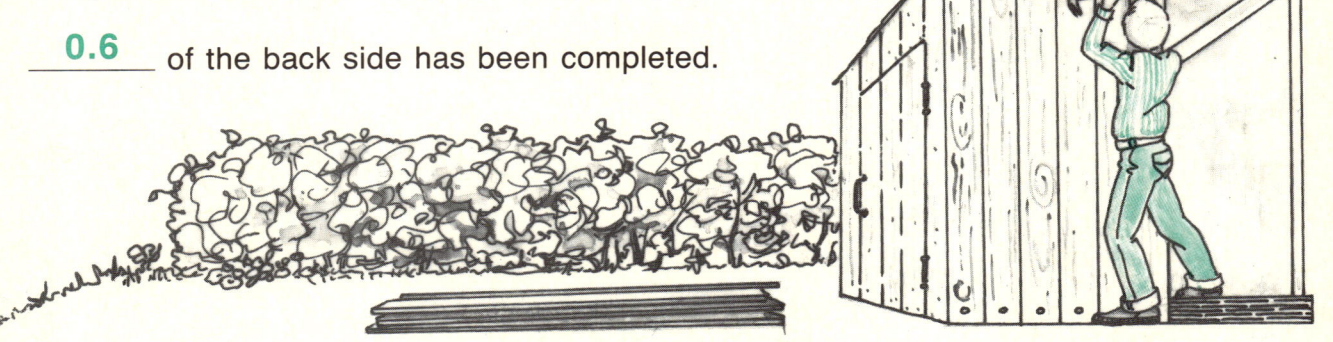

__0.6__ of the back side has been completed.

73

Objective: Students will read and write decimals to hundredths.

Instructional Model: Direct students' attention to the illustrations at the top of the page. Explain that the square is divided into 100 sections and *one hundredth* is shaded. Write the word *hundred* on the chalkboard and add *th* with colored chalk. Have students read *hundredth*. Draw a place-value chart divided into *ones*, *tenths*, and *hundredths* on the chalkboard. Make sure the decimal point is clearly visible. Write *0.01* in the chart and point out that the first *0* means *no ones*, and the second *0* means *no tenths*. Distribute copies of *Hundredths*, the blackline master on page T27. Dictate various decimals in hundredths and have students

Hundredths

When a whole is divided into 100 equal parts, each part is 1 **hundredth** of the whole.

1

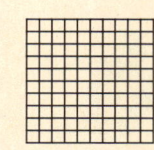

Each part is 1 hundredth.
1 hundredth = 0.01

1 whole = 100 hundredths

A place-value chart can help show decimal places.

tens	ones		tenths	hundredths
	2	.	3	7

↑
decimal point

The drawing below shows that 2 and 37 hundredths are shaded.

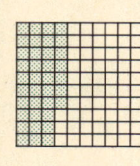

The number in the chart is 2.37.
Read this number as 2 and 37 hundredths.

2   and   0.37

Guided Practice

◆ Write each decimal.

1. 3 hundredths = __0.03__
2. 5 hundredths = __0.05__
3. 26 hundredths = __0.26__
4. 1 and 52 hundredths = __1.52__
5. 19 and 78 hundredths = __19.78__
6. 72 and 8 hundredths = __72.08__

shade the appropriate number of squares. Have volunteers write each decimal in the place-value chart on the chalkboard. Explain that *100 hundredths* is written *1.0*. Review the example of *2.37* on the page.
Guided Practice: Work through the problems with students. Stress the use of zero as a placeholder where needed.

Practice: Have students complete the problems independently.
Using Math: Explain to students that money is written as a decimal. Tell them that *1 cent* is *0.01* of a dollar or *$0.01*. Work the problem as a group.
Blackline Master: *Hundredths*, page T27.

Practice

◆ Write each decimal.

1. 6 hundredths = __0.06__
2. 8 hundredths = __0.08__
3. 4 hundredths = __0.04__
4. 10 hundredths = __0.10__
5. 15 hundredths = __0.15__
6. 29 hundredths = __0.29__
7. 63 hundredths = __0.63__
8. 88 hundredths = __0.88__
9. 100 hundredths = __1.0__
10. 1 and 1 hundredth = __1.01__
11. 10 and 15 hundredths = __10.15__
12. 22 and 8 hundredths = __22.08__
13. 56 and 19 hundredths = __56.19__
14. 2 and 5 hundredths = __2.05__
15. 14 and 10 hundredths = __14.10__
16. 79 and 22 hundredths = __79.22__
17. 83 and 7 hundredths = __83.07__
18. 5 and 25 hundredths = __5.25__
19. 33 and 1 hundredth = __33.01__
20. 15 and 28 hundredths = __15.28__

Using Math

◆ One dollar is equal to 100 cents. Cindy has 42 cents. Write 42 cents as a decimal part of one dollar.

__$0.42__

75

Objective: Students will compare two decimals using the inequality symbols > or <.
Instructional Model: Explain to students that we can *compare* two decimals to see which has the greater value. Review the symbols > and <. Go over the explanation in the text for comparing *0.4* and *0.5*. Then, show students how to compare *0.8* and *0.6* by lining up the decimals in a place-value chart on the chalkboard. Select a volunteer to write *0.8* and *0.6* with the correct symbol and read the answer aloud. Next, have students compare *1.3* and *1.7* using the same procedure. Remind students to start at the left and proceed to the tenths' place, comparing each digit. Work through the steps in the text for comparing *2.47* and *2.49* with students.
Guided Practice: Work through the problems with

3

Comparing Decimals

Is the decimal 0.4 greater than or less than 0.5? Count the green parts of each figure to answer the question.

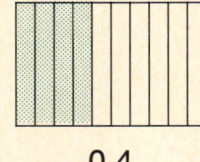

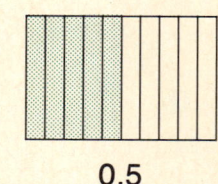

0.4   0.5

0.4 is less than 0.5 because 4 is less than 5.

> The symbol for **less than** is <. The symbol for **greater than** is >.
> 0.4 < 0.5

Which number is greater, 2.47 or 2.49? Start at the left and compare.

2.47	2.49	**Step 1**	Compare the ones. 2 ones and 2 ones are the same, so compare the next digit.
2.47	2.49	**Step 2**	Compare the tenths. 4 tenths and 4 tenths are the same, so compare the next digit.
2.47	2.49	**Step 3**	Compare the hundredths. 9 hundredths is greater than 7 hundredths, so 2.49 > 2.47.

Guided Practice

◆ Compare the decimals. Write > or <.

1. 0.3 __>__ 0.1
2. 0.6 __<__ 0.9
3. 0.4 __<__ 0.7

4. 21.3 __>__ 21.1
5. 2.35 __<__ 2.39
6. 7.42 __>__ 7.40

7. 12.44 __>__ 12.41
8. 26.32 __<__ 26.38
9. 74.36 __>__ 74.22

10. 0.5 __>__ 0.2
11. 3.01 __<__ 3.08
12. 87.19 __<__ 87.91

students, reminding them to start at the left and compare the digits in each place. Have students line up the decimal points and compare the numbers vertically if needed.
Practice: Have students complete the problems independently.
Using Math: Work the problem with students. Have them write the two prices as a number sentence using > or <.

Then have them write the correct name to complete the sentence.
Blackline Master: Reinforce the skills in this lesson with *Tenths* and *Hundredths* on pages T26–T27. Dictate two decimals and have students shade two pictures to illustrate the two decimals. Then have them write > or < between the two pictures.
Practice Book E: Pages 21–22.

Practice

◆ Compare the decimals. Write > or <.

1. 0.6 __>__ 0.2
2. 0.3 __<__ 0.8
3. 0.9 __>__ 0.5
4. 1.4 __>__ 1.2
5. 2.6 __<__ 2.8
6. 4.8 __<__ 4.9
7. 6.2 __<__ 6.4
8. 9.7 __>__ 9.3
9. 10.2 __<__ 10.8
10. 14.6 __<__ 14.9
11. 23.2 __>__ 23.1
12. 41.5 __<__ 41.7
13. 1.63 __>__ 1.62
14. 3.85 __>__ 3.81
15. 7.96 __<__ 7.98
16. 25.26 __<__ 25.28
17. 13.23 __<__ 13.31
18. 72.86 __>__ 72.66
19. 34.81 __<__ 34.82
20. 40.09 __>__ 40.08
21. 10.00 __<__ 10.01
22. 0.8 __>__ 0.1
23. 5.1 __<__ 5.8
24. 7.7 __>__ 7.6
25. 0.34 __>__ 0.31
26. 9.19 __>__ 9.11
27. 8.44 __<__ 8.46
28. 19.52 __<__ 19.56
29. 69.16 __<__ 69.66
30. 55.04 __>__ 55.01

Using Math

◆ George spent $27.43 for a new radio. Sue spent $27.47 for a new watch. Who spent more money?

____Sue____ spent more money.

77

Objective: Students will add decimals.
Instructional Model: Use flash cards to review the basic addition facts with students. Then ask students how they would solve the problem, "Tony bought 2 rugs for his hallway. The first one is 1.42 meters long and the second one is 2.39 meters long. How long are the 2 rugs all together?" Write the problem on the chalkboard, stressing that we always line up the decimal points when adding decimals. Explain that we add decimals the same way we add whole numbers, by starting at the right and regrouping each sum of 10 or more. Discuss the addition steps with students. In Step 1, explain that we can regroup 11 hundredths as 1 tenth 1 hundredth. In Step 2, have students add the tenths. Stress writing the decimal point in the

4

Adding Decimals

When you add decimals, always line up the decimal points of each number.

Add 1.42 and 2.39.

Step 1 Add the hundredths. Regroup if you need to.	Step 2 Add the tenths. Write the decimal point in the answer.	Step 3 Add the ones.
1 1.42 + 2.39 ——— 1	1 1.42 + 2.39 ——— .81	1 1.42 + 2.39 ——— 3.81

Adding decimals is just like adding whole numbers. Remember to write the decimal point in the answer.

Guided Practice

◆ Add.

1.	2.	3.	4.	5.
1 6.8 2 +1.3 5 ——— 8.17	2.5 3 +1.4 2 ——— 3.9 5	1 4.7 3 + 2.1 6 ——— 1 6.8 9	3.9 1 +6.3 4 ——— 1 0.2 5	1 2.5 3 +1 1.4 2 ——— 2 3.9 5

answer, and finally adding the ones. It may help students line up decimal points by working problems on lined paper turned so the holes are at the top.
Guided Practice: Work through the problems with students. Check to see that students regroup where needed and align the digits correctly. Students may wish to write a decimal point before they add.

Practice: Have students complete the problems independently.
Using Math: Explain that adding dollars and cents is the same as adding whole numbers and hundredths. Remind students to use a dollar sign and decimal point in the answer.

Practice

◆ Add.

1. 4.27 + 3.16 = **7.43**	2. 5.04 + 3.14 = **8.18**	3. 5.03 + 2.17 = **7.20**	4. 2.36 + 1.23 = **3.59**	5. 5.63 + 4.28 = **9.91**
6. 6.51 + 3.62 = **10.13**	7. 8.59 + 2.63 = **11.22**	8. 9.67 + 3.66 = **13.33**	9. 11.29 + 7.16 = **18.45**	10. 10.85 + 9.76 = **20.61**
11. 12.47 + 6.13 = **18.60**	12. 14.64 + 8.52 = **23.16**	13. 18.57 + 2.64 = **21.21**	14. 23.61 + 4.76 = **28.37**	15. 17.62 + 8.51 = **26.13**
16. 14.72 + 11.65 = **26.37**	17. 25.94 + 15.62 = **41.56**	18. 19.04 + 11.73 = **30.77**	19. 32.74 + 12.68 = **45.42**	20. 13.75 + 16.75 = **30.50**

Using Math

◆ Terri baby-sat one weekend. On Saturday she earned $6.25. On Sunday she earned $8.75. How much did she earn in all?

She earned ___**$15.00**___ in all.

Work here.

Objective: Students will subtract decimals.
Instructional Model: Use flash cards to review the basic subtraction facts with students. Read the following problem to students. "Margaret enters a 4.85 mile bike race. She has ridden 2.37 miles. How many more miles does she have to go?" Write the problem on the chalkboard, emphasizing that we always line up the decimal points when subtracting decimals. Explain that we subtract decimals the same way we subtract whole numbers. Remind students that we need to regroup in subtraction when the top digit is smaller than the bottom digit. Discuss the subtraction steps with students. In Step 1, explain that we can regroup 8 tenths 5 hundredths as 7 tenths 15 hundredths. In Step 2, have students subtract the tenths. Stress writing the decimal

5

Subtracting Decimals

When you subtract decimals, always line up the decimal points.
Subtract 2.37 from 4.85.

Step 1: Subtract the hundredths. Regroup if you need to.	Step 2: Subtract the tenths. Write the decimal point in the answer.	Step 3: Subtract the ones.

7 15
4.8̸5̸
− 2.3 7
          8
	7 15
	4.8̸5̸
	− 2.3 7
	    .4 8
		7 15
		4.8̸5̸
		− 2.3 7
		  2.4 8

Guided Practice

◆ Subtract.

1. 3 12 8.4̸2̸ − 6.1 6 **2.2 6**	2. 3.9 6 − 2.7 5 **1.2 1**	3. 7.5 4 − 3.8 2 **3.7 2**	4. 5.5 4 − 3.2 4 **2.3 0**	5. 6.9 1 − 1.9 6 **4.9 5**
6. 1 9.5 2 − 1 0.0 1 **9.5 1**	7. 5 5.5 5 − 1 1.4 6 **4 4.0 9**	8. 3 9.7 7 − 1 8.8 6 **2 0.9 1**	9. 1 0.6 5 − 4.2 7 **6.3 8**	10. 1 2.3 7 − 1 0.5 2 **1.8 5**

80

point in the answer, and finally subtracting the ones. It may help students line up decimal points by working problems on lined paper turned so the holes are at the top.
Guided Practice: Work through the problems with students. Check to see that students cross out the appropriate digits and regroup correctly. Students may wish to write a decimal point before they subtract.

Practice: Spot check students' work as they complete the problems independently.
Using Math: Have students solve the problem independently. Have each student write a subtraction money problem to exchange with a partner to solve. Remind them to line up decimal points and to use one in the answer.

Practice

◆ Subtract.

1. 6.75 − 2.41 = 4.34	2. 9.63 − 8.42 = 1.21	3. 4.96 − 1.85 = 3.11	4. 3.84 − 0.32 = 3.52	5. 7.46 − 2.17 = 5.29
6. 8.45 − 5.16 = 3.29	7. 2.76 − 1.28 = 1.48	8. 5.93 − 2.75 = 3.18	9. 6.47 − 2.72 = 3.75	10. 9.84 − 3.91 = 5.93
11. 7.66 − 2.84 = 4.82	12. 9.62 − 6.71 = 2.91	13. 11.62 − 3.51 = 8.11	14. 10.86 − 4.67 = 6.19	15. 14.83 − 6.91 = 7.92
16. 18.45 − 5.72 = 12.73	17. 17.83 − 14.26 = 3.57	18. 27.65 − 11.28 = 16.37	19. 19.76 − 12.92 = 6.84	20. 31.65 − 16.52 = 15.13

Using Math

◆ Mark had $15.25 in the bank. He took out $9.17 for a new fish tank. How much money does he have left?

He has ___$6.08___ left.

Work here.

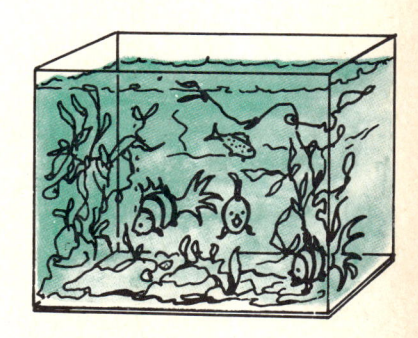

81

Objective: Students will add and subtract decimals that have a different number of decimal points.

Instructional Model: Write *2.6* on the chalkboard. Add *0* to make *2.60*. Explain that *6 tenths* is the same as *60 hundredths*. Add *0* to other decimals with tenths and emphasize that writing *0* after the last digit in a decimal does not change the value of the decimal. Next, show students how to change a whole number to a decimal by adding a decimal point and zeros. Dictate whole numbers and decimals with tenths and hundredths for students to write in place-value charts (tens through hundredths). Have students add zeros to even off the columns in the chart. Then, review the addition and subtraction steps in the text with students. Point out that adding zeros to a number helps keep the

6

Adding and Subtracting Decimals

Can you add 1.4 and 1.35? Yes, you can add numbers that have different place values. You can change 1.4 to hundredths by writing a zero after the 4 to make 1.40. Writing a zero after the last digit in a decimal does not change the value of the decimal.

Step 1 Line up the decimal points.	Step 2 Write a zero.	Step 3 Add.
1.4 + 1.3 5	1.4 0 + 1.3 5	1.4 0 + 1.3 5 2.7 5

You can also subtract decimals that have different place values. Subtract 3.62 from 8.7.

Step 1 Line up the decimal points.	Step 2 Write a zero.	Step 3 Subtract.
8.7 − 3.6 2	8.7 0 − 3.6 2	6 10 8.7̸ 0̸ − 3.6 2 5.0 8

You can write a whole number as a decimal by writing a decimal point and one or more zeros after the whole number. 10 = 10.0 = 10.00

Guided Practice

◆ Write the zeros. Then add or subtract.

| 1. 3.2 6
   +1.1 0
   4.3 6 | 2. 2 5.8 0
   +1 6.2 7
   4 2.0 7 | 3. 6.8 0
   − 4.6 3
   2.1 7 | 4. 3 7.8 2
   − 2 3.6 0
   1 4.2 2 | 5. 4 5.0
   − 2.8
   4 2.2 |

digits in place, prevents errors in computation, and doesn't change the value of the number. Stress the importance of lining up the decimal points.
Guided Practice: Work through the problems with students. Make sure that students add the appropriate number of zeros. Check to see that the decimal point and the digits are correctly aligned in the answers.

Practice: Remind students to watch for the "+" and "−" signs. Instruct students to complete the problems independently, stressing careful computation and correct regrouping.
Problem Solving: Work *Problem Solving* as a group. Remind students to add a decimal and two zeros to $10 before they complete step 2. After students have solved the problem, review answers with them.
Practice Book E: Pages 23–26.

Practice

◆ Write the zeros. Then add or subtract.

1. 6.7 8 +1.4 8.1 8	2. 5.2 9 +3.4 8.6 9	3. 7.6 7 +4.8 1 2.4 7	4. 8.8 1 +6 1 4.8 1	5. 1 9.6 +1 4.2 5 3 3.8 5
6. 2 5.9 +1 4.8 6 4 0.7 6	7. 1 6.6 +1 4.7 9 3 1.3 9	8. 3 2.2 +1 5.5 3 4 7.7 3	9. 9.8 2 +6.5 1 6.3 2	10. 3 2.3 +2 9.0 2 6 1.3 2
11. 9.7 3 −7.2 2.5 3	12. 1 1.8 4 − 6.9 4.9 4	13. 1 3.3 2 − 6.7 6.6 2	14. 1 2.9 7 −1 1.6 1.3 7	15. 8.4 −6.5 7 1.8 3
16. 9.4 −6.8 4 2.5 6	17. 1 3.8 −1 0.6 5 3.1 5	18. 7 6.9 −2 5.4 3 5 1.4 7	19. 9.6 4 −2.7 6.9 4	20. 4 5 −4 1.3 9 3.6 1

Problem Solving

◆ Use two steps to solve.

Simon bought parts for his bicycle. The parts cost $7.32 and $1.08. He paid with a $10 bill. How much change did Simon receive?

Step 1	Step 2
$7.32 + $1.08 $8.40	$10.00 − $ 8.40 $ 1.60 change

83

Milliliters and Liters

You learned that liquids can be measured using cups, pints, or quarts. Liquids can also be measured using metric measures. **Liters** and **milliliters** are used to measure liquids.

A raindrop is about 1 milliliter of liquid.

1 milliliter

A carton of orange juice is about 1 liter of liquid.

1 liter

1,000 milliliters = 1 liter

Guided Practice

Ring the unit of measure you would use.

1. a glass of water (milliliter) liter	2. a jug of apple cider milliliter (liter)
3. medicine in a spoon (milliliter) liter	4. water in a swimming pool milliliter (liter)
5. formula in a baby's bottle (milliliter) liter	6. a large carton of milk milliliter (liter)
7. water in a birdbath milliliter (liter)	8. bottle of vanilla flavoring (milliliter) liter

Remind them that milliliters are used to measure small amounts of liquid and liters are used to measure larger amounts of liquid.
Practice: Have students complete the exercises independently.

Using Math: Discuss the problem with students. Explain why 4 milliliters is not enough water to wash hair. Have students guess a more logical amount of water for hair washing.

Practice

◆ Ring the unit of measure you would use.

1. water in a bathtub milliliter (liter)	2. perfume in a bottle (milliliter) liter
3. sunscreen lotion in a bottle (milliliter) liter	4. a bottle of fingernail polish (milliliter) liter
5. gasoline in a tank milliliter (liter)	6. a can of house paint milliliter (liter)
7. a sink full of water milliliter (liter)	8. a bowl of soup (milliliter) liter
9. dew on a flower (milliliter) liter	10. a bottle of cooking oil milliliter (liter)

Using Math

◆ Kate and Lorraine were camping. Kate wanted to wash her hair. She asked Lorraine to get some water. Lorraine was glad to help. She put 4 milliliters of water into a container. Then she took the water to Kate.

Did Kate have enough water to wash her hair? __No__

Objective: Students will solve two-step problems involving addition and subtraction of numbers with decimals.
Instructional Model: Review two-step problems with students. Read the problem and steps in the instructional model with students, reminding them that adding and subtracting problems with decimals is like adding and subtracting whole numbers. It may help students line up decimal points by working on lined paper turned horizontally so that all decimals are in one column.
Guided Practice: Work through *Guided Practice* with the students. Ask students to explain how they found the answers. Review their answers with them.
Practice Book E: Pages 25–26.

Problem Solving 8

Two-Step Problems

Carina had $21.34 in the bank. She took out $7.00 to buy a poster. The next day, Carina put $5.12 more in the bank. How much money did Carina have in the bank then?

> This is a two-step problem.
> You will use more than one operation to solve it.

Step 1 Read the problem to find what you need first. Solve for that part.

Carina had $21.34 in the bank.
She took out $7.00 to buy a poster.

$21.34
− $ 7.00
$14.34

Step 2 Read the problem to find the next fact. Use the answer from Step 1 to solve.

The next day Carina put $5.12 more in the bank.

$14.34
+ $ 5.12
$19.46

Guided Practice

◆ Use two steps to solve.

		Step 1	Step 2
1.	Raymond got a shirt for $32.98 and a hat for $15.87. He gave the clerk $50.00. How much change did Raymond get back?	$32.98 +$15.87 $48.85	$50.00 −$48.85 $ 1.15
2.	Jeri had $17.34 in her pocket. Ms. Sanchez paid her $10.00 to mow the lawn. Then Jeri spent $4.26 for lunch. How much money did Jeri have left?	$17.34 + $10.00 $27.34	$27.34 − $ 4.26 $23.08

Practice: Have students complete the problems independently. Then review their answers with them. You may wish to have students check their answers with a calculator, telling them to first check the placement of decimals when their answers and the calculator do not match.

Practice Book E: Pages 25–26.

Practice

◆ Use two steps to solve.

	Step 1	Step 2
1. Emily had $3.68. She got $5.00 for her birthday. Then she spent $1.98 for poster paint. How much money did Emily have left?	$ 3.68 + $ 5.00 ——— $ 8.68	$ 8.68 − $ 1.98 ——— $ 6.70
2. Jiro had $12.58 in one pocket and $9.45 in another pocket. He bought a model sports car for $13.04. How much money did Jiro have left?	$12.58 + $ 9.45 ——— $22.03	$22.03 − $13.04 ——— $ 8.99
3. Jack earned $10.00 for mowing lawns and $12.50 for raking leaves. Then he spent $6.57 for a bicycle tire. How much money did Jack have left?	$10.00 + $12.50 ——— $22.50	$22.50 − $ 6.57 ——— $15.93
4. Thao had $14.64. He spent $2.50 for a sandwich. Then Thao got $5.00 for washing Mr. Kwan's car. How much money did Thao have then?	$14.64 − $ 2.50 ——— $12.14	$12.14 + $ 5.00 ——— $17.14
5. Bianca had $4.25 and Maria had $3.70. They put their money together to buy Ms. Lopez a gift. The gift cost $6.98. How much money did Bianca and Maria have left?	$ 4.25 + $ 3.70 ——— $ 7.95	$ 7.95 − $ 6.98 ——— $ 0.97
6. Erin had $20.00. She bought a skirt and a blouse for $14.76. Later that day, Erin took back the skirt and got back $7.50 for it. How much money did Erin have then?	$20.00 − $14.76 ——— $ 5.24	$ 5.24 + $ 7.50 ——— $12.74

Review

◆ Write each decimal. pages 72–73

1. 7 tenths = __0.7__
2. 3 tenths = __0.3__
3. 1 tenth = __0.1__
4. 8 and 8 tenths = __8.8__
5. 1 and 4 tenths = __1.4__
6. 12 and 9 tenths = __12.9__

pages 74–75

7. 2 hundredths = __0.02__
8. 9 hundredths = __0.09__
9. 1 hundredth = __0.01__
10. 1 and 25 hundredths = __1.25__
11. 4 and 3 hundredths = __4.03__
12. 26 and 19 hundredths = __26.19__

◆ Compare the decimals. Write > or <. pages 76–77

13. 0.4 __<__ 0.6
14. 0.5 __>__ 0.2
15. 4.7 __>__ 4.2
16. 26.03 __<__ 26.08
17. 19.45 __>__ 19.42
18. 6.08 __<__ 6.09

◆ Add. pages 78–79

19. 3.17 +2.42 = **5.59**	20. 5.37 +2.84 = **8.21**	21. 7.06 +3.14 = **10.20**	22. 9.53 +2.61 = **12.14**	23. 8.35 +4.74 = **13.09**
24. 14.81 + 3.63 = **18.44**	25. 18.17 + 6.09 = **24.26**	26. 36.72 +12.31 = **49.03**	27. 45.39 +26.48 = **71.87**	28. 15.23 +12.64 = **27.87**

88

difficulty with any of the problems, use the page numbers to diagnose where their difficulties are occurring. By looking back at the pages, you can identify the skills that have not been mastered. It is important that you reteach these skills to students before allowing them to move ahead. After you have diagnosed student deficiencies and have retaught those skills, have students complete the *Extra Practice* for Chapter 4 on page 169.

CHAPTER 4

◆ Subtract. pages 80–81

29. 7.63 − 4.52 = 3.11	30. 3.75 − 0.23 = 3.52	31. 8.54 − 4.72 = 3.82	32. 5.84 − 1.25 = 4.59	33. 6.32 − 2.81 = 3.51
34. 14.72 − 6.56 = 8.16	35. 16.37 − 4.62 = 11.75	36. 27.87 − 10.68 = 17.19	37. 36.52 − 29.38 = 7.14	38. 40.35 − 12.91 = 27.44

◆ Write the zeros. Then add or subtract. pages 82–83

39. 6.42 + 1.3 = 7.72	40. 3.1 + 4.26 = 7.36	41. 25.6 + 12.72 = 38.32	42. 17.34 + 26.5 = 43.84	43. 10.7 + 5 = 15.7
44. 9.23 − 7.4 = 1.83	45. 11.8 − 6.75 = 5.05	46. 13.42 − 10.6 = 2.82	47. 36.5 − 13.26 = 23.24	48. 9 − 4.32 = 4.68

◆ Ring the unit of measure you would use. pages 84–85

49. a cup of soup (milliliter) liter	50. a fish tank full of water milliliter (liter)
51. a bucket of water milliliter (liter)	52. a bottle of cough syrup (milliliter) liter

89

Review

CHAPTER 4

◆ Use two steps to solve.
pages 86–87

	Step 1	Step 2
53. Mita had $4.95. She got a gift of $5.00. Then she bought a book for $6.98. How much money did Mita have left?	$ 4.95 + $ 5.00 $ 9.95	$ 9.95 − $ 6.98 $ 2.97
54. Tomas had saved $15.69. He bought a game for $9.18. Then he saved $17.00 more. How much money did Tomas have then?	$15.69 − $ 9.18 $ 6.51	$ 6.51 + $17.00 $23.51
55. Donetta bought a pen for $1.29 and a stapler for $6.97. She gave the store clerk $10.00. How much change did Donetta get back?	$ 1.29 + $ 6.97 $ 8.26	$10.00 − $ 8.26 $ 1.74
56. Mr. Zhang bought running shoes for $39.95 and socks for $4.50. He gave the sales clerk $50.00. How much change did Mr. Zhang get in return?	$39.95 + $ 4.50 $44.45	$50.00 − $44.45 $ 5.55
57. Ms. Cruz had $42.00 in her wallet. She bought a model plane for her son for $17.08. Then she cashed a check for $30.00 more. How much money did Ms. Cruz have then?	$42.00 − $17.08 $24.92	$24.92 + $30.00 $54.92

90

Chapter Test: Before testing be sure students can read all the directions on the page. Remind them to watch the "+" and "−" signs. It may be necessary to divide the test into sections that can be completed at different times. You may find that providing a marker helps them keep their place. You can use the page references, printed only in the Teacher's Edition, to diagnose where students need help.

It is important to reteach skills that have not been mastered before proceeding to the next chapter. After reteaching the skills students did not master on the *Chapter Test*, have students complete *Chapter 4 Checkup*, the blackline master on page T18.
Blackline Master: *Chapter 4 Checkup,* page T18.

Test CHAPTER 4

◆ Write each decimal. pages 72–75

1. 5 tenths = __0.5__
2. 8 hundredths = __0.08__

◆ Compare the decimals. Write > or <. pages 76–77

3. 0.8 __>__ 0.3
4. 1.4 __<__ 1.7
5. 8.76 __<__ 8.79

◆ Add. pages 78–79

6.	7.	8.	9.	10.
6.26	8.45	15.37	22.83	5.38
+3.13	+6.26	+ 2.56	+15.92	+7.44
9.39	14.71	17.93	38.75	12.82

◆ Subtract. pages 80–81

11.	12.	13.	14.	15.
3.94	7.64	15.83	25.94	32.15
−2.83	−2.81	− 6.21	−10.65	−14.61
1.11	4.83	9.62	15.29	17.54

◆ Write the zeros. Then add or subtract. pages 82–83

16.	17.	18.	19.	20.
7.26	23.1	12.9	27.72	4.5
+2.4	+12.57	− 6.34	−11.2	−1.26
9.66	35.67	6.56	16.52	3.24

◆ Ring the unit of measure you would use. pages 84–85

21. ink in a pen

    (milliliter)   liter

22. punch in a punch bowl

    milliliter   (liter)

91

Test

CHAPTER 4

◆ Use two steps to solve.
pages 86–87

		Step 1	Step 2
23.	Li had $6.86. She earned $8.50 babysitting. Then she spent $7.75 on a cassette tape. How much money did Li have left?	$ 6.86 + $ 8.50 $15.36	$15.36 – $ 7.75 $ 7.61
24.	Jill saved $21.06. She spent $6.50 on a baseball cap. Then she got $14.00 for her birthday. How much money did Jill have then?	$21.06 – $ 6.50 $14.56	$14.56 + $14.00 $28.56
25.	Luis bought a magazine for $1.98 and a sandwich for $2.49. He gave the clerk $5.00. How much change did Luis get back?	$ 1.98 + $ 2.49 $ 4.47	$ 5.00 – $ 4.47 $ 0.53
26.	Henry bought a shirt for $11.99 and a pair of shorts for $7.80. Henry had $20.00 he could spend. How much of that money did he have left?	$11.99 + $ 7.80 $19.79	$20.00 – $19.79 $ 0.21
27.	Karl earned $9.75 for babysitting the Valdez children and $11.00 for babysitting the Rendon children. Then he spent $15.03 on a music video. How much money did Karl have left?	$ 9.75 + $11.00 $20.75	$20.75 – $15.03 $ 5.72

92

Name _____

CHAPTER 5

Discuss the photograph with students. Read aloud the sentences on the page. Remind students that numbers with decimals can be rounded to whole numbers to use estimation. Make sure students consider the cost of 4 movie tickets, remembering to count Mr. Lopez. Have students make up other multiplication and division problems about the picture or what the people might spend inside the movie theater. Then explain to students that they will learn how to multiply decimals in this chapter.

Multiplying Decimals

Mr. Lopez and his friends stood in line a long time to see a movie about dinosaurs. The movie tickets were $6.25 each. Did it cost Mr. Lopez and his 3 friends more than or less than $30.00 in all for movie tickets? How can you estimate to find out?

93

Objective: Students will read and write decimals to thousandths.

Instructional Model: Review the concept of tenths and hundredths. Explain that if we divide one hundredth into 10 equal parts, each part is 1 *thousandth*. Write *thousand* on the chalkboard and add *th* with colored chalk. Have students read *thousandth*. Write *0.1, 0.01,* and *0.001* in a place-value chart on the chalkboard. Stress that we must always use 3 digits to write numbers in the thousandths, since the thousandths' column is 3 places to the right of the decimal point. Direct students' attention to the page. Read with them the numbers in the place-value chart. Dictate various decimals and have volunteers write them in the place-value chart on the chalkboard as the other students

1

Decimal Place Value to Thousandths

The value of a digit in a decimal depends on its place in the number. You can use a place-value chart to find the value of a digit in a decimal.

tens	ones	.	tenths	hundredths	thousandths
	0	.	3		
	5	.	1	6	
1	7	.	0	4	9

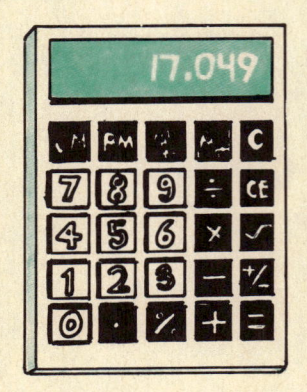

= 0.3 = 3 tenths
= 5.16 = 5 and 16 hundredths
= 17.049 = 17 and 49 **thousandths**

Write a zero when there are no ones, tenths, or hundredths in the number.

5 tenths   = 0.5 ← no ones
5 hundredths   = 0.05 ← no ones, no tenths
5 thousandths = 0.005 ← no ones, no tenths, no hundredths

Guided Practice

◆ Write each decimal.

1. 127 thousandths = __0.127__
2. 45 thousandths = __0.045__
3. 5 and 2 tenths = __5.2__
4. 3 hundredths = __0.03__
5. 875 thousandths = __0.875__
6. 12 and 5 thousandths = __12.005__

write the decimals at their desks. Have students take turns reading the decimals aloud.
Guided Practice: Work through the problems with students. Stress the correct placement of the decimal point and the use of *0* as a placeholder where needed.
Practice: Have students complete the problems independently.
Using Math: Explain that the farther to the right a digit is from the decimal point, the smaller its value. Direct students to make the smallest number possible using the 7 and 4. Have them use the zeros as placeholders. Then, have students write the largest number possible.

Practice

◆ Write each decimal.

1. 1 and 6 tenths = __1.6__
2. 4 and 12 hundredths = __4.12__
3. 8 and 247 thousandths = __8.247__
4. 3 and 496 thousandths = __3.496__
5. 9 and 28 hundredths = __9.28__
6. 15 and 8 hundredths = __15.08__
7. 27 and 13 thousandths = __27.013__
8. 9 and 726 thousandths = __9.726__
9. 52 and 4 tenths = __52.4__
10. 28 and 19 hundredths = __28.19__
11. 75 and 7 tenths = __75.7__
12. 427 thousandths = __0.427__
13. 239 thousandths = __0.239__
14. 9 tenths = __0.9__
15. 17 and 29 thousandths = __17.029__
16. 4 and 3 thousandths = __4.003__
17. 13 and 81 hundredths = __13.81__
18. 7 tenths = __0.7__
19. 18 thousandths = __0.018__
20. 4 and 1 hundredth = __4.01__

Using Math

◆ Use all the digits below to write the smallest decimal possible. Write the digits in the boxes on the calculator.

0　　7　　4　　0

0　0　4　7

Objective: Students will multiply a decimal through hundredths by a whole number.

Instructional Model: Write the problem *1.6 + 1.6 + 1.6* in vertical form on the chalkboard. Select a student to do the computation, emphasizing the placement of the decimal point in the sum. Review the concept of multiplication as repeated addition and have a student rewrite the problem as *4 × 1.6*. Explain that we can multiply a decimal by a whole number the same way we multiply two whole numbers. Work through the problem step-by-step with students. First, have students disregard the decimal point and multiply *4 × 16*. Remind students to regroup where needed and to add the regrouped numbers. Then, point out that since there is 1 decimal place in the factors

2

Multiplying a Decimal by a Whole Number

You already know how to multiply whole numbers. Now you can multiply a decimal by a whole number.

```
  1
  5.4 2
×     3
  1 6 2 6
```

Step 1 Multiply as if you were multiplying whole numbers.

```
  5.4 2   ← 2 decimal places
×     3
  1 6 2 6
```

Step 2 Start at the right and count the number of decimal places in the factors.

```
  5.4 2
×     3
  1 6.2 6  ← 2 decimal places
```

Step 3 Start at the right and count the same number of decimal places you counted in Step 2. Write the decimal point in the answer.

Guided Practice

◆ Multiply.

1. 0.8 × 6 **4.8**	2. 4.1 × 2 **8.2**	3. 2.7 × 4 **10.8**	4. 7.12 × 3 **21.36**	5. 0.59 × 2 **1.18**
6. 2.1 × 5 **10.5**	7. 12.33 × 2 **24.66**	8. 0.87 × 7 **6.09**	9. 3.12 × 8 **24.96**	10. 3.4 × 9 **30.6**

96

(1.6), there must be 1 decimal place in the product. Show students where to place the decimal point in the product by counting the appropriate number of places from right to left. Direct students to the steps in the lesson, reviewing the process.

Guided Practice: Work through the problems with students, stressing the correct placement of the decimal point in the products.

Practice: Spot check students' work for the correct number of decimal places as they complete the problems independently.

Using Math: Discuss and solve the problem as a group activity. Have students make up similar problems using grocery store advertisements.

Practice Book E: Pages 27–28.

Practice

◆ Multiply.

1. 4.7 × 2 = 9.4	2. 3.8 × 4 = 15.2	3. 5.1 × 6 = 30.6	4. 0.5 × 7 = 3.5	5. 6.9 × 2 = 13.8
6. 7.81 × 5 = 39.05	7. 8.9 × 8 = 71.2	8. 3.72 × 9 = 33.48	9. 4.2 × 6 = 25.2	10. 8.63 × 7 = 60.41
11. 5.5 × 3 = 16.5	12. 7.8 × 4 = 31.2	13. 9.14 × 3 = 27.42	14. 2.6 × 8 = 20.8	15. 7.46 × 4 = 29.84
16. 8.3 × 7 = 58.1	17. 0.56 × 8 = 4.48	18. 8.3 × 3 = 24.9	19. 7.62 × 6 = 45.72	20. 4.82 × 2 = 9.64

Using Math

◆ Art bought 3 books. Each book cost $1.25. How much did Art pay in all?

He paid ___$3.75___ in all.

Work here.

97

Objective: Students will multipy 2 decimals with tenths.
Instructional Model: Write the problem *0.6 × 0.4* on the chalkboard. Solve the problem step-by-step with students. First, have students disregard the decimal point and multiply *6 × 4*. Then, emphasize that since there are 2 decimal places in the factors (*0.6* and *0.4*), there must be 2 decimal places in the product. Have a volunteer demonstrate where to place the decimal point in the product by counting 2 places from the right.
Guided Practice: Work through the problems with students, stressing correct alignment of the digits and proper placement of the decimal point. Have students draw

3

Multiplying Tenths

When you multiply two decimals in tenths, the product is in hundredths.

Step 1 Multiply.

```
   0.4
 ×0.6
─────
  0 2 4
```

Step 2 Count the number of decimal places in the two factors. Write the decimal point in the product.

```
   0.4    — 1 decimal place
 ×0.6    —+1 decimal place
─────
  0.2 4  — 2 decimal places
```

Guided Practice

◆ Multiply.

1. 1.4 ×2.1 ───── 14 +280 ───── 2.94	2. 3.6 ×2.4 ───── 8.6 4	3. 0.5 ×0.3 ───── 0.1 5	4. 6.7 ×3.8 ───── 2 5.4 6	5. 2.9 ×0.5 ───── 1.4 5
6. 2.1 ×1.2 ───── 2.5 2	7. 0.7 ×0.8 ───── 0.5 6	8. 3.4 ×0.3 ───── 1.0 2	9. 5.5 ×3.9 ───── 2 1.4 5	10. 8.1 ×1.8 ───── 1 4.5 8

vertical lines or turn the paper sideways, if needed. Remind students to write a *0* in the ones' place when the product is less than 1.
Practice: Have students complete the problems independently, stressing correct regrouping and careful computation.
Using Math: Have volunteers work the problem on the chalkboard while the others solve it independently. For further practice, vary the distance and the time.

Practice

◆ Multiply.

1. 1.6 × 2.3 = 3.68	2. 0.8 × 0.4 = 0.32	3. 3.7 × 2.1 = 7.77	4. 6.5 × 4.5 = 29.25	5. 0.7 × 0.5 = 0.35
6. 6.4 × 3.1 = 19.84	7. 5.7 × 3.2 = 18.24	8. 3.6 × 5.2 = 18.72	9. 8.2 × 1.1 = 9.02	10. 7.6 × 4.9 = 37.24
11. 8.2 × 1.3 = 10.66	12. 5.1 × 0.2 = 1.02	13. 3.2 × 3.2 = 10.24	14. 1.8 × 1.4 = 2.52	15. 6.3 × 0.6 = 3.78

Using Math

◆ Juan runs 6.2 miles in an hour. How far can he run in 1.5 hours?

He can run __9.3__ miles.

Work here.

Objective: Students will multiply decimals with hundredths by decimals with tenths.

Instructional Model: Write 0.9×0.23 on the chalkboard. Discuss the steps for multiplying two decimals. Stress the placement of the decimal point in the product 3 places from the right because there are a total of 3 decimal places in the factors. Next, present students with the problem, "Ben's dog weighs 3.56 pounds. Marie's dog weighs 2.4 times as much. How much does Marie's dog weigh?" Write the problem on the chalkboard and solve it step-by-step with students. First, have students multiply 3.56×2.4. Then, tell students to count the number of decimal places in the factors to determine the placement of the decimal point in

4

Multiplying Tenths and Hundredths

Multiply 3.56 by 2.4.

```
    3.5 6   — 2 decimal places
  ×   2.4   — +1 decimal place
    1 4 2 4
  +7 1 2 0
    8.5 4 4 — 3 decimal places
```

Multiply 8.46 by 3.5.

```
    8.4 6   — 2 decimal places
  ×   3.5   — +1 decimal place
    4 2 3 0
  +2 5 3 8 0
    2 9.6 1 0 — 3 decimal places
```
  — Drop 0.   29.610 = 29.61

If the last digit is a zero, you can drop it. Dropping the last zero in a decimal does not change the value of the number.

Guided Practice

◆ Multiply.

1. 2.3 5 × 2.7 1645 +4700 6.345	2. 5.2 4 × 3.1 1 6.2 4 4	3. 8.2 5 × 0.2 1.6 5 0 or 1.6 5	4. 2.3 5 × 2.6 6.1 1 0 or 6.1 1	5. 2 6.5 2 × 1.8 4 7.7 3 6
6. 2.0 1 × 1.2 2.4 1 2	7. 3.2 4 × 3.3 1 0.6 9 2	8. 9.1 4 × 6.1 5 5.7 5 4	9. 7.2 2 × 0.5 3.6 1 0 or 3.6 1	10. 4.5 6 × 0.4 1.8 2 4

Emphasize that since the last digit in the product is zero, we drop it *after* writing the decimal point. Explain that it does not change the value of the number.
Guided Practice: Work through the problems with students.
Practice: Spot check students' work as they complete the problems independently.
Using Math: Have students work in pairs to solve the problem. Remind them to use a dollar sign and a decimal point and to drop the zero after writing the decimal point in the answer.
Practice Book E: Pages 29–30.

Practice

◆ Multiply.

1. 2.47 × 3.5 = 8.645	2. 5.38 × 0.2 = 1.076	3. 4.96 × 2.4 = 11.904	4. 5.15 × 6.8 = 35.020 or 35.02	5. 4.19 × 3.6 = 15.084
6. 2.56 × 1.7 = 4.352	7. 3.53 × 6.1 = 21.533	8. 4.48 × 2.8 = 12.544	9. 29.30 × 0.5 = 14.650 or 14.65	10. 6.25 × 3.4 = 21.250 or 21.25
11. 6.71 × 1.3 = 8.723	12. 8.72 × 9.4 = 81.968	13. 9.73 × 4.6 = 44.758	14. 8.05 × 0.9 = 7.245	15. 6.39 × 2.8 = 17.892

Using Math

◆ Cheese costs $2.98 for one pound. How much does 1.5 pounds cost?

It costs ___$4.47___.

Work here.

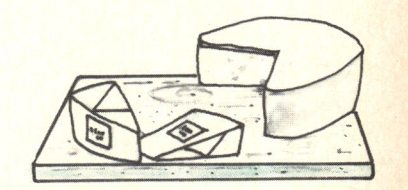

101

Objective: Students will write zeros in the products when multiplying decimals.
Instructional Model: Present students with the problem, "Pam lives 0.2 miles from school. Kate lives 0.4 times that distance from school. How far does Kate live from school?" Write the problem on the chalkboard and discuss the steps for multiplying 2 decimals. Remind students that since there are 2 decimal places in the factors, there must be 2 decimal places in the product. Explain that we must write 0 to the left of the 8 so that the product can have 2 decimal places. Stress the importance of 0 as a placeholder. Substitute 0.4 × 0.2 with 0.2 × 0.03 in the problem. Explain that since there are 3 decimal places in the factors, we must write 2 zeros to the left of the 6 so that the

5

Zeros in the Product

Sometimes you have to write one or more zeros in the product when multiplying decimals.

Multiply 0.2 by 0.4.

$$
\begin{array}{r}
0.2 \leftarrow \text{1 decimal place} \\
\times 0.4 \leftarrow \underline{+\text{1 decimal place}} \\
\hline
0.08 \leftarrow \text{2 decimal places}
\end{array}
$$

↳ Write a zero in the product so that you can have **2** decimal places.

Multiply 0.03 by 0.2.

$$
\begin{array}{r}
0.03 \leftarrow \text{2 decimal places} \\
\times \ 0.2 \leftarrow \underline{+\text{1 decimal place}} \\
\hline
0.006 \leftarrow \text{3 decimal places}
\end{array}
$$

↳↳ Write two zeros in the product so that you can have **3** decimal places.

Guided Practice

◆ Multiply.

| 1. 0.0 2
× 0.1
―――
0.002 | 2. 0.3 6
× 0.2
―――
0.0 7 2 | 3. 0.3
× 0.3
―――
0.0 9 | 4. 0.0 2
× 4
―――
0.0 8 | 5. 0.0 1 7
× 5
―――
0.0 8 5 |
|---|---|---|---|---|
| 6. 0.0 1
× 6
―――
0.0 6 | 7. 0.4
× 0.2
―――
0.0 8 | 8. 0.0 0 5
× 3
―――
0.0 1 5 | 9. 0.3 4
× 0.2
―――
0.0 6 8 | 10. 0.0 9
× 0.5
―――
0.0 4 5 |

product can have 3 decimal places.
Guided Practice: Work through the problems with students, reminding them to count the number of decimal places in both factors. Make sure that students write the proper number of zeros in the product and place the decimal point correctly.

Practice: Have students complete the problems independently. Tell students to read their answers aloud as you check their work.
Using Math: Have students solve the problem independently. After checking their work, have students compute the total cost of the notebook.
Practice Book E: Pages 31–34.

Practice

◆ Multiply.

1. 0.03 × 0.3 = 0.009	2. 0.34 × 0.2 = 0.068	3. 0.15 × 0.3 = 0.045	4. 0.06 × 0.8 = 0.048	5. 0.03 × 0.5 = 0.015
6. 0.01 × 0.9 = 0.009	7. 0.2 × 0.3 = 0.06	8. 0.9 × 0.1 = 0.09	9. 0.2 × 0.2 = 0.04	10. 0.6 × 0.1 = 0.06
11. 0.01 × 5 = 0.05	12. 0.03 × 2 = 0.06	13. 0.01 × 7 = 0.07	14. 0.026 × 3 = 0.078	15. 0.039 × 2 = 0.078
16. 0.08 × 0.8 = 0.064	17. 0.05 × 1 = 0.05	18. 0.02 × 2 = 0.04	19. 0.027 × 3 = 0.081	20. 0.04 × 0.4 = 0.016

Using Math

◆ Helen is buying a notebook that costs $2. She has to pay sales tax on the notebook. The tax is $0.04 for each dollar. How much sales tax does she have to pay?

She has to pay ___$0.08___ sales tax.

Work here.

103

Objective: Students will multiply decimals by 10, 100, and 1,000.
Instructional Model: Explain that we can easily multiply decimals by *10, 100,* or *1,000* by moving the decimal point to the right. Write the problem *10 × 0.842* in vertical form on the chalkboard and select a volunteer to solve it. Stress the placement of the decimal point in the product 3 places from the right. Remind students that we can drop the last zero in a decimal without changing the value of the number. Then, rewrite the problem horizontally and explain the shortcut for multiplying a decimal by 10. Point out that since there is *1 zero* in *10*, we move the decimal point 1 place

6

Multiplying Decimals by 10, 100, and 1,000

When you multiply a decimal by 10, 100, or 1,000, the decimal becomes greater in value.

```
  0.842   ← 3 decimal places
×    10
  8.420   ← 3 decimal places
  8.42    Drop zero.
```

See the pattern:

Multiplying a decimal by 10 moves the decimal point **one place** to the right.
There is **one zero** in **10**.

$$10 \times 0.842 = 8.42$$

```
   0.842   ← 3 decimal places
×    100
  84.200   ← 3 decimal places
  84.2     Drop zeros.
```

Multiplying a decimal by 100 moves the decimal point **two places** to the right.
There are **two zeros** in **100**.

$$100 \times 0.842 = 84.2$$

```
    0.842   ← 3 decimal places
× 1,000
  842.000   ← 3 decimal places
  842       Drop zeros.
```

Multiplying a decimal by 1,000 moves the decimal point **three places** to the right.
There are **three zeros** in **1,000**.

$$1{,}000 \times 0.842 = 842$$

Guided Practice

◆ Multiply.

1. 100 × 3.92 = __392__

2. 10 × 7.1 = __71__

3. 1,000 × 0.497 = __497__

4. 100 × 0.046 = __4.6__

5. 10 × 2.368 = __23.68__

6. 1,000 × 1.786 = __1,786__

to the right. Repeat the procedure for multiplying *0.842* by *100;* then by *1,000.*
Guided Practice: Work through the problems with students. Make sure that students move the decimal points the correct number of places to the right.
Practice: Spot check students' work for the correct placement of the decimal point as they complete the problems independently. Review all answers.
Problem Solving: Work *Problem Solving* as a group. Remind students to line up decimals in a column before adding or subtracting. Encourage students to work independently, then review answers with them.

Practice

◆ Multiply.

1. 10 × 8.9 = __89__
2. 10 × 6.4 = __64__
3. 10 × 0.7 = __7__
4. 10 × 3.965 = __39.65__
5. 100 × 6.91 = __691__
6. 100 × 7.22 = __722__
7. 100 × 0.87 = __87__
8. 100 × 2.396 = __239.6__
9. 1,000 × 1.429 = __1,429__
10. 1,000 × 9.795 = __9,795__
11. 1,000 × 0.535 = __535__
12. 1,000 × 6.317 = __6,317__
13. 100 × 1.04 = __104__
14. 10 × 2.9 = __29__
15. 1,000 × 3.303 = __3,303__
16. 100 × 16.68 = __1,668__
17. 10 × 1.7 = __17__
18. 1,000 × 8.293 = __8,293__
19. 100 × 6.91 = __691__
20. 10 × 4.5 = __45__

Problem Solving

◆ Use two steps to solve.

Kendra bought a shirt for $12.99 and a pair of shoes for $19.95. She gave the sales clerk $40.00. How much change did Kendra get back?

Step 1	Step 2
$12.99	$40.00
+ $19.95	− $32.94
$32.94	$ 7.06

Objective: Students will decide whether an object is weighed in ounces or pounds.

Instructional Model: Explain to students that we can find out how heavy or light an object is by weighing it. Ask students if they can name any units of weight (ounce, pound, ton, etc.). Give a volunteer a feather and a small rock. Ask which is heavy and which is light. Explain that exact units of measurement can help us find the weight of an object. Read the Instructional Model with students. If possible, provide two scales, one that measures in ounces and one that measures in pounds, for students to weigh various objects.

Guided Practice: Work through the exercises with

7

Ounces and Pounds

You measure how light or heavy an object is to find its **weight**. Two units of weight are the **ounce** and the **pound**. Light objects are measured in ounces. Heavier objects are measured in pounds.

A letter weighs about 1 ounce.

A loaf of bread weighs about 1 pound.

1 ounce

1 pound

16 ounces = 1 pound

Guided Practice

◆ Ring the word that completes each sentence.

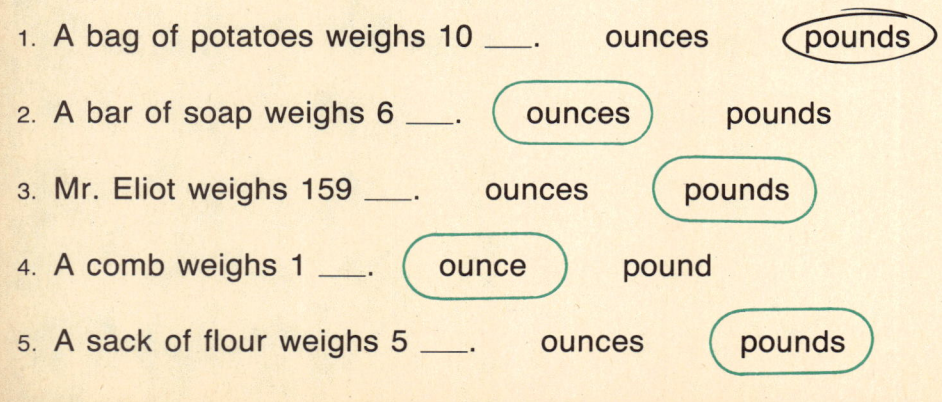

1. A bag of potatoes weighs 10 ___.   ounces   (pounds)

2. A bar of soap weighs 6 ___.   (ounces)   pounds

3. Mr. Eliot weighs 159 ___.   ounces   (pounds)

4. A comb weighs 1 ___.   (ounce)   pound

5. A sack of flour weighs 5 ___.   ounces   (pounds)

Practice

◆ Ring the word that completes each sentence.

1. A loaf of bread weighs 1 ___.   ounce   (pound)
2. A pencil weighs 1 ___.   (ounce)   pound
3. A turkey weighs 11 ___.   ounces   (pounds)
4. A desk weighs 17 ___.   ounces   (pounds)
5. One orange weighs 8 ___.   (ounces)   pounds
6. Sam's collie weighs 30 ___.   ounces   (pounds)
7. A slice of toast weighs 1 ___.   (ounce)   pound
8. A pair of scissors weighs 3 ___.   (ounces)   pounds

Using Math

◆ Juan took his pig, Spot, to the vet for a checkup. First the doctor listened to Spot's heartbeat. Then she looked at Spot's teeth. Then she looked at Spot's eyes and ears. Next the doctor decided to weigh Spot. Juan helped the doctor lift Spot onto the scale.
Was Spot's weight measured in ounces or pounds?

Spot's weight was measured in

___**pounds**___.

Objective: Students will choose an operation to solve problems.
Instructional Model: Have students use their own words to describe when it is best to add, subtract, multiply, and divide. Then read through the instructional model with students, making sure students understand why the correct operation is division. Checking reasonableness of answers will help students decide whether adding, subtracting, multiplying, or dividing was the correct choice.
Guided Practice: Work through *Guided Practice* with the students. Manipulatives may be used if students are having trouble checking the reasonableness of their

Problem Solving 8

Choose an Operation

Ms. Lee got a free book for every 6 books that her students ordered. The students ordered 144 books. How many free books did Ms. Lee get?

$$\begin{array}{r}144\\+6\\\hline 150\text{ books}\end{array}\qquad\begin{array}{r}144\\-6\\\hline 138\text{ books}\end{array}\qquad\begin{array}{r}144\\\times6\\\hline 864\text{ books}\end{array}\qquad\underset{\text{(circled)}}{6\overline{)144}\;\;24\text{ books}}$$

Add to put things together.
Subtract to take things away.
Multiply to combine groups.
Divide to separate groups.

Guided Practice

◆ Ring the correct problem.

1. Rick Vasca sells tickets at Cinema 8. He sells 200 tickets each day. He works 5 days every week. How many tickets does Rick sell in a week?

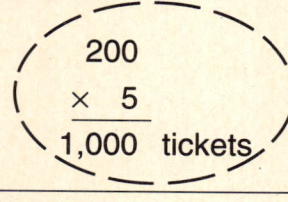

$$\begin{array}{r}200\\+5\\\hline 205\text{ tickets}\end{array}\qquad\begin{array}{r}200\\-5\\\hline 195\text{ tickets}\end{array}\qquad\underset{\text{(circled)}}{\begin{array}{r}200\\\times5\\\hline 1{,}000\text{ tickets}\end{array}}\qquad 5\overline{)200}\;\;40\text{ tickets}$$

2. Melody Brown has 28 video game tokens. Her best friend, Jasmine Lewis, has 14 video game tokens. How many video game tokens do Melody and Jasmine have together?

$$\underset{\text{(circled)}}{\begin{array}{r}28\\+14\\\hline 42\text{ tokens}\end{array}}\qquad\begin{array}{r}28\\-14\\\hline 14\text{ tokens}\end{array}\qquad\begin{array}{r}28\\\times 14\\\hline 392\text{ tokens}\end{array}\qquad 14\overline{)28}\;\;2\text{ tokens}$$

answers. Help students understand that although adding could be used to complete number 1, multiplying to find the answer is much faster.

Practice: Read the directions aloud with students. Have students complete the problems independently. Then review answers with them.

Practice Book E: Pages 33–34.

Practice

◆ Ring the correct problem.

1. In a zoo, the Indian elephant eats 32 pounds of grain mix each day. How many pounds of grain mix does the zoo need each day for 8 elephants?

32	32	(32	4 pounds
+ 8	− 8	× 8	8)32
40 pounds	24 pounds	256 pounds)	

2. One sea lion eats 11 pounds of fish each day. Another one eats 9 pounds of fish each day. How many pounds of fish in all do these sea lions eat in one day?

(11	11	11	1 R2 pounds
+ 9	− 9	× 9	9)11
20 pounds)	2 pounds	99 pounds	

3. The zoo had 350 pounds of oats. The zoo keeper fed the animals 50 pounds of oats. How many pounds of oats were left?

350	(350	350	7 pounds
+ 50	− 50	× 50	50)350
400 pounds	300 pounds)	17,500 pounds	

4. Polar bears in the zoo eat 15 pounds of bear chow each day. How many polar bears can the zoo feed with 180 pounds of bear chow?

180	180	180	(12 bears
+ 15	− 15	× 15	15)180)
195 bears	165 bears	2,700 bears	

109

Chapter Review: Tell students that the exercises on these pages will help them review the math in Chapter 5. Point out the page numbers printed above each group of exercises, and explain that students should look back at these pages if they need help. Be sure students understand all the directions. Encourage them to work independently. When students complete the *Review*, go over their answers. If students have difficulty with any of the problems, use the

Review

◆ Write each decimal. pages 94–95

1. 2 and 8 tenths = __2.8__
2. 3 and 2 thousandths = __3.002__
3. 423 thousandths = __0.423__
4. 1 and 5 hundredths = __1.05__
5. 2 and 4 tenths = __2.4__
6. 17 and 22 thousandths = __17.022__

◆ Multiply.

pages 96–97

| 7. 3.6 × 4 = 14.4 | 8. 5.2 × 3 = 15.6 | 9. 6.95 × 5 = 34.75 | 10. 0.76 × 8 = 6.08 | 11. 4.62 × 9 = 41.58 |

pages 98–99

| 12. 1.4 × 2.6 = 3.64 | 13. 0.7 × 0.5 = 0.35 | 14. 7.3 × 1.9 = 13.87 | 15. 5.9 × 4.3 = 25.37 | 16. 6.4 × 7.2 = 46.08 |

pages 100–101

| 17. 3.92 × 4.1 = 16.072 | 18. 6.87 × 0.3 = 2.061 | 19. 9.36 × 6.5 = 60.840 or 60.84 | 20. 8.21 × 3.2 = 26.272 | 21. 4.56 × 7.2 = 32.832 |

110

page numbers to diagnose where their difficulties are occurring. By looking back at the pages, you can identify the skills that have not been mastered. It is important that you reteach these skills to students before allowing them to move ahead. After you have diagnosed student deficiencies and have retaught those skills, have students complete the *Extra Practice* for Chapter 5 on page 171.

CHAPTER 5

◆ Multiply.

pages 100–101				
22.　1.2 1 × 　5.5 ————— 6.6 5 5	23.　2.1 3 × 　0.7 ————— 1.4 9 1	24.　2.0 5 × 　1.8 ————— 3.6 9 0 or 3.6 9	25.　5.6 7 × 　1.1 ————— 6.2 3 7	26.　7.1 1 × 　2.4 ————— 1 7.0 6 4

pages 102–103				
27.　0.0 2 × 　　2 ————— 0.0 4	28.　0.1 4 × 　0.2 ————— 0.0 2 8	29.　0.3 ×0.3 ————— 0.0 9	30.　0.0 1 2 × 　　　8 ————— 0.0 9 6	31.　0.0 5 × 　0.7 ————— 0.0 3 5
32.　0.3 6 × 　0.1 ————— 0.0 3 6	33.　0.0 0 9 × 　　　9 ————— 0.0 8 1	34.　0.1 4 × 　0.3 ————— 0.0 4 2	35.　0.2 ×0.4 ————— 0.0 8	36.　0.0 5 × 　0.5 ————— 0.0 2 5

pages 104–105

37. 10 × 7.6 = __76__　　　　　38. 100 × 4.83 = __483__

39. 1,000 × 6.925 = __6,925__　　40. 1,000 × 9.822 = __9,822__

41. 10 × 100.2 = __1,002__　　　42. 100 × 0.99 = __99__

◆ Ring the word that completes each sentence.　pages 106–107

43. A football player weighs 215 ___.　　ounces　　(pounds)

44. An egg weighs 4 ___.　　(ounces)　　pounds

45. 18 pennies weigh about 2 ___.　　(ounces)　　pounds

111

Review

CHAPTER 5

◆ Ring the correct problem.
pages 108–109

46. Scouts entered 246 cars in the pinewood derby.

   6 cars raced at a time. How many races in all were held?

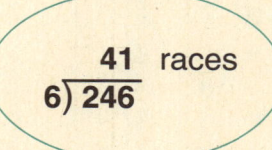

246	246	246	41 races
+ 6	− 6	× 6	6)246
252 races	240 races	1,476 races	*(ringed)*

47. Ms. Garcia took 129 students to an art show.

   Only 43 students could be in the building at a time.

   How many students had to wait while the first group went in?

129	129	129	3 students
+ 43	− 43	× 43	43)129
172 students	86 students *(ringed)*	5,547 students	

48. Martin Luther King Elementary sent 9 classes to the science fair.

   Each class had 27 students.

   How many students in all went to the science fair?

27	27	27	3 students
+ 9	− 9	× 9	9)27
36 students	18 students	243 students *(ringed)*	

49. Keisha had a collection of 70 sea shells.

   She found 35 more.

   How many shells in all did Keisha have then?

70	70	70	2 shells
+ 35	− 35	× 35	35)70
105 shells *(ringed)*	35 shells	2,450 shells	

Chapter Test: Before testing be sure students can read all the directions on the page. It may be necessary to divide the test into sections that can be completed at different times. You may find that providing a marker helps them keep their place. You can use the page references, printed only in the Teacher's Edition, to diagnose where students need help. It is important to reteach skills that have not been mastered before proceeding to the next chapter. After reteaching the skills students did not master on the *Chapter Test*, have students complete *Chapter 5 Checkup*, the blackline master on page T19.

Blackline Master: *Chapter 5 Checkup*, page T19.

Test

CHAPTER 5

◆ Write each decimal.   pages 94–95

1. 426 thousandths = __0.426__
2. 8 and 72 thousandths = __8.072__
3. 5 and 3 tenths = __5.3__
4. 16 and 24 hundredths = __16.24__

◆ Multiply.

pages 96–99

5.   0.5
   × 9
   ———
   4.5

6.   4.6 3
   ×   6
   ———
   2 7.7 8

7.   9.2
   × 0.4
   ———
   3.6 8

8.   3.7
   × 6.9
   ———
   2 5.5 3

pages 100–103

9.   2.3 9
   × 3.1
   ———
   7.4 0 9

10.   4.6 2
    × 4.5
    ———
    2 0.7 9 0
    or
    2 0.7 9

11.   0.1 3
    × 0.2
    ———
    0.0 2 6

12.   0.0 4
    ×   2
    ———
    0.0 8

pages 104–105

13. 10 × 2.6 = __26__
14. 100 × 1.49 = __149__
15. 1,000 × 8.623 = __8,623__
16. 100 × 7.94 = __794__

◆ Ring the word that completes each sentence.   pages 106–107

17. A sack of potatoes weighs 10 ___.   ounces   (pounds)

18. A package of sliced cheese weighs 10 ___.   (ounces)   pounds

113

Test

CHAPTER 5

◆ Ring the correct problem.
pages 108–109

19. Che used 108 popsicle sticks to build one fort.
    He built a fort for each of his 3 brothers.
    How many popsicle sticks did he use?

108	108	(108	36 sticks
+ 3	− 3	× 3)	3)108
111 sticks	105 sticks	324 sticks	

   (third option circled)

20. In one month, LaShonda read a 125-page book on famous women chemists.
    She read a 25-page book on Sally Ride, the astronaut.
    How many pages in all did she read?

(125	125	125	25 pages
+ 25)	− 25	× 25	5)125
150 pages	100 pages	3,125 pages	

   (first option circled)

21. Vinny earned $459 on a paper route. He spent $51 on a video game
    and saved the rest. How much did Vinny save?

$459	($459	$ 459	$ 9 saved
+ $ 51	− $ 51)	× $ 51	$51)$459
$510 saved	$408 saved	$23,409 saved	

   (second option circled)

22. Ms. Stein's band had 49 trumpet players. She put 7 trumpet players
    in each group. How many groups did Ms. Stein make?

49	49	49	(7 groups
+ 7	− 7	× 7	7)49)
56 groups	42 groups	343 groups	

   (fourth option circled)

114

Name _____

CHAPTER 6

Discuss the photograph with students. Read aloud the sentences on the page. Ask students to tell about a time they have seen people try to figure out what each person owes in a restaurant. Help students understand that Jeremy and his friends probably used division to find out what each of them should pay. Work through the division problem on the chalkboard with students. Then explain to students that they will learn how to divide decimals in this chapter.

Dividing Decimals by Whole Numbers

Jeremy and his friends ate together at the China Hut restaurant yesterday. All 5 boys ordered the same lunch special. The total bill was $24.40. Did Jeremy and his friends have to multiply or divide to find out what each person owed?

Objective: Students will divide a decimal with tenths by a 1-digit whole number.

Instructional Model: Ask students how they would solve the problem, "John bought 9.6 meters of rope. He needs to cut it into 4 equal pieces. How long will each piece be?" Direct students' attention to the page and explain that we can divide a decimal the same way we divide a whole number.

In Step 1, emphasize the placement of the decimal point in the quotient directly above the decimal point in the dividend. In Step 2, point out that the 2 is written in the ones' place because we divide *9 ones* by *4*. Stress the proper alignment of the digits as they multiply *4* by *2 ones* and subtract. Remind students that we compare the remainder with the divisor before bringing down the *6 tenths*. In Step 3,

1

Dividing Tenths

The line to the right is 9.6 centimeters long. Can you divide the line into 4 equal parts? Yes.

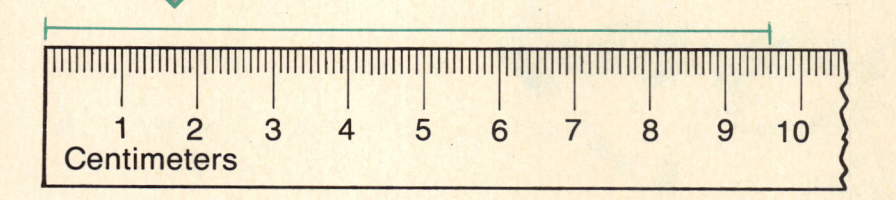

Divide 9.6 by 4.   4)9.6

Step 1

Write the decimal point in the quotient directly above the decimal point in the dividend.

$$4\overline{)9.6}^{\,.}$$

Step 2

Divide as you would with whole numbers.

Divide 9 ÷ 4
  Write 2 in the ones' place.
Multiply 2 × 4
Subtract 9 − 8

$$\begin{array}{r}2.\\4\overline{)9.6}\\-8\\\hline 1\end{array}$$

Step 3

Bring down the 6 tenths.
Divide 16 ÷ 4
  Write 4 in the tenths' place.
Multiply 4 × 4
Subtract 16 − 16

$$\begin{array}{r}2.4\\4\overline{)9.6}\\-8\downarrow\\\hline 16\\-16\\\hline 0\end{array}$$

Check the answer by multiplying.

$$\begin{array}{r}\overset{1}{}\\2.4\\\times4\\\hline 9.6\end{array}$$

2.4 — 1 decimal place
9.6 — 1 decimal place

Guided Practice

◆ Divide.

1. $$\begin{array}{r}5.9\\3\overline{)17.7}\\-15\\\hline 27\\-27\\\hline 0\end{array}$$

2. $$\begin{array}{r}3.1\\6\overline{)18.6}\end{array}$$

3. $$\begin{array}{r}4.7\\2\overline{)9.4}\end{array}$$

4. $$\begin{array}{r}2.3\\3\overline{)6.9}\end{array}$$

stress the placement of the 4 in the tenths' place because we divide *16 tenths* by *4*. Explain to students that they can check the answer to a division problem by multiplying the quotient by the divisor. Review the method to determine the placement of the decimal point in the product.

Guided Practice: Work through the problems with students.

Practice: Instruct students to complete the problems independently.

Using Math: Discuss and solve the problem as a group activity. Vary the distance and number of hours for further practice.

Practice

◆ Divide.

1. 5)49.5 = 9.9	2. 3)3.9 = 1.3	3. 8)72.8 = 9.1	4. 2)7.2 = 3.6
5. 9)56.7 = 6.3	6. 6)49.8 = 8.3	7. 4)12.8 = 3.2	8. 7)50.4 = 7.2
9. 2)18.6 = 9.3	10. 3)14.1 = 4.7	11. 5)37.5 = 7.5	12. 8)22.4 = 2.8

Using Math

◆ Sally can ride her bicycle 20.1 miles in 3 hours. How far can she ride in 1 hour?

She can ride __6.7__ miles in one hour.

Work here.

117

Objective: Students will divide a decimal with hundredths by a 1-digit whole number.

Instructional Model: Present students with the problem, "At the farmer's market, 20.96 pounds of tomatoes were equally divided among 4 baskets. How many pounds of tomatoes were in each basket?" Direct students attention to the page and discuss the steps for dividing a decimal with hundredths. In Step 1, emphasize the correct placement of the decimal point in the quotient. Then remind students that they divide the same way they would divide whole numbers. Work through the division steps with students. Review the method for checking the answers to division problems.

2

Dividing Hundredths

Divide 20.96 by 4.   4)20.96

Step 1
Write the decimal point in the quotient.

$$4\overline{)20.96}$$ (with decimal point in quotient)

Step 2
Divide 20 ÷ 4
   Write 5 in the ones' place.
Multiply 5 × 4
Subtract 20 − 20

$$\begin{array}{r} 5. \\ 4\overline{)20.96} \\ -20 \\ \hline 0 \end{array}$$

Step 3
Bring down the 9 tenths.
Divide 9 ÷ 4
   Write 2 in the tenths' place.
Multiply 2 × 4
Subtract 9 − 8

$$\begin{array}{r} 5.2 \\ 4\overline{)20.96} \\ -20\downarrow \\ \hline 09 \\ -8 \\ \hline 1 \end{array}$$

Step 4
Bring down the 6 hundredths.
Divide 16 ÷ 4
   Write 4 in the hundredths' place.
Multiply 4 × 4
Subtract 16 − 16
Check the answer by multiplying.

$$\begin{array}{r} 5.24 \\ 4\overline{)20.96} \\ -20 \\ \hline 09 \\ -8\downarrow \\ \hline 16 \\ -16 \\ \hline 0 \end{array}$$

Guided Practice

◆ Divide.

1.
$$\begin{array}{r} 3.75 \\ 2\overline{)7.50} \\ -6 \\ \hline 15 \\ -14 \\ \hline 10 \\ -10 \\ \hline 0 \end{array}$$

2.
$$\begin{array}{r} 4.11 \\ 4\overline{)16.44} \end{array}$$

3.
$$\begin{array}{r} 12.46 \\ 7\overline{)87.22} \end{array}$$

4.
$$\begin{array}{r} 5.29 \\ 3\overline{)15.87} \end{array}$$

Guided Practice: Work through the problems with students. Make sure that students write the decimal point in the quotient and align the digits in the problems correctly. Remind students to compare the remainders with the divisors before bringing down the next number.
Practice: Spot check students' work for the correct placement of the decimal point in the quotient as they complete the problems independently.
Using Math: Have students solve the problem independently. Have students exchange their own division problems with a partner to solve and check.

Practice

◆ Divide.

1. $9\overline{)18.99}$ = **2.11**	2. $2\overline{)4.84}$ = **2.42**	3. $7\overline{)82.95}$ = **11.85**	4. $6\overline{)9.84}$ = **1.64**
5. $5\overline{)14.20}$ = **2.84**	6. $3\overline{)12.69}$ = **4.23**	7. $4\overline{)90.72}$ = **22.68**	8. $9\overline{)65.07}$ = **7.23**
9. $2\overline{)89.56}$ = **44.78**	10. $5\overline{)26.05}$ = **5.21**	11. $6\overline{)81.24}$ = **13.54**	12. $8\overline{)28.72}$ = **3.59**

Using Math

◆ Mary has $11.31. She wants to buy presents for her 3 friends. She wants to spend the same amount for each present. How much can she spend for each present?

Work here.

She can spend __$3.77__ for each present.

Objective: Students will divide a decimal by a whole number to obtain a quotient less than one.

Instructional Model: Ask students how they would solve the problem, "Russ bought 1.26 pounds of ground beef. He divided the meat into 3 patties. How much did each patty weigh?" Solve the problem step-by-step with students. In Step 1, stress the correct placement of the decimal point in the quotient. Then, explain that since we cannot divide 1 one by 3, we must write 0 in the ones' place. In Step 2, remind students that since *1 whole = 10 tenths,* we can think of *1 one 2 tenths* as *12 tenths.* In Step 3, point out that 4 is written in the tenths' place because we divide *12 tenths* by 3. Emphasize the proper alignment of the digits as students multiply and subtract. Have students compare the

3

Regrouping Whole Numbers as Tenths

When you divide a decimal by a whole number, sometimes you need to regroup whole numbers as tenths.

Divide 1.26 by 3.   3)1.26

Step 1 Write the decimal point in the quotient. Can you divide 1 by 3? No. Write a zero over the 1. This is the ones' place.	0. 3)1.26	**Step 2** Regroup the whole 1 and 2 tenths as 12 tenths. 1.2 = 12 tenths

Step 3
 	
Divide 12 tenths by 3.
   Write 4 in the tenths' place.
Multiply 4 × 3
Subtract 12 − 12
	0.4
	3)1.26
	−1 2
	⎯⎯
	0
		Step 4
		
		Bring down the 6 hundredths. 0.42
		Divide 6 ÷ 3 3)1.26
		   Write 2 in the hundredths' −1 2
		   place. ⎯⎯
		Multiply 2 × 3 06
		Subtract 6 − 6 − 6
		Check the answer by multiplying. ⎯⎯
		                                              0

Guided Practice

◆ Divide.

1.
0.85
5)4.25
−40
⎯⎯
25
−25
⎯⎯
0

2.
0.9 4
9)8.4 6

3.
0.8 3
7)5.8 1

4.
0.5 2
3)1.5 6

remainder with the divisor. In Step 4, remind students to bring down the *6 hundredths*. Explain that we write *2* in the hundredths' place because we divide *6 hundredths* by *3*. Have a volunteer check the answer by multiplying 3×0.42.

Guided Practice: Work through the problems with students. Remind students to write *0* in the ones' place when the quotient is less than 1.

Practice: Instruct students to complete the problems independently.

Using Math: Have students work the problem independently. After students have solved the problem, ask them if they know another way to write $0.73 (73¢).

Practice Book E: Pages 35–36.

Practice

◆ Divide.

1. $0.9\,6$ $4\overline{)3.8\,4}$	2. $0.6\,8$ $7\overline{)4.7\,6}$	3. $0.7\,4$ $2\overline{)1.4\,8}$	4. $0.4\,3$ $5\overline{)2.1\,5}$
5. $0.8\,8$ $8\overline{)7.0\,4}$	6. $0.7\,6$ $3\overline{)2.2\,8}$	7. $0.2\,2$ $6\overline{)1.3\,2}$	8. $0.9\,5$ $2\overline{)1.9\,0}$
9. $0.2\,4$ $6\overline{)1.4\,4}$	10. $0.4\,3$ $7\overline{)3.0\,1}$	11. $0.6\,2$ $3\overline{)1.8\,6}$	12. $0.3\,5$ $8\overline{)2.8\,0}$

Using Math

◆ Kim has 4 more days before she will receive her allowance. She has $2.92. If she spends an equal amount each of the 4 days, how much money can Kim spend each day?

Kim can spend ____$0.73____ each day.

Work here.

121

Objective: Students will divide a decimal by a whole number, writing zeros in the quotient.
Instructional Model: Write the problem 3)12.021 on the chalkboard. Explain that sometimes we need to write zeros in the quotient as placeholders when dividing decimals. Discuss the division steps as volunteers do the computation on the chalkboard. In Step 1, emphasize the correct placement of the decimal point in the quotient. Then, have students divide 12 by 3. In Step 2, point out that since we cannot divide 0 by 3, we write 0 in the tenths place to indicate that there are no groups of 3 in 0. In Step 3, remind students to bring down the 2 hundredths. Emphasize the importance of writing 0 in the hundredths' place to indicate

4

Zeros in the Quotient

Sometimes you have to write zeros in the quotient when dividing decimals.

Step 1		Step 2	

Write the decimal point in the quotient. **Divide** 12 ÷ 3 Write 4 in the ones' place. **Multiply** 4 × 3 **Subtract** 12 − 12	4.
	3)12.021
	−12
	  0
		Bring down the 0 tenths. Can you divide 0 by 3? No. Write 0 in the tenths' place. **Multiply** 0 × 3 **Subtract** 0 − 0	4.0
			3)12.021
			−12 ↓
			  0 0
			  − 0
			    0

Step 3		Step 4	

Bring down the 2 hundredths. Can you divide 2 by 3? No. Write 0 in the hundredths' place. **Multiply** 0 × 3 **Subtract** 2 − 0	4.00
	3)12.021
	−12
	  0 0
	  − 0
	   0 2
	   − 0
	     2
		Bring down the 1 thousandth. Can you divide 21 by 3? Yes. **Divide** 21 ÷ 3 **Multiply** 7 × 3 **Subtract** 21 − 21 Check the answer by multiplying.	4.007
			3)12.021
			−12
			  0 0
			  − 0
			   0 2
			   − 0 ↓
			    21
			   −21
			     0

Guided Practice

◆ Divide.

	1. 0.006
	     8)0.048
	       −48
	         0
		2. 0.0 8 6
		     7)0.6 0 2
			3. 2.0 6
			     3)6.1 8
				4. 5.0 0 9
				     4)2 0.0 3 6

that there are *no* groups of *3* in *2*. Have students divide *21 thousandths* by *3*, placing the 7 in the thousandths' place. Review the procedure for checking division problems.

Guided Practice: Work through the problems with students. Stress the writing of zeros in the quotient whenever there are not enough ones, tenths, or hundredths to divide.

Practice: Spot check students' work for the correct placement of the decimal point in the quotient as they complete the problems on their own.

Using Math: Instruct students to solve the problem independently. Have students make up their own division problems using different money-making ideas.

Practice Book E: Pages 37–38.

Practice

◆ Divide.

1. 0.0 6 4 6)0.3 8 4	2. 0.0 0 9 2)0.0 1 8	3. 0.0 2 8)0.1 6	4. 0.0 9 7 5)0.4 8 5
5. 6.0 1 3)1 8.0 3	6. 0.0 9 2 9)0.8 2 8	7. 0.0 9 4)0.3 6	8. 1.0 9 1 7)7.6 3 7
9. 3.8 0 7 8)3 0.4 5 6	10. 0.0 4 2 2)0.0 8 4	11. 0.0 5 3 4)0.2 1 2	12. 0.6 0 9 6)3.6 5 4

Using Math

◆ Three friends formed a company called Saturday Yard Service. One Saturday, they earned $105.15. They divided the money evenly. How much did each person earn?

Work here.

Each person earned _____$35.05_____.

123

Objective: Students will divide a decimal by a 1-digit whole number, writing zeros in the dividend.
Instructional Model: Write *9.4* on the chalkboard. Add a zero to make *9.40* and explain to students that adding zeros after the last digit in a decimal does not change its value. Write *18.200*, *0.10*, and *0.59000* on the chalkboard. Have volunteers write equivalent decimals without zeros beside each decimal on the chalkboard (*18.2, 0.1, 0.59*). Write 4)9.4 on the chalkboard. Review the division step-by-step with students. Explain that we must add zeros in the dividend and divide until a remainder of zero is obtained. Show students how to write a whole number as a decimal. Write 8)6 on the chalkboard. Explain that since we cannot divide *6* by *8*, we write zero and a decimal point in the divi-

5

Writing Zeros in the Dividend

Sometimes when you are dividing decimals, you need to write one or more zeros in the dividend to complete the division. Remember that writing one or more zeros **after** the last digit in a decimal does not change its value.

Divide 9.4 by 4.   4)9.4

Step 1		**Step 2**	
Divide until you have used each digit in the dividend.	$$\begin{array}{r} 2.3 \\ 4\overline{)9.4} \\ -8 \\ \hline 1\,4 \\ -1\,2 \\ \hline 2 \end{array}$$	Write a zero after the last digit in the dividend. Complete the division. Check by multiplying.	$$\begin{array}{r} 2.35 \\ 4\overline{)9.40} \\ -8 \\ \hline 1\,4 \\ -1\,2 \\ \hline 20 \\ -20 \\ \hline 0 \end{array}$$

You can change a whole number to a decimal by writing a decimal point and one or more zeros after the whole number.   3 = 3.0 = 3.00

Divide 6 by 8.   8)6
Can you divide 6 by 8? No.

Step 1		**Step 2**	
Write a decimal point and a zero in the dividend. Divide until you have used each digit in the dividend.	$$\begin{array}{r} 0.7 \\ 8\overline{)6.0} \\ -5\,6 \\ \hline 4 \end{array}$$	Write a zero after the last digit in the dividend. Complete the division. Check by multiplying.	$$\begin{array}{r} 0.75 \\ 8\overline{)6.00} \\ -5\,6 \\ \hline 40 \\ -40 \\ \hline 0 \end{array}$$

dend to indicate that there are no groups of 8 in 6. Review the division step-by-step with students. Remind students to check the answer by multiplying.
Guided Practice: Work through the problems with students.
Practice: Have students complete the problems independently.
Using Math: Make up real-life situations that involve dividing a decimal by a 1-digit whole number. For example, "At a garage sale, John bought 8 books for $2. All the books cost the same amount. How much did each book cost?" ($0.25) Have students set up and solve the problems.

Guided Practice

◆ Divide.

1.
```
      1.25
   8)10.00
     -8
     ──
      20
     -16
     ───
       40
      -40
      ───
        0
```

2. 3.64 / 5)18.20

3. 0.025 / 4)0.100

4. 0.5 / 6)3.0

Practice

◆ Divide.

1. 0.075 / 8)0.600

2. 0.295 / 2)0.590

3. 0.65 / 6)3.90

4. 0.05 / 4)0.20

5. 0.44 / 5)2.20

6. 0.125 / 4)0.500

7. 0.45 / 8)3.60

8. 5.2 / 5)26.0

9. 1.35 / 2)2.70

10. 8.6 / 5)43.0

11. 1.5 / 6)9.0

12. 8.25 / 4)33.00

Objective: Students will divide whole numbers and decimals by 10, 100, and 1,000.

Instructional Model: Direct students' attention to the problems at the top of the page as you review the steps for dividing 842 by 10, 100, and 1,000. Stress the correct placement of the decimal point and the additional zeros in the dividends. Explain the shortcut for dividing numbers by 10, 100, or 1,000 by moving the decimal point to the left. Direct students' attention to the horizontal division problems in the middle of the page. In each shortcut, help students see the correlation between the number of zeros in the divisor and the number of places the decimal point is moved

6

Dividing by 10, 100, and 1,000

When you divide by 10, 100, or 1,000, the number becomes smaller in value.
Divide 842 by 10, 100, and 1,000.

```
      84.2              8.42             0.842
 10)842.0         100)842.00       1,000)842.000
   -80              -800              -800 0
    42               42 0              42 00
   -40              -40 0             -40 00
     2 0              2 00              2 000
    -2 0             -2 00             -2 000
      0                 0                 0
```

Dividing by 10, 100, or 1,000 moves the decimal point **to the left**. Move one decimal place for each zero in the divisor. Divide.	Multiplying by 10, 100, or 1,000 moves the decimal point **to the right**. Move one decimal place for each zero in the factor. Check by multiplying.
523.7 ÷ 10 = 52.37	52.37 × 10 = 523.7
523.7 ÷ 100 = 5.237	5.237 × 100 = 523.7
523.7 ÷ 1,000 = 0.5237	0.5237 × 1,000 = 523.7

Guided Practice

◆ Divide. Then check your answer by multiplying.

1. 68 ÷ 100 = __0.68__
   100 × __0.68__ = __68__

2. 36.9 ÷ 10 = __3.69__
   10 × __3.69__ = __36.9__

126

to the left. Show students how to check the answers to the division problems by multiplying using the shortcut.
Guided Practice: Work through the problems with students. Make sure that students move the decimal points the correct number of places to the *left* when *dividing* and to the *right* when *multiplying*. Students may wish to use arrows to move the decimal point.

Practice: Have students complete the problems independently.
Problem Solving: Read the directions with the students. Remind students that thinking about whether or not an answer makes sense will help them choose the operation for solving the problem.

Practice

◆ Divide. Then check your answer by multiplying.

1. 78.6 ÷ 10 = __7.86__ 10 × __7.86__ = __78.6__	2. 78.6 ÷ 100 = __0.786__ 100 × __0.786__ = __78.6__
3. 836 ÷ 100 = __8.36__ 100 × __8.36__ = __836__	4. 836 ÷ 1,000 = __0.836__ 1,000 × __0.836__ = __836__
5. 3.62 ÷ 10 = __0.362__ 10 × __0.362__ = __3.62__	6. 36.2 ÷ 100 = __0.362__ 100 × __0.362__ = __36.2__
7. 94 ÷ 100 = __0.94__ 100 × __0.94__ = __94__	8. 2 ÷ 10 = __0.2__ 10 × __0.2__ = __2__
9. 143 ÷ 1,000 = __0.143__ 1,000 × __0.143__ = __143__	10. 6 ÷ 10 = __0.6__ 10 × __0.6__ = __6__

Problem Solving

◆ Ring the correct problem.

There are 21 steps in each flight of stairs to Jerry's apartment.
Jerry climbs 7 flights of stairs to his apartment.
How many steps in all does Jerry climb?

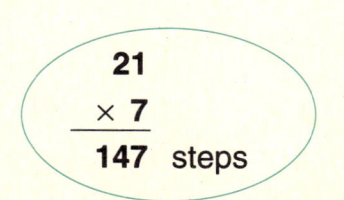

| 21
+ 7
28 steps | 21
− 7
14 steps | (21
× 7
147 steps) | 3 steps
7)21 |

127

Objective: Students will decide whether an object is weighed in grams or kilograms.
Instructional Model: Review ounces and pounds as two units used to measure weight. Explain that weight can also be measured in metric units. Read the *Instructional Model* with students. Have students take turns holding a paper clip and one volume of an encyclopedia to get an idea of how heavy a gram and a kilogram are. If possible, provide scales that measure grams and kilograms for students to weigh various objects.
Guided Practice: Work through the exercises with students. Remind them that light objects are measured in

7

Grams and Kilograms

Weight can be measured using metric measures. Light objects are measured in **grams**. Heavier objects are measured in **kilograms**.

A paper clip weighs about 1 gram.   A large book weighs about 1 kilogram.

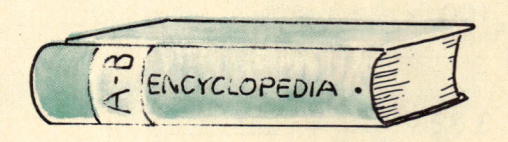

1 gram   1 kilogram

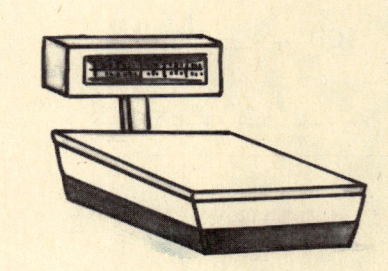

1,000 grams = 1 kilogram

Guided Practice

◆ Ring the word that completes each sentence.

1. An egg weighs 5 ___. (grams) kilograms

2. A dog weighs 12 ___. grams (kilograms)

3. A baseball bat weighs 1 ___. gram (kilogram)

4. A hammer weighs 1 ___. gram (kilogram)

5. A nickel weighs 5 ___. (grams) kilograms

128

Practice

◆ Ring the word that completes each sentence.

1. A hippopotamus weighs 2,600 ___.   grams   (kilograms)
2. A light bulb weighs 6 ___.   (grams)   kilograms
3. A dollar bill weighs 1 ___.   (gram)   kilogram
4. A lion weighs 160 ___.   grams   (kilograms)
5. An apple weighs 250 ___.   (grams)   kilograms
6. A penny weighs 3 ___.   (grams)   kilograms
7. A car weighs 975 ___.   grams   (kilograms)
8. A child weighs 30 ___.   grams   (kilograms)

Using Math

◆ Michelle has a new job. She works in the shipping department of a stereo store. The store has 2 scales. One scale measures weight in kilograms. The other scale measures weight in grams. As each package is given to Michelle, she decides which scale to use.

Draw a line to match each object to the scale Michelle should use.

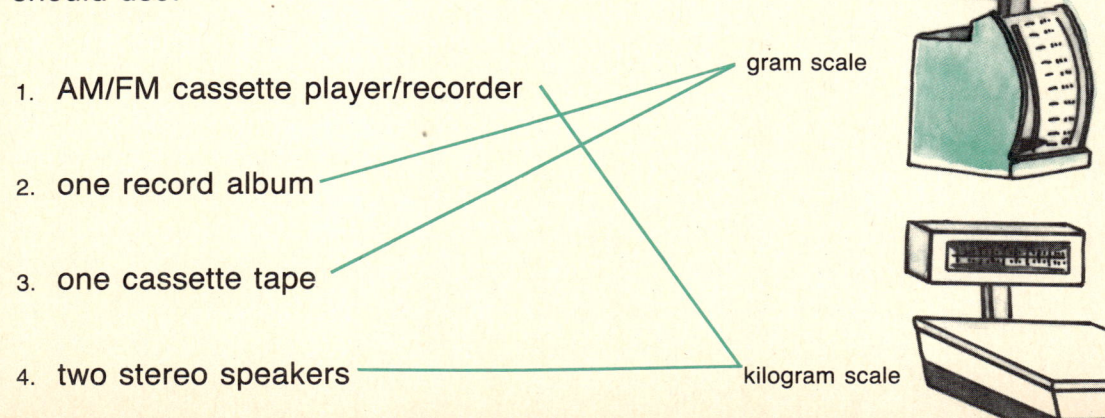

1. AM/FM cassette player/recorder
2. one record album
3. one cassette tape
4. two stereo speakers

gram scale

kilogram scale

Objective: Students will identify extraneous information in word problems to solve for what is needed.

Instructional Model: Begin the lesson by giving students this example of extra information. Say, "When a stranger in town asked for directions to the post office, he was told, 'Go two blocks past Main Street, turn right onto Oak Street. That's where the street fair will be next week. Then turn left and you will see the post office on the right.'" Although the information about the street fair may have been interesting, it will not help the stranger know how to find the post office. Explain to students that sometimes a problem can also have extra information like this.

Problem Solving 8

Identify Extra Information

Sometimes a problem gives you more information than you need to solve it.

Lucy stacked 6 rows of boxes. Each row had 18 boxes. There were 5 boxes with prizes inside. How many boxes in all did Lucy stack?

Step 1 Find the **facts you need.**

Lucy stacked 6 rows of boxes.

Each row had 18 boxes.

Step 2 Cross out the **facts you do not need.**

~~There are 5 boxes with prizes inside.~~

Step 3 Solve the problem.

$$\begin{array}{r} 18 \\ \times\ 6 \\ \hline 108 \end{array}$$

Lucy stacked **108** boxes in all.

◆ Cross out the fact you do not need.
Then solve the problem.

1. Adrian has 40 videos.
   Each case holds 10 videos.
   ~~The cases cost $5.49 each.~~
   How many cases did Adrian buy?

   $10\overline{)40}$ **4** cases

2. Su Ling bought 6 packs of basketball cards.
   There were 4 cards in each pack. ~~Su saw that 3 of the cards shown were for players on her favorite team.~~
   How many basketball cards did Su get?

   $$\begin{array}{r} 6 \\ \times 4 \\ \hline 24 \end{array}$$ cards

Read through the instructional model with students and help them identify the extra information in the problem. Ask students to explain why the information about the prizes is not needed to solve the problem.
Guided Practice: Work through *Guided Practice* with the students. Have students explain why the cost of the cases is not needed in problem 1. Review their answers with them after both problems have been completed.
Practice: Read the directions aloud with students. Have students complete the problems independently, one section at a time. Make sure students understand how to choose the operation needed in each problem. Then review the answers with them.
Practice Book E: Pages 39–40.

Practice

◆ Cross out the fact you do not need.
Then solve the problem.

1. Angela packed 24 bags of cookies.
   ~~Each bag cost $1.50.~~
   These are 6 cookies in each bag.
   How many cookies in all did Angela pack?

   $$\begin{array}{r} 24 \\ \times\ 6 \\ \hline 144 \end{array}$$ cookies

2. Ben put potatoes into 50-pound bags.
   ~~He put carrots into 10-pound bags.~~
   He has 800 pounds of potatoes. How many bags of potatoes did Ben have?

   16 bags
   50)800

3. ~~Ying has a 30-foot tree in her yard.~~
   She wants to put up a fence that has 8-foot sections. The fence will be 280 feet long around her backyard. How many sections of fence will Ying need to fence in her backyard?

   35 sections
   8)280

4. Maria bought 6 garden hoses. Each hose is 50 feet long. ~~She bought 8 packages of seeds.~~ How long will the garden hoses be if she joins them?

   $$\begin{array}{r} 50 \\ \times\ 6 \\ \hline 300 \end{array}$$ feet

5. Jose must sell 108 tickets to a school play. He puts the tickets into groups of six. ~~He plans to buy one set of tickets.~~ How many groups of tickets did Jose make?

   18 tickets
   6)108

131

Chapter Review: Tell students that the exercises on these pages will help them review the math in Chapter 6. Point out the page numbers printed above each group of exercises, and explain that students should look back at these pages if they need help. Be sure students understand all the directions. Encourage them to work independently. When students complete the *Review*, go over their answers. If students have difficulty with any of the problems, use the

Review

◆ Divide.

pages 116–117

1. 6)9.6 = 1.6
2. 5)20.5 = 4.1
3. 8)42.4 = 5.3
4. 3)13.2 = 4.4

pages 118–119

5. 7)46.97 = 6.71
6. 4)7.32 = 1.83
7. 8)48.96 = 6.12
8. 3)42.84 = 14.28

pages 120–121

9. 2)1.34 = 0.67
10. 5)1.15 = 0.23
11. 4)1.92 = 0.48
12. 6)5.16 = 0.86

pages 122–123

13. 4)0.376 = 0.094
14. 6)24.546 = 4.091
15. 9)9.45 = 1.05
16. 5)0.065 = 0.013

page numbers to diagnose where their difficulties are occurring. By looking back at the pages, you can identify the skills that have not been mastered. It is important that you reteach these skills to students before allowing them to move ahead. After you have diagnosed student deficiencies and have retaught those skills, have students complete the *Extra Practice* for Chapter 6 on page 172.

CHAPTER 6

◆ **Divide.**   pages 124–125

17. $0.9\,5$ $8)\overline{7.6\,0}$	18. 1.6 $5)\overline{8.0}$	19. $0.4\,2\,5$ $4)\overline{1.7\,0\,0}$	20. $0.0\,6\,5$ $2)\overline{0.1\,3\,0}$

◆ **Divide. Then check your answer by multiplying.**   pages 126–127

21. 926 ÷ 1,000 = __0.926__ 1,000 × __0.926__ = __926__	22. 79.53 ÷ 10 = __7.953__ 10 × __7.953__ = __79.53__
23. 85 ÷ 100 = __0.85__ 100 × __0.85__ = __85__	24. 9 ÷ 10 = __0.9__ 10 × __0.9__ = __9__
25. 94 ÷ 100 = __0.94__ 100 × __0.94__ = __94__	26. 125 ÷ 1,000 = __0.125__ 1,000 × __0.125__ = __125__

◆ **Ring the word that completes each sentence.**   pages 128–129

27. A typewriter weighs 7 ___.   grams   (kilograms)

28. A spoon weighs 30 ___.   (grams)   kilograms

29. A letter weighs 25 ___.   (grams)   kilograms

30. A telephone weighs 2 ___.   grams   (kilograms)

133

Review   CHAPTER 6

Practice

◆ Cross out the fact you do not need.
Then solve the problem. pages 130–131

31. ~~Paul's garden is 28 feet long.~~
    He will plant 14 rows of beans.
    He will plant 30 beans in each row.
    How many beans will Paul plant?

    $$\begin{array}{r} 14 \\ \times\ 30 \\ \hline 420 \end{array}$$ beans

32. ~~Bev picked 17 baskets of oranges.~~
    She picked 12 baskets of apples. There
    are 9 apples in each basket. How
    many apples in all did Bev pick?

    $$\begin{array}{r} 12 \\ \times\ 9 \\ \hline 108 \end{array}$$ apples

33. Alberto bought 24 packages of squash
    seeds. ~~He bought 19 packages of corn
    seeds.~~ There are 5 seeds in each package.
    How many squash seeds does Alberto have?

    $$\begin{array}{r} 24 \\ \times\ 5 \\ \hline 120 \end{array}$$ squash seeds

34. Lee has 210 pounds of onions.
    ~~He has 12 boxes.~~ He packed all the
    onions in 6 boxes. How many pounds
    of onions did he pack in each box?

    $6\overline{)210}$ 35 pounds

35. ~~Tanya has 50 flower pots.~~ She plants
    3 flower seeds in each pot. She sold
    41 pots. How many flower seeds in all
    were in the pots she sold?

    $$\begin{array}{r} 41 \\ \times\ 3 \\ \hline 123 \end{array}$$ flower seeds

Chapter Test: Before testing be sure students can read all the directions on the page. It may be necessary to divide the test into sections that can be completed at different times. You may find that providing a marker helps them keep their place. You can use the page references, printed only in the Teacher's Edition, to diagnose where students need help. It is important to reteach skills that have not been mastered before proceeding to the next chapter. After reteaching the skills students did not master on the *Chapter Test*, have students complete *Chapter 6 Checkup*, the blackline master on page T20.

Blackline Master: *Chapter 6 Checkup*, page T20.

Test   CHAPTER 6

◆ Divide.

pages 116–119			
1. 4)17.2 = 4.3	2. 7)52.5 = 7.5	3. 5)26.35 = 5.27	4. 3)14.91 = 4.97
pages 120–125			
5. 5)2.65 = 0.53	6. 6)6.048 = 1.008	7. 8)0.680 = 0.085	8. 4)4.300 = 1.075

◆ Divide. Then check your answer by multiplying.   pages 126–127

9. 18 ÷ 100 = __0.18__ 100 × __0.18__ = __18__	10. 24.2 ÷ 10 = __2.42__ 10 × __2.42__ = __24.2__
11. 4,383 ÷ 1,000 = __4.383__ 1,000 × __4.383__ = __4,383__	12. 10.52 ÷ 100 = __0.1052__ 100 × __0.1052__ = __10.52__

◆ Ring the word that completes each sentence.   pages 128–129

13. A paintbrush weighs 60 ___.   (**grams**)   kilograms

14. A watermelon weighs 4 ___.   grams   (**kilograms**)

135

Test

CHAPTER 6

Practice

◆ Cross out the fact you do not need.
The solve the problem. pages 130–131

15. There are 154 band members that will march in a parade. ~~14 of the band members play the trumpet.~~ The band director puts 7 members in each row. How many rows in all will the band make?

$$7\overline{)154} = 22 \text{ rows}$$

16. The marching band has 18 drummers. Each drummer has 2 drumsticks. ~~11 of the drummers can play the piano.~~ How many drumsticks does the marching band have?

$$18 \times 2 = 36 \text{ drumsticks}$$

17. There are 78 chairs in the band room. The chairs are in 3 rows. ~~59 band members came to practice.~~ How many chairs are in each row?

$$3\overline{)78} = 26 \text{ chairs}$$

18. ~~The marching band plays 17 songs.~~ They practiced playing 8 of the songs on Tuesday. They practiced each song for 12 minutes. How many minutes did the band practice on Tuesday?

$$12 \times 8 = 96 \text{ minutes}$$

19. The band director put 6 band members in a row at the football game. ~~There were 4 rows of flutes.~~ There were 12 rows of band members in all. How many band members in all were in rows?

$$12 \times 6 = 72 \text{ members}$$

136

Name _____

CHAPTER 7

Discuss the photograph with students. Read aloud the sentences on the page. For students who need help answering the question, ask them to first tell what ⅕ of 5 sandwiches would be. Show students how to write several fractions on the chalkboard. Then ask volunteers to write fractions on the chalkboard as you name them. Explain to students that in this chapter they will learn about fractions.

Understanding Fractions

Uncle Alan packed a big lunch for a family picnic. When Jeff got hungry, Uncle Alan told him that he could eat $\frac{1}{5}$ of the sandwiches in the basket. There were 10 sandwiches. How could Jeff figure out the number of sandwiches that were his?

Objective: Students will write fractions for parts of a whole.
Instructional Model: Present students with the problem, "A stick of butter is equal to 8 tablespoons. A recipe for mashed potatoes calls for 4 tablespoons of butter. What part of a stick of butter is used to make the mashed potatoes?" On the chalkboard draw a rectangle divided into 8 equal parts. Shade 4 parts. Tell students that a *fraction* is a number that names equal parts of a whole. Ask students how many parts there are in the stick of butter. Write *8* under a fraction line. Then ask how many parts were used in the mashed potatoes. Write *4* above the fraction line. Read the fraction $\frac{4}{8}$ to students. Read the *Instructional Model* with students. Write various fractions on the chalkboard. Have students practice reading the fractions

1

Parts of a Whole

A **fraction** is a number that names equal parts of one whole.

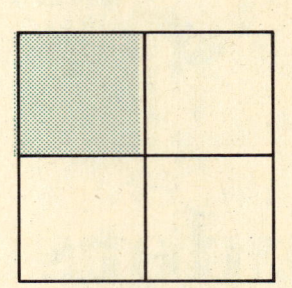

What fraction of the square is green?

Step 1 Count the number of equal parts.
Write the number **below** the line. $\overline{4}$

Step 2 Count the number of green parts.
Write the number **above** the line. $\frac{1}{4}$

$\frac{1}{4}$ of the square is green.

The top number of a fraction is the **numerator**.
The numerator tells us how many of the parts are counted.
The bottom number of a fraction is the **denominator**.
The denominator tells the total number of parts in the whole.

$\frac{1}{4}$ ← numerator
← denominator

Guided Practice

◆ Write the denominator for each fraction.

1. 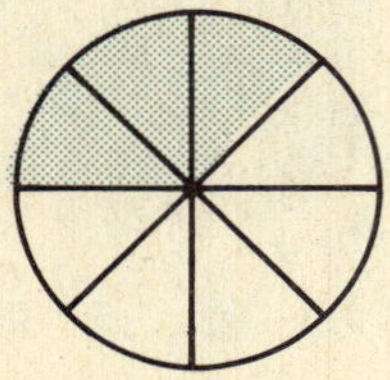 $\frac{3}{8}$

2. 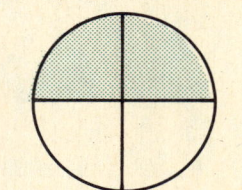 $\frac{2}{4}$

3. 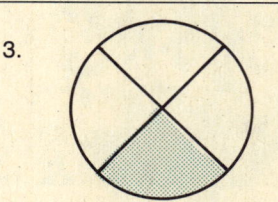 $\frac{1}{4}$

◆ Write the numerator for each fraction.

4. 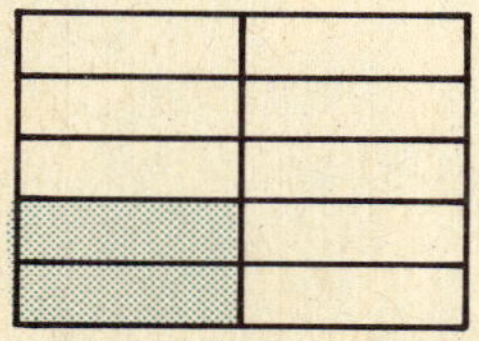 $\frac{2}{10}$

5. 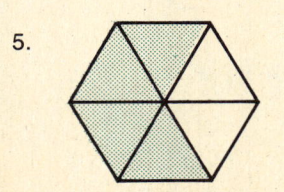 $\frac{4}{6}$

6. 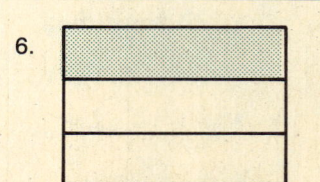 $\frac{1}{3}$

aloud. Emphasize the correct pronunciation for each fraction (*half, thirds, fourths,* etc.). You may wish to post a chart with fraction names spelled out for students to use as a reference.
Guided Practice: Work through the problems with students. Have students read each fraction aloud.
Practice: Have students complete the problems independently. Distribute copies of *Fractions*, the blackline master on page T28. Have students shade various sections of each figure. Then have them exchange papers with a partner and write the fraction for each shaded part.
Using Math: Discuss and solve the problem as a group.
Blackline Master: *Fractions,* page T28.

Practice

◆ Write a fraction in each box. Remember to count the number of equal parts first and write it below the line.

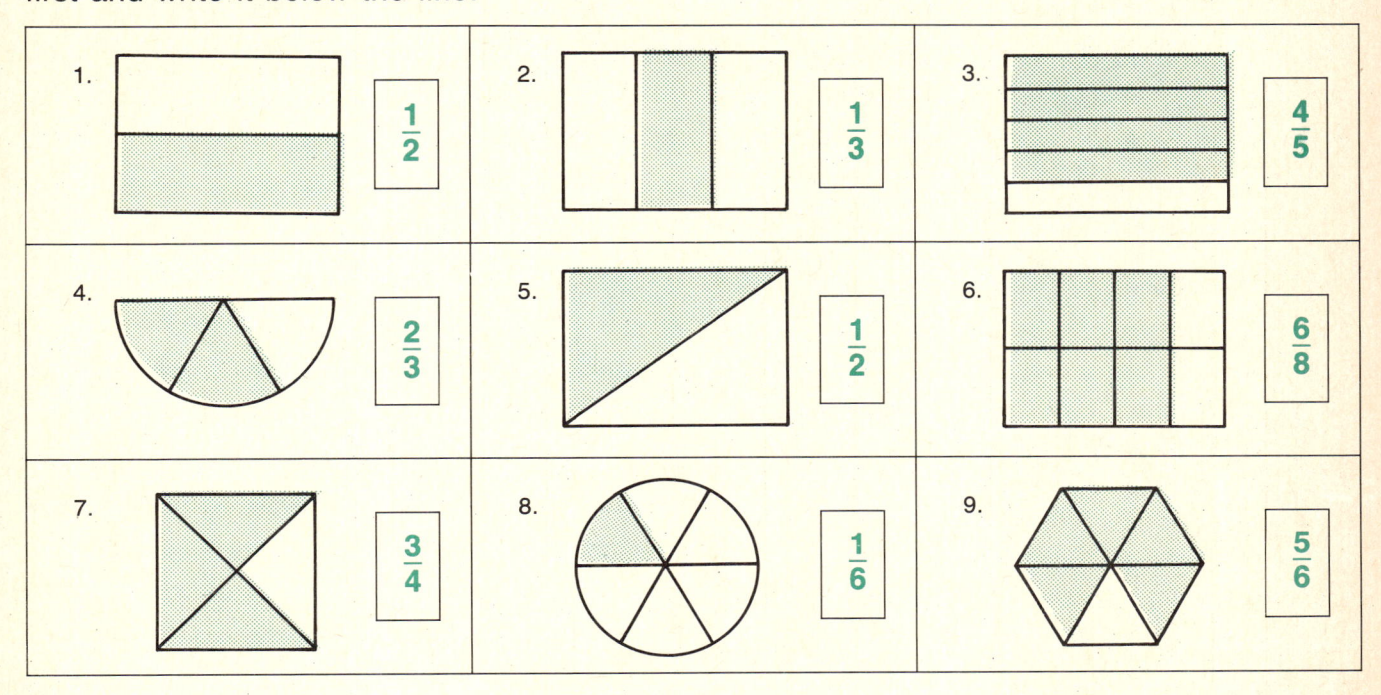

1. $\frac{1}{2}$	2. $\frac{1}{3}$	3. $\frac{4}{5}$
4. $\frac{2}{3}$	5. $\frac{1}{2}$	6. $\frac{6}{8}$
7. $\frac{3}{4}$	8. $\frac{1}{6}$	9. $\frac{5}{6}$

Using Math

◆ Michael ordered a pizza for dinner. It was cut in 8 equal pieces. Michael ate 5 pieces.

What fraction of the pizza did he eat? $\frac{5}{8}$

What fraction of the pizza did he have left? $\frac{3}{8}$

139

Objective: Students will write fractions for parts of a group.
Instructional Model: Have 3 students hold pencils and stand at the front of the room. Then have 3 students without pencils stand with the group. Explain that a fraction can name a part of a group. Discuss with students what fraction of the group has pencils. Remind students that the denominator is the bottom number in a fraction which names the total number in the group. Then remind them that the numerator is the top number in a fraction which counts a particular part of the group. Direct different groups of students to illustrate fractions while students practice writing the fractions on the chalkboard. Continue to review

2

Fractional Parts of a Group

You can write a fraction to name a part of a group.

What fraction of the group is green?

Step 1 Count the number in the group.
Write it as the denominator. $\overline{5}$

Step 2 Count the green circles.
Write it as the numerator. $\frac{1}{5}$

$\frac{1}{5}$ of the group is green.

Guided Practice

◆ Write each fraction in the box to answer the question.

1. What fraction of the group is white?

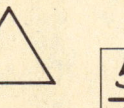

   $\frac{5}{8}$

2. What fraction of the flowers is tall?

   $\frac{3}{5}$

3. What fraction of the money is dimes?

   $\frac{1}{3}$

4. What fraction of the glasses is empty?

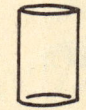

   $\frac{1}{4}$

the 2-step *Instructional Model* for each example.
Guided Practice: Work through the *Guided Practice* with students. Have students read their answers aloud, saying them in complete sentences. (For example, "*1.* ⅚ of the group is white.")
Practice: Have students complete the exercise in-dependently. For further practice, have them write a fraction for the remaining objects in each illustration.
Using Math: Discuss and solve the problem as a group activity. Then help students find what fraction of the group did not bring flashlights.

Practice

◆ Write each fraction in the box to answer the question.

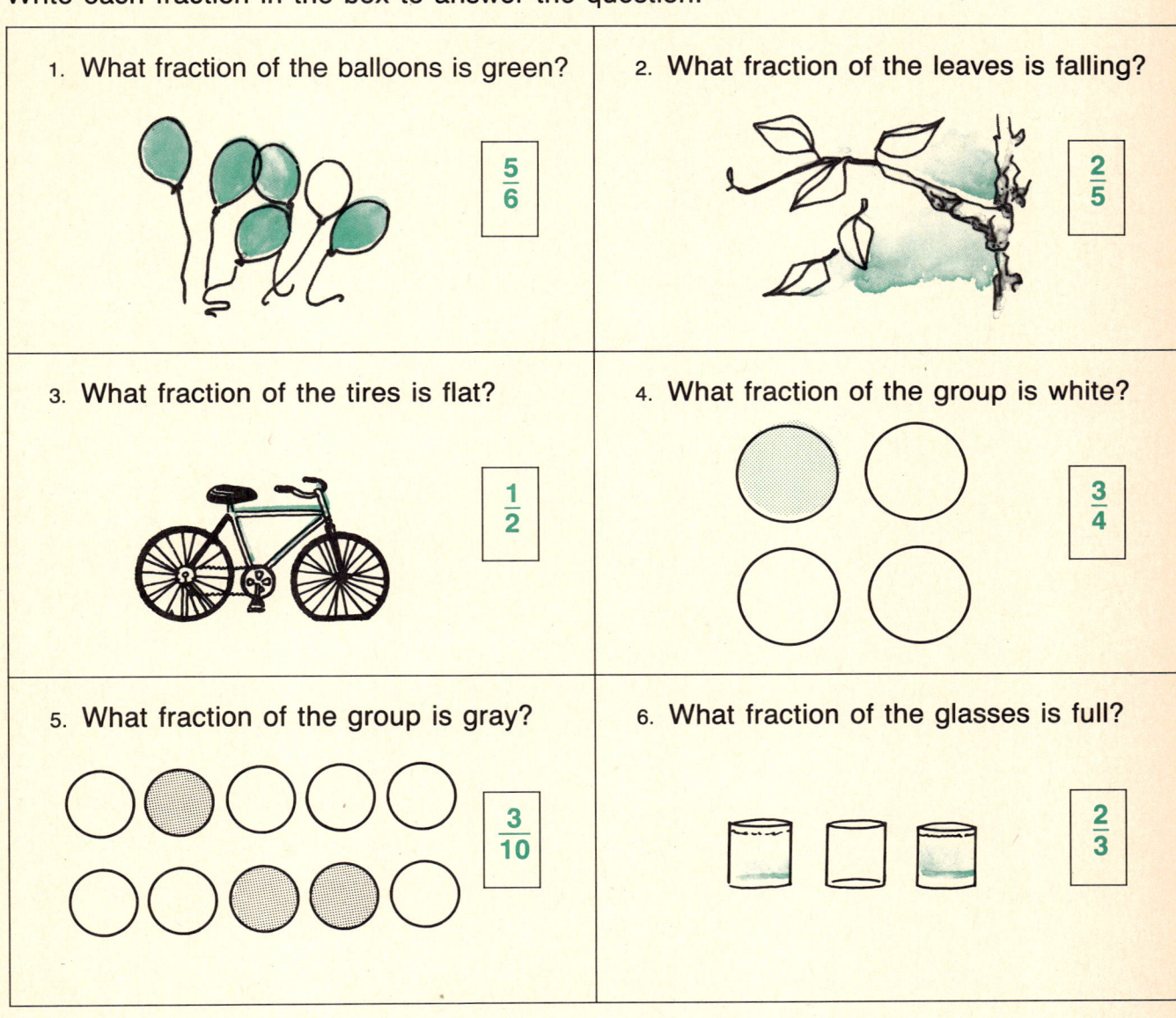

1. What fraction of the balloons is green?

   $\frac{5}{6}$

2. What fraction of the leaves is falling?

   $\frac{2}{5}$

3. What fraction of the tires is flat?

   $\frac{1}{2}$

4. What fraction of the group is white?

   $\frac{3}{4}$

5. What fraction of the group is gray?

   $\frac{3}{10}$

6. What fraction of the glasses is full?

   $\frac{2}{3}$

Using Math

◆ 12 Girl Scouts went on a hike. 7 girls brought flashlights on the hike. What fraction of the group brought flashlights?

$\frac{7}{12}$ of the group brought flashlights.

141

Objective: Students will compare two fractions with the same denominator.

Instructional Model: Present students with the problem, "Amy and Tom ordered pizzas for lunch. Amy ate $\frac{5}{8}$ of her pizza; Tom ate $\frac{7}{8}$ of his. Who ate more pizza?" Draw 2 "pizzas," on the chalkboard, each divided into eighths, and label them *Amy* and *Tom*. Have volunteers write the correct fraction below each pizza and shade in the corresponding number of "slices." Point out that since both pizzas are divided into eighths, all the pieces are the same size. Explain that when the denominators are the same, we simply compare the numerators to find the greater fraction. Remind students that > means *is greater than* and < means *is less than*. Show students that since 7 is greater than 5,

3

Comparing Fractions

Which fraction is greater, $\frac{4}{5}$ or $\frac{2}{5}$?

$\frac{4}{5}$

$\frac{2}{5}$

Compare the fractions.
   The denominators are the same.
   There are more shaded parts in $\frac{4}{5}$ than $\frac{2}{5}$.

Since 4 is greater than 2, then $\frac{4}{5} > \frac{2}{5}$.

To compare fractions having the same denominator, you compare the numerators. The fraction with the greater numerator is the greater fraction.

Guided Practice

◆ Compare the fractions. Write > or < in the box.

1. $\frac{2}{3}$ > $\frac{1}{3}$

2. $\frac{1}{4}$ < $\frac{2}{4}$

3. $\frac{2}{6}$ < $\frac{4}{6}$

4. $\frac{5}{8}$ > $\frac{4}{8}$

5. $\frac{5}{10}$ > $\frac{3}{10}$

6. $\frac{1}{7}$ < $\frac{6}{7}$

7. $\frac{1}{5}$ < $\frac{4}{5}$

8. $\frac{5}{9}$ > $\frac{4}{9}$

then ⅞ > ⅝. Read through the *Instructional Model* with students.
Guided Practice: Work through the problems with students. Remind students to compare the numerators, which represent the green parts of each illustration.

Practice: Spot check students' work for the correct use of the inequality symbols as they complete the problems independently. It may help students to draw an illustration for each fraction to compare.
Using Math: Have students solve the problem independently.

Practice

◆ Compare the fractions. Write > or < in the box.

1. $\frac{1}{4}$ < $\frac{2}{4}$	2. $\frac{3}{5}$ > $\frac{2}{5}$	3. $\frac{7}{8}$ > $\frac{1}{8}$
4. $\frac{6}{10}$ < $\frac{7}{10}$	5. $\frac{5}{6}$ > $\frac{1}{6}$	6. $\frac{1}{3}$ < $\frac{2}{3}$
7. $\frac{10}{12}$ > $\frac{5}{12}$	8. $\frac{3}{6}$ < $\frac{5}{6}$	9. $\frac{4}{5}$ > $\frac{2}{5}$
10. $\frac{5}{8}$ > $\frac{3}{8}$	11. $\frac{1}{8}$ < $\frac{2}{8}$	12. $\frac{5}{7}$ > $\frac{3}{7}$
13. $\frac{3}{4}$ > $\frac{1}{4}$	14. $\frac{7}{9}$ < $\frac{8}{9}$	15. $\frac{10}{12}$ > $\frac{1}{12}$

Using Math

◆ Bryan's bus ride takes $\frac{3}{4}$ of an hour. Angela's bus ride takes $\frac{1}{4}$ of an hour. Whose ride takes longer?
Ring the answer.   (Bryan's)   Angela's

Objective: Students will write an equivalent fraction for a given fraction.
Instructional Model: Draw and cut out 3 identical oaktag circles. Divide the first circle into thirds and cut each out. Divide and cut the second circle into sixths. Then divide and cut the last circle into ninths. Display the first two circles (thirds and sixths) and ask students how many sixths will cover the same areas as one third. Have a volunteer place $\frac{2}{6}$ onto the $\frac{1}{3}$ section to show equality. Write $\frac{1}{3} = \frac{2}{6}$ on the chalkboard. Repeat the procedure to find how many ninths equal $\frac{1}{3}$. Direct students' attention to the page. Review the examples pictured.

4

Finding Equivalent Fractions

Equivalent fractions are fractions that are equal.

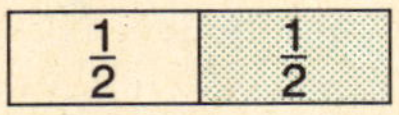

$\frac{1}{2}$ green

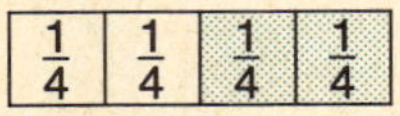

$\frac{2}{4}$ green $\frac{1}{2} = \frac{2}{4} = \frac{4}{8}$

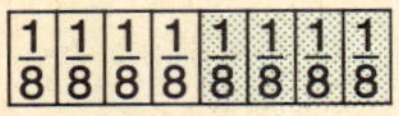

$\frac{4}{8}$ green

Look at the two circles. The same part of each circle is green. The fractions are equivalent.

$\frac{1}{3} = \frac{2}{6}$

Guided Practice

◆ Write an equivalent fraction in the box.

1. $\frac{2}{8} = \boxed{\frac{1}{4}}$

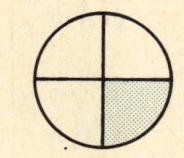

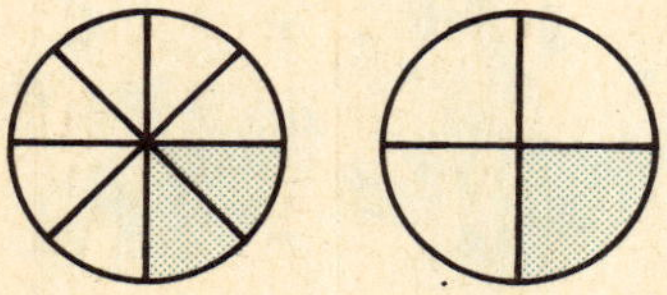

2. $\frac{1}{2} = \boxed{\frac{4}{8}}$

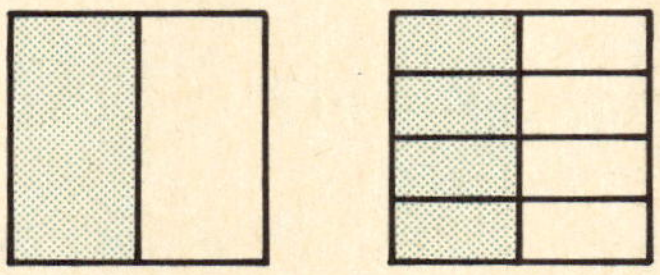

3. $\frac{3}{9} = \boxed{\frac{1}{3}}$

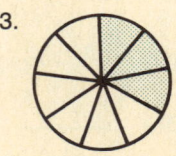

Guided Practice: Work through the problems with students, stressing careful comparison of the green areas in each pair of illustrations.
Practice: Have students complete the problems independently. Remind them that the total number of parts is the denominator and the total number of green parts is the numerator.
Problem Solving: Read the directions with the students. Remind students that reading the question first and working backwards will help them identify the information that is not needed. Review answers with them.

Practice

◆ Write an equivalent fraction in the box.

1. 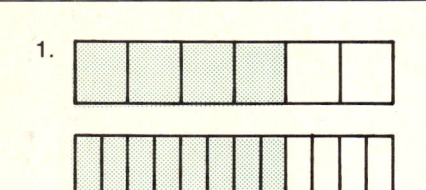 $\dfrac{4}{6} = \dfrac{8}{12}$

2. 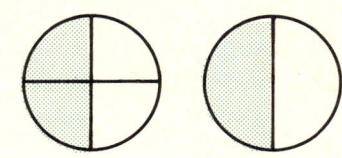 $\dfrac{2}{4} = \dfrac{1}{2}$

3. 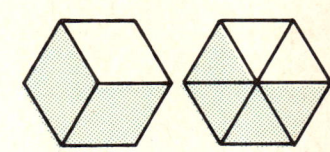 $\dfrac{2}{3} = \dfrac{4}{6}$

4. 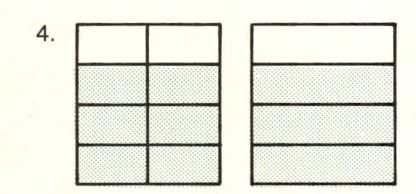 $\dfrac{6}{8} = \dfrac{3}{4}$

5. 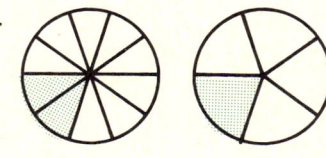 $\dfrac{2}{10} = \dfrac{1}{5}$

6. 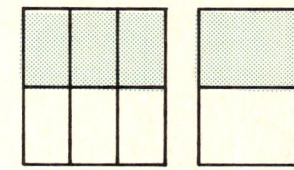 $\dfrac{3}{6} = \dfrac{1}{2}$

7. 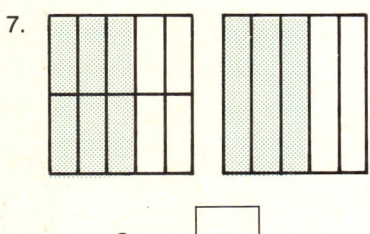 $\dfrac{6}{10} = \dfrac{3}{5}$

8. 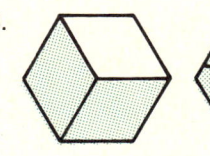 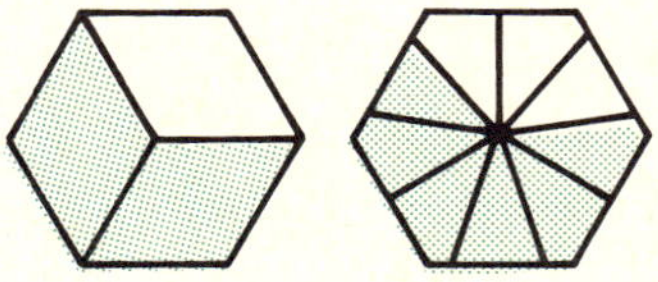 $\dfrac{2}{3} = \dfrac{6}{9}$

9.  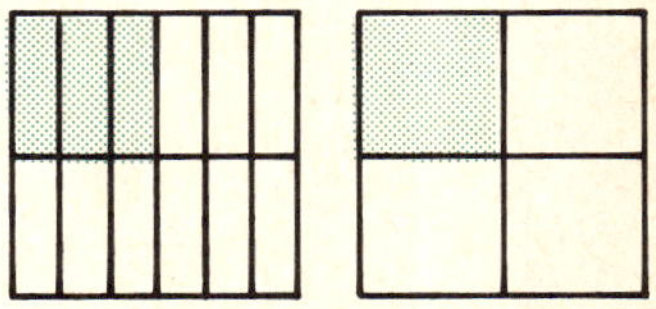 $\dfrac{3}{12} = \dfrac{1}{4}$

Problem Solving

◆ Cross out the fact you do not need.
Then solve the problem.

~~Alfonso bought 4 packs of baseball cards.~~ He bought 6 packs of football cards. There were 6 cards in each pack. How many football cards did Alfonso buy?

$$\begin{array}{r} 6 \\ \times\ 6 \\ \hline 36 \end{array}$$ cards

145

Objective: Students will write an equivalent fraction in lowest terms for a given fraction.
Instructional Model: Explain to students that they can tell an equivalent fraction by looking at a picture. Tell them they can also tell an equivalent fraction by dividing both the numerator and the denominator by the same number.

Direct students attention to the page. Demonstrate the division $3 \div 3$ and $6 \div 3$. Show students that the illustration shows $\frac{3}{6} = \frac{1}{2}$. Tell students that the numerator and denominator of a fraction are called the *terms* of a fraction. Explain that they can check if a fraction is in *lowest terms* if it can only be divided by *1*. Demonstrate the division $1 \div 1$ and $2 \div 1$ to show that $\frac{1}{2}$ is in lowest terms.

5

Fractions in Lowest Terms

You can find equivalent fractions by dividing both the numerator and the denominator by the same number.

$$\frac{3}{6} = \frac{3 \div 3}{6 \div 3} = \frac{1}{2}$$

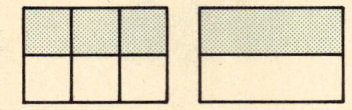

$$\frac{3}{6} = \frac{1}{2}$$

A fraction is in **lowest terms** if the numerator and denominator can only be divided by 1.

$$\frac{1}{2} = \frac{1 \div 1}{2 \div 1} = \frac{1}{2}$$ The fraction $\frac{1}{2}$ is in lowest terms.

Guided Practice

◆ Write an equivalent fraction in lowest terms in the box.

1. $\frac{6}{8} = \frac{6 \div 2}{8 \div 2} = \boxed{\frac{3}{4}}$

2. $\frac{4}{10} = \frac{4 \div 2}{10 \div 2} = \boxed{\frac{2}{5}}$

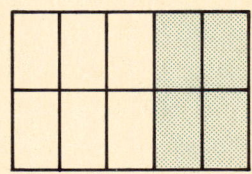

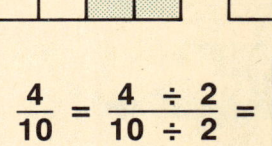

3. $\frac{3}{12} = \frac{3 \div 3}{12 \div 3} = \boxed{\frac{1}{4}}$

4. $\frac{6}{9} = \frac{6 \div 3}{9 \div 3} = \boxed{\frac{2}{3}}$

5. $\frac{8}{16} = \frac{8 \div 8}{16 \div 8} = \boxed{\frac{1}{2}}$

Guided Practice: Work through the problems with students. Have students divide each answer by *1* to see that the fraction is in its lowest terms.
Practice: Spot check students' work for correct division as they complete the problems independently. After reviewing the answers, have students illustrate the equivalent fractions for selected problems.
Using Math: Have volunteers work the problem on the chalkboard while others solve it independently.
Practice Book E: Pages 41–44.

Practice

◆ Write an equivalent fraction in lowest terms in the box.

1. $\dfrac{15}{20} = \dfrac{15 \div 5}{20 \div 5} = \boxed{\dfrac{3}{4}}$

2. $\dfrac{5}{10} = \dfrac{5 \div 5}{10 \div 5} = \boxed{\dfrac{1}{2}}$

3. $\dfrac{8}{12} = \dfrac{8 \div 4}{12 \div 4} = \boxed{\dfrac{2}{3}}$

4. $\dfrac{2}{8} = \dfrac{2 \div 2}{8 \div 2} = \boxed{\dfrac{1}{4}}$

5. $\dfrac{4}{8} = \dfrac{4 \div 4}{8 \div 4} = \boxed{\dfrac{1}{2}}$

6. $\dfrac{2}{6} = \dfrac{2 \div 2}{6 \div 2} = \boxed{\dfrac{1}{3}}$

7. $\dfrac{12}{14} = \dfrac{12 \div 2}{14 \div 2} = \boxed{\dfrac{6}{7}}$

8. $\dfrac{9}{27} = \dfrac{9 \div 9}{27 \div 9} = \boxed{\dfrac{1}{3}}$

9. $\dfrac{2}{12} = \dfrac{2 \div 2}{12 \div 2} = \boxed{\dfrac{1}{6}}$

10. $\dfrac{3}{15} = \dfrac{3 \div 3}{15 \div 3} = \boxed{\dfrac{1}{5}}$

11. $\dfrac{7}{21} = \dfrac{7 \div 7}{21 \div 7} = \boxed{\dfrac{1}{3}}$

12. $\dfrac{8}{10} = \dfrac{8 \div 2}{10 \div 2} = \boxed{\dfrac{4}{5}}$

13. $\dfrac{9}{12} = \dfrac{9 \div 3}{12 \div 3} = \boxed{\dfrac{3}{4}}$

14. $\dfrac{6}{18} = \dfrac{6 \div 6}{18 \div 6} = \boxed{\dfrac{1}{3}}$

15. $\dfrac{10}{24} = \dfrac{10 \div 2}{24 \div 2} = \boxed{\dfrac{5}{12}}$

Using Math

◆ The race was 4 laps around the track.
After 2 laps, Lee's car had a flat tire.

What fraction of the race did he finish? $\dfrac{2}{4}$

What is the equivalent fraction in lowest terms? $\dfrac{1}{2}$

Work here.

$\boxed{} = \dfrac{\boxed{} \div 2}{\boxed{} \div 2} = \boxed{}$

147

Objective: Students will write a mixed number for a given illustration.

Instructional Model: Present students with the problem, "After camping out overnight, the Boy Scouts ate 4 full boxes of cereal and ¾ of another box. How many boxes of cereal did the Boy Scouts eat for breakfast?" Explain that sometimes we need to represent quantities that are made up of a whole number *and* a fraction. Tell students that these are called *mixed numbers*. Draw 5 identical rectangles on the chalkboard. Have a volunteer shade in the number of rectangles that represent the full boxes of cereal eaten. Then, divide the last rectangle into fourths. Choose a student to shade in the fractional part of the other box of cereal that was eaten. Write 4¾ on the chalkboard and explain that we read the mixed number as "4 *and* ¾." Review the example in the *Instructional Model* with students.

6

Mixed Numbers

$3\frac{1}{2}$ is a **mixed number**. A mixed number is a whole number and a fraction.

There are three full glasses of juice and $\frac{1}{2}$ glass of juice. The mixed number is written $3\frac{1}{2}$ glasses of juice.

Guided Practice

◆ Write a mixed number for each picture.

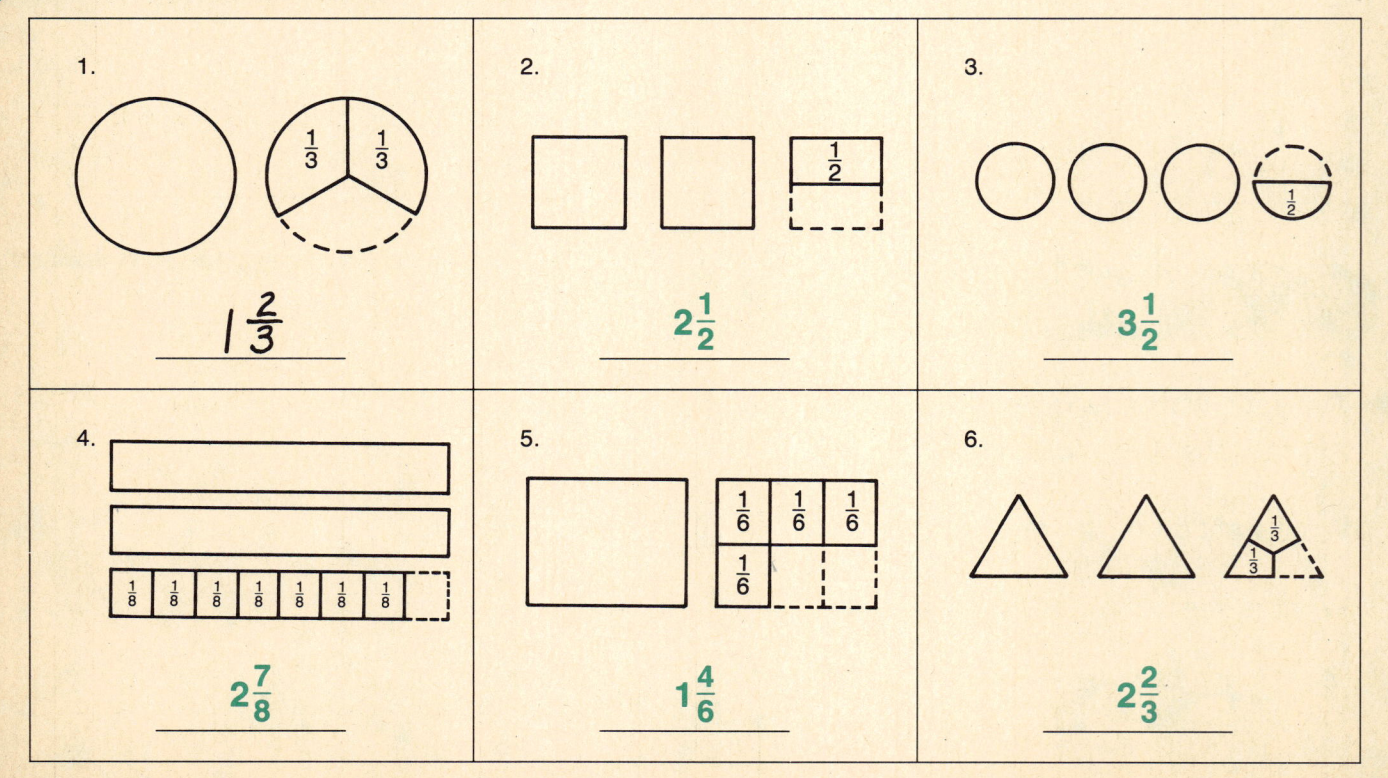

1. $1\frac{2}{3}$

2. $2\frac{1}{2}$

3. $3\frac{1}{2}$

4. $2\frac{7}{8}$

5. $1\frac{4}{6}$

6. $2\frac{2}{3}$

Guided Practice: Discuss the illustrations before working through the problems with students. Remind students to first write the number of whole objects and then the number of fractional parts shown.
Practice: Have students complete the problems independently. As a class activity, have students collect mixed numbers from various sources such as recipes, sewing patterns, and the stock-market and sports pages from the newspaper.
Using Math: Have students solve the problem independently. Then have each student make up a problem to read to the class. Choose volunteers to write the mixed numbers on the chalkboard.

Practice

◆ Write a mixed number for each picture.

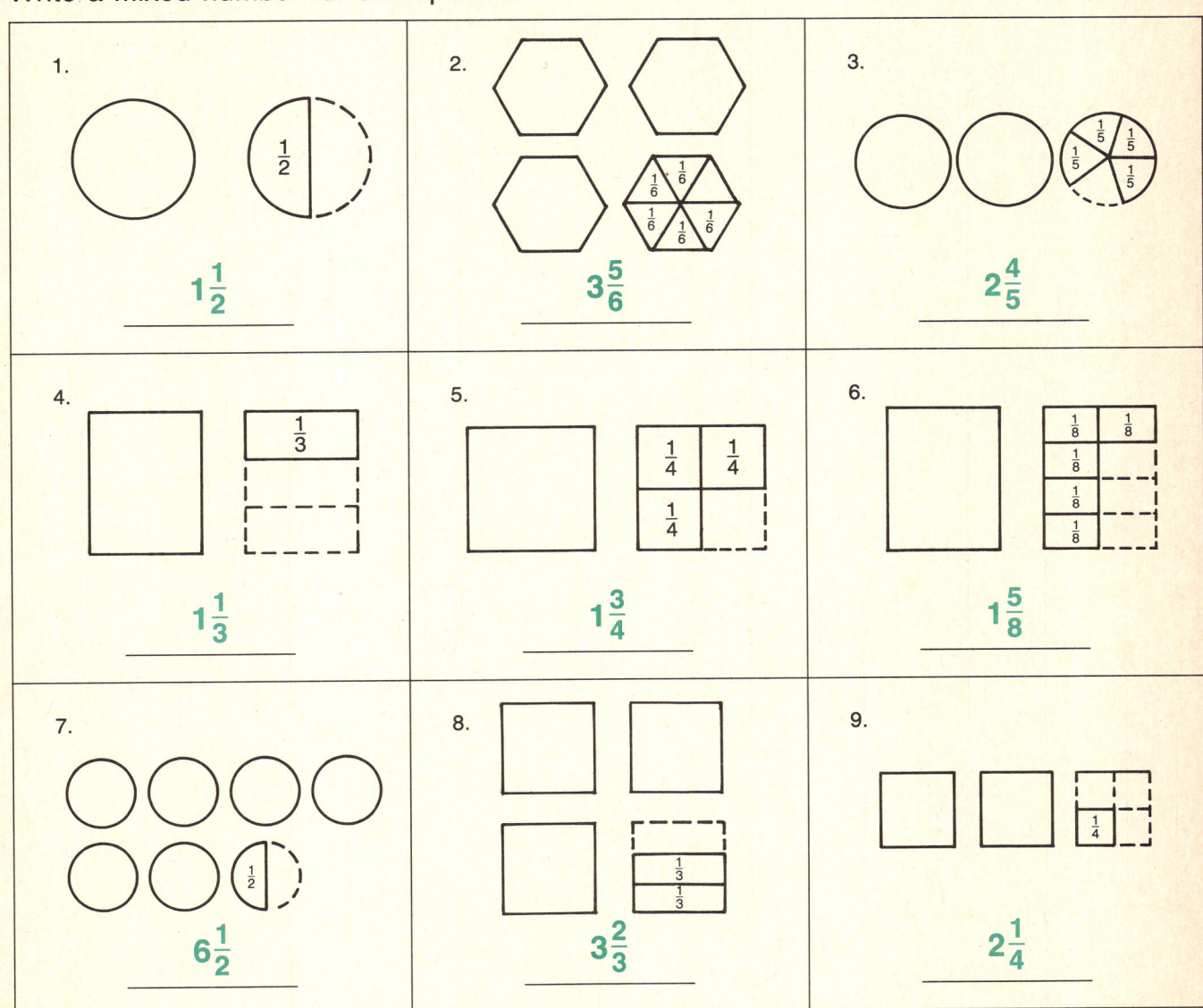

1. $1\frac{1}{2}$

2. $3\frac{5}{6}$

3. $2\frac{4}{5}$

4. $1\frac{1}{3}$

5. $1\frac{3}{4}$

6. $1\frac{5}{8}$

7. $6\frac{1}{2}$

8. $3\frac{2}{3}$

9. $2\frac{1}{4}$

Using Math

◆ Margaret was swimming laps. A lap is one time across the pool. Margaret swam across the pool 4 times. Then she swam $\frac{1}{2}$ way across the pool and stopped. How many laps did Margaret swim?

Margaret swam ____$4\frac{1}{2}$____ laps.

149

Objective: Students will choose the appropriate unit of measurement for an object.
Instructional Model: Review the units of measurement introduced in this book (inches, feet, centimeters, meters, cups, pints, grams, kilograms). Review the definitions of *length*, *capacity*, and *weight*. Give each student 3 index cards. Have each student write *length* on the first card, *capacity* on the second, and *weight* on the third. Have one student name something he/she wants to measure. (For example, "I want to find out how heavy an elephant is.") Instruct the other students to hold up one of their three cards to indicate whether they want to measure length, capacity,

7

Choosing Measurement

Before you can measure something, you must decide whether you want to measure its length, capacity, or weight.

Customary Measurement

Length	Capacity	Weight
inches feet	cups pints quarts	ounces pounds

Metric Measurement

Length	Capacity	Weight
centimeters meters	milliliters liters	grams kilograms

Guided Practice

◆ Ring the word that completes each sentence.

1. To measure the amount of milk for a recipe use ___.   (**cups**)   inches

2. To measure the weight of a cat use ___.   centimeters   (**kilograms**)

3. To measure the length of a room use ___.   (**feet**)   quarts

4. To measure the length of your finger use ___.   milliliters   (**centimeters**)

5. To measure the amount of water in a swimming pool use ___.   (**liters**)   kilograms

or weight. After everyone has had a turn, direct their attention to the page and review the charts.
Guided Practice: Work through the *Guided Practice* with students. Tell students to refer to the chart when necessary.
Practice: Have students complete the *Practice* section independently.

Using Math: Have students complete the problem independently. Discuss with students why inches or centimeters could be used to measure the frog's length. Discuss why ounces or grams could be used to measure the frog's weight.

Practice

◆ Ring the word that completes each sentence.

1. To measure the weight of a baby use ___.   (pounds)   pints

2. To measure the height of a door use ___.   liters   (meters)

3. To measure the amount of milk you will drink at lunch use ___.   (pints)   meters

4. To measure the length of a shoestring use ___.   ounces   (inches)

5. To measure formula for a baby's bottle use ___.   centimeters   (milliliters)

6. To measure the amount of orange juice in a pitcher use ___.   (quarts)   pounds

7. To weigh a letter use ___.   (ounces)   pints

8. To weigh a hamster use ___.   meters   (grams)

Using Math

◆ Ronald volunteered to help the science teacher after school. The first thing Ms. Beeker asked him to do was measure a frog to record its growth. First Ronald measured the frog's length. He measured it in __inches or centimeters__.

Next, he measured the frog's weight. He measured it in __ounces or grams__.

Objective: Students will identify extraneous information in word problems to solve for what is needed.
Instructional Model: Before you begin the lesson, review fractions with students. Draw 8 circles on the board and shade 3 of them. Tell students that they will be finding out what fraction of the circles is shaded. Draw a small horizontal fraction bar on the chalkboard. Ask students to name the number of circles in all. Write 8 under the fraction line and label it *circles in all*. Then ask how many circles are shaded. Write 3 above the line and label it *circles shaded*. Tell the students that 3/8 of the circles are shaded. Read through the instructional model with the

Problem Solving 8

Identify Extra Information

Sometimes a problem gives you more information than you need to solve it.

John painted 8 model cars.
He painted 3 cars red. He painted
5 cars blue. What fraction of the
cars are red?

Step 1 Find the **facts you need**.

　　　　John painted 8 model cars.
　　　　He painted 3 cars red.

Step 2 Cross out the **fact you do not need**.

　　　　He painted 5 cars blue.

Step 3 Solve the problem.

$$\frac{3 \text{ cars are red}}{8 \text{ cars in all}}$$

John painted $\frac{3}{8}$ of the cars red.

Guided Practice

◆ Cross out the fact you do not need.
Then solve the problem.

1. Carl bought 6 books. ~~2 of Carl's books are about horses.~~ 4 books are about cats.
What fraction of books are about cats?　　$\frac{4}{6}$ of the books

152

students. Review the steps for identifying extra information in a problem.
Guided Practice: Work through *Guided Practice* with students. Have students explain how they knew what information was not needed. Then review their answers with them.

Practice: Read the directions aloud with students. Have students complete the problems independently. If students need help identifying the extra information in each problem, have them read the final question and work backwards to find what they do need to answer that question. Then review their answers with them.
Practice Book E: Pages 43–44.

Practice

◆ Cross out the fact you do not need.
Then solve the problem.

1. Oscar cut a pizza into 9 slices. He ate 4 slices of pizza. ~~He gave a friend 5 slices of pizza.~~ What fraction of pizza did Oscar eat?

   $\frac{4}{9}$ of the pizza

2. Terry made 12 sandwiches. ~~5 of the sandwiches were turkey.~~ 7 of the sandwiches were ham. What fraction of sandwiches were ham?

   $\frac{7}{12}$ of the sandwiches

3. ~~Tru has 7 friends coming over.~~ Tru made a pie and cut it into 8 pieces. She ate 1 piece. What fraction of the pie did Tru eat?

   $\frac{1}{8}$ of the pie

4. Jack baked 8 cakes. 5 of the cakes were chocolate and ~~3 of the cakes were white~~. What fraction of cakes Jack baked were chocolate?

   $\frac{5}{8}$ of the cakes

5. ~~Rosa had 8 chocolate chip cookies.~~ She had 5 oatmeal cookies. She ate 3 oatmeal cookies. What fraction of oatmeal cookies did Rosa eat?

   $\frac{3}{5}$ of the oatmeal cookies

153

Chapter Review: Tell students that the exercises on these pages will help them review the math in Chapter 7. Point out the page numbers printed above each group of exercises, and explain that students should look back at these pages if they need help. Be sure students understand all the directions. Encourage them to work independently. When students complete the *Review*, go over their answers. If students have difficulty with any of the problems, use the

Review

◆ Write a fraction in each box. pages 138–139

1. 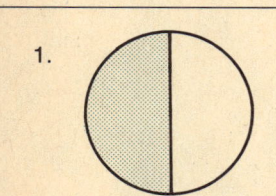 $\frac{1}{2}$

2. 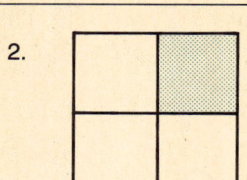 $\frac{1}{4}$

3. 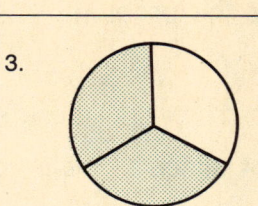 $\frac{2}{3}$

◆ Write a fraction in the box to answer the question. pages 140–141

4. What fraction of the balls is white? $\frac{5}{6}$

5. What fraction of the money is pennies? $\frac{2}{3}$

◆ Compare the fractions. Write > or < in the box. pages 142–143

6. $\frac{3}{5}$ > $\frac{1}{5}$

7. $\frac{3}{7}$ < $\frac{4}{7}$

8. $\frac{6}{8}$ > $\frac{3}{8}$

◆ Write an equivalent fraction in the box. pages 144–145

9. 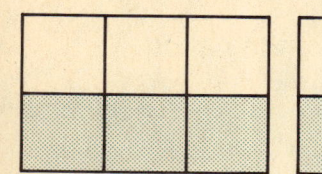 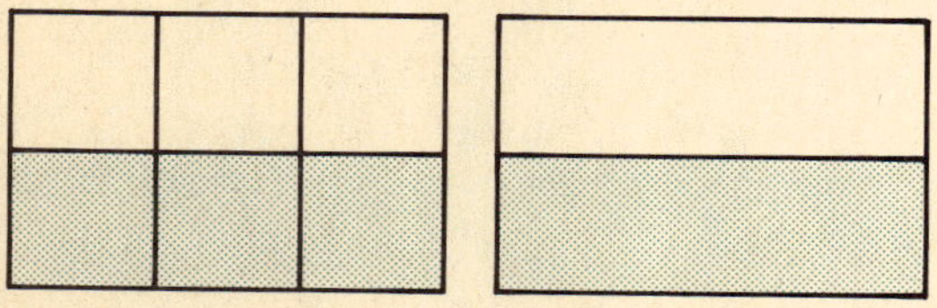 $\frac{3}{6} = \frac{1}{2}$

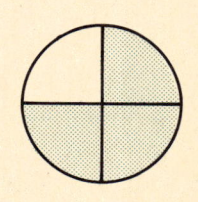

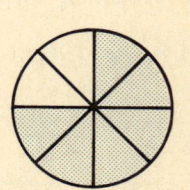

10. $\frac{3}{4} = \frac{6}{8}$

CHAPTER 7

◆ Write an equivalent fraction in lowest terms in the box.   pages 146–147

11. $\dfrac{8}{12} = \dfrac{8 \div 4}{12 \div 4} = \boxed{\dfrac{2}{3}}$

12. $\dfrac{3}{12} = \dfrac{3 \div 3}{12 \div 3} = \boxed{\dfrac{1}{4}}$

13. $\dfrac{2}{16} = \dfrac{2 \div 2}{16 \div 2} = \boxed{\dfrac{1}{8}}$

◆ Write a mixed number for each picture.   pages 148–149

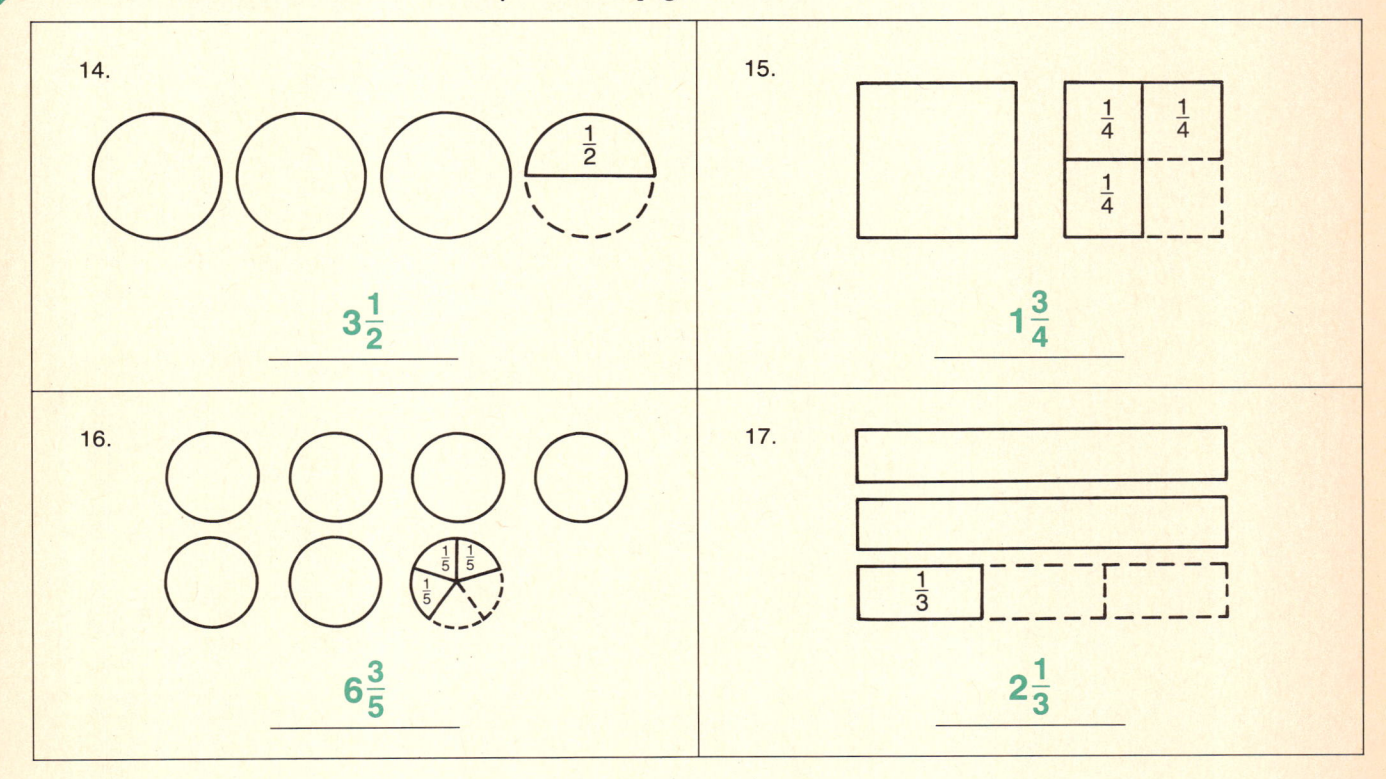

14. $3\dfrac{1}{2}$

15. $1\dfrac{3}{4}$

16. $6\dfrac{3}{5}$

17. $2\dfrac{1}{3}$

◆ Ring the word that completes each sentence.   pages 150–151

18. To measure the height of a tree use ___.   (meters)   liters

19. To measure the weight of a necklace use ___.   cups   (ounces)

20. To measure the amount of water to make gravy use ___.   (cups)   feet

21. To measure the length of a clothes line use ___.   pounds   (feet)

155

Review

CHAPTER 7

Practice

◆ Cross out the fact you do not need.
Then solve the problem. pages 152–153

22. Kenya has 8 fish. She has 3 angelfish. ~~She has 5 goldfish~~. What fraction of Kenya's fish are angelfish?

    $\dfrac{3}{8}$ of the fish

23. Glenn has 4 pets. ~~He has 1 dog.~~ He has 3 cats. What fraction of Glenn's pets are cats?

    $\dfrac{3}{4}$ of the pets

24. Rico has 12 rabbits. ~~2 of the rabbits are fully grown.~~ 10 of the rabbits are babies. What fraction of Rico's rabbits are babies?

    $\dfrac{10}{12}$ of the rabbits

25. Ms. King has 5 horses. 2 horses are black. ~~3 horses are brown~~. What fraction of Ms. King's horses are black?

    $\dfrac{2}{5}$ of the horses

26. Becky had 9 parrots. She sold 3 parrots. ~~She kept 6 parrots.~~ What fraction of her parrots did Becky sell?

    $\dfrac{3}{9}$ of the parrots

Chapter Test: Before testing be sure students can read all the directions on the page. It may be necessary to divide the test into sections that can be completed at different times. You may find that providing a marker helps them keep their place. You can use the page references, printed only in the Teacher's Edition, to diagnose where students need help. It is important to reteach skills that have not been mastered before proceeding to the next chapter. After reteaching the skills students did not master on the *Chapter Test*, have students complete *Chapter 7 Checkup*, the blackline master on page T21.

Blackline Master: *Chapter 7 Checkup*, page T21.

Test CHAPTER 7

◆ Write a fraction in each box to name the green part.   pages 138–141

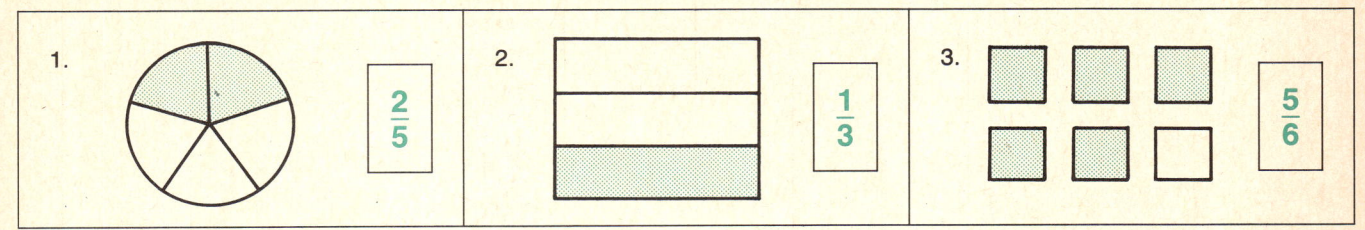

1. $\frac{2}{5}$
2. $\frac{1}{3}$
3. $\frac{5}{6}$

◆ Compare the fractions. Write > or < in the box.   pages 142–143

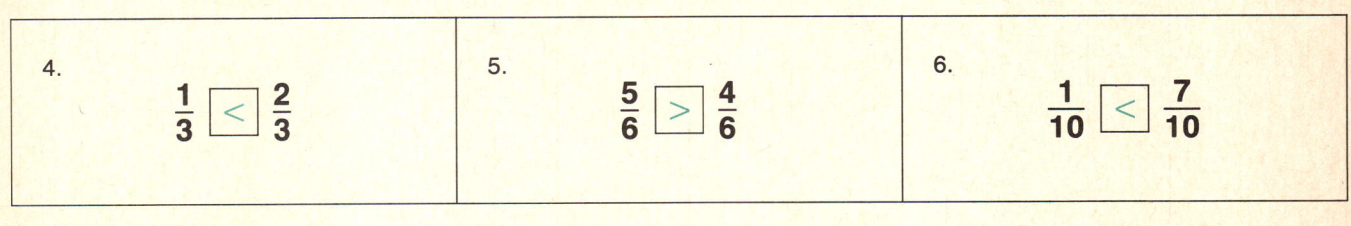

4. $\frac{1}{3} < \frac{2}{3}$
5. $\frac{5}{6} > \frac{4}{6}$
6. $\frac{1}{10} < \frac{7}{10}$

◆ Write an equivalent fraction in lowest terms in the box.   pages 144–147

7. $\frac{2}{4} = \frac{2 \div 2}{4 \div 2} = \frac{1}{2}$
8. $\frac{5}{10} = \frac{5 \div 5}{10 \div 5} = \frac{1}{2}$
9. $\frac{12}{16} = \frac{12 \div 4}{16 \div 4} = \frac{3}{4}$

◆ Write a mixed number for each picture.   pages 148–149

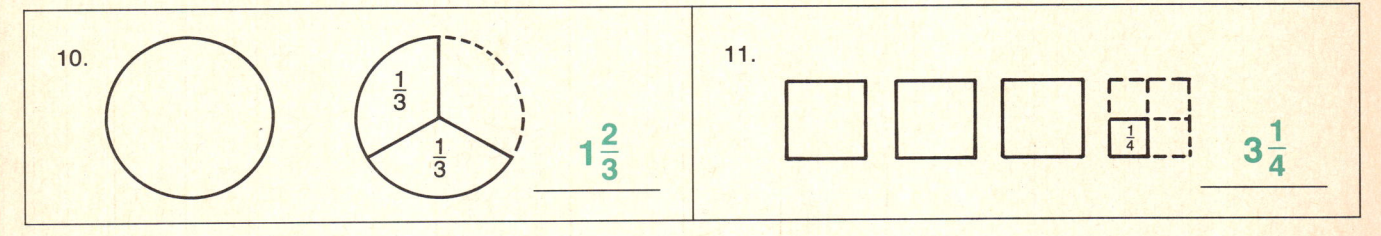

10. $1\frac{2}{3}$
11. $3\frac{1}{4}$

◆ Ring the word that completes each sentence.   pages 150–151

12. To measure the weight of a sack of dog food use ___.

    quarts   (pounds)

13. To measure the amount of orange juice needed to make punch use ___.

    kilograms   (liters)

157

Test

CHAPTER 7

Practice

◆ Cross out the fact you do not need. Then solve the problem. pages 152–153

14. Clara made 10 pizzas. 7 pizzas were made with pepperoni. ~~3 pizzas were made with sausage.~~ What fraction of pizzas were made with pepperoni?

    $\frac{7}{10}$ of the pizzas

15. Rubin bought 12 doughnuts. 6 doughnuts were plain. ~~6 doughnuts were cherry.~~ What fraction of doughnuts were plain?

    $\frac{6}{12}$ of the doughnuts

16. Carl made 9 breadsticks. ~~He ate 4 breadsticks.~~ He gave 5 breadsticks to friends. What fraction of breadsticks did Carl give away?

    $\frac{5}{9}$ of the breadsticks

17. Rita bought 4 apples. She ate 1. ~~She saved 3 apples to eat later.~~ What fraction of apples did Rita eat?

    $\frac{1}{4}$ of the apples

18. Sam baked 7 muffins. ~~He gave 4 muffins to his teacher.~~ He gave 3 muffins to a friend. What fraction of muffins did Sam's friend get?

    $\frac{3}{7}$ of the muffins

Cumulative Review — CHAPTER 4

Write each decimal. pages 72–75

1. 1 and 5 tenths = __1.5__
2. 3 and 4 hundredths = __3.04__

Compare the decimals. Write > or <. pages 76–77

3. 0.3 __<__ 0.5
4. 5.6 __>__ 5.5
5. 7.06 __<__ 7.09

Add. pages 78–79

6. 4.19 + 3.43 = 7.62
7. 8.42 + 2.84 = 11.26
8. 9.03 + 2.32 = 11.35
9. 45.83 + 16.25 = 62.08
10. 54.93 + 27.84 = 82.77

Subtract. pages 80–81

11. 9.64 − 4.41 = 5.23
12. 3.85 − 0.14 = 3.71
13. 28.86 − 10.69 = 18.17
14. 63.25 − 28.37 = 34.88
15. 40.25 − 13.93 = 26.32

Write the zeros. Then add or subtract. pages 82–83

16. 4.41 + 1.4 = 5.81
17. 2.6 + 4.28 = 6.88
18. 29.8 + 13.62 = 43.42
19. 47.5 − 14.28 = 33.22
20. 8 − 3.76 = 4.24

Ring the unit of measure you would use. pages 84–85

21. a pitcher of lemonade — milliliter / **(liter)**
22. milk in a cup — **(milliliter)** / liter

CHAPTER 5

◆ Write each decimal. pages 94–95

1. 3 and 6 tenths = __3.6__
2. 4 and 5 thousandths = __4.005__
3. 324 thousandths = __0.324__
4. 7 and 5 hundredths = __7.05__

◆ Multiply.

pages 96–99

5. 3.7 × 4 = __14.8__	6. 6.4 × 3 = __19.2__	7. 0.9 × 0.5 = __0.45__	8. 8.4 × 2.9 = __24.36__	9. 4.6 × 3.4 = __15.64__

pages 100–103

10. 4.93 × 4.2 = __20.706__	11. 8.46 × 6.5 = __54.99__	12. 0.03 × 2 = __0.06__	13. 0.3 × 0.3 = __0.09__	14. 0.04 × 0.6 = __0.024__

pages 104–105

15. 10 × 8.5 = __85__
16. 100 × 6.75 = __675__
17. 1,000 × 7.813 = __7,813__
18. 1,000 × 4.621 = __4,621__
19. 10 × 100.7 = __1,007__
20. 100 × 0.98 = __98__

◆ Ring the word that completes each sentence. pages 106–107

21. A bag of apples weighs 5 ___.   ounces   (**pounds**)
22. A wedding ring weighs 2 ___.   (**ounces**)   pounds

CHAPTERS 4–5

◆ Use two steps to solve. pages 86–87

	Step 1	Step 2
1. Javier had $8.14. He earned $12.00 helping at Mr. Webber's store. Then he paid $7.25 for a haircut. How much money did Javier have then?	$ 8.14 + $12.00 $20.14	$20.14 − $ 7.25 $12.89
2. Abby bought a roll of film for $2.69 and a magazine for $2.50. She gave the sales clerk $10.00. How much change did Abby get back?	$ 2.69 + $ 2.50 $ 5.19	$10.00 − $ 5.19 $ 4.81

◆ Ring the correct problem. pages 108–109

3. All the sixth-graders at Feldman Middle School are going on a field trip. 210 students and teachers will go. Each bus will carry 42 people. How many buses will they need?

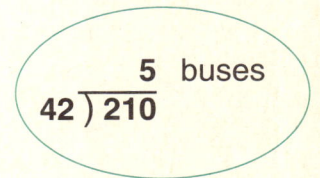

   210   210   210   5 buses
   + 42   − 42   × 42   42) 210
   252 buses   168 buses   8,820 buses

4. Ms. Macelli bought 7 tickets to the theme park. Each ticket cost $28. How much money in all did Ms. Macelli spend on tickets?

   $28 $28 $28 $4 in all
   + 7   − 7   × 7   7) $28
   $35 in all $ 21 in all $196 in all

161

CHAPTER 6

◆ Divide.

pages 116–119

1. 5)2 5.5 = **5.1**
2. 3)1 8.6 = **6.2**
3. 7)4 7.0 4 = **6.7 2**
4. 8)4 2.0 8 = **5.2 6**

pages 120–125

5. 2)1.3 8 = **0.6 9**
6. 6)0.5 7 6 = **0.0 9 6**
7. 4)9.0 0 = **2.2 5**
8. 4)1.7 0 0 = **0.4 2 5**

◆ Divide. Then check your answer by multiplying.   pages 126–127

9. 815 ÷ 1,000 = **0.815**
    1,000 × **0.815** = **815**

10. 76.42 ÷ 10 = **7.642**
    10 × **7.642** = **76.42**

11. 7 ÷ 10 = **0.7**
    10 × **0.7** = **7**

12. 324 ÷ 100 = **3.24**
    100 × **3.24** = **324**

◆ Ring the word that completes each sentence.   pages 128–129

13. A dime weighs 2 ___.   (**grams**)   kilograms

14. A book weighs 1 ___.   gram   (**kilogram**)

162

CHAPTER 7

◆ Write a fraction in each box to name the green part. pages 138–141

1.  $\dfrac{1}{3}$

2. 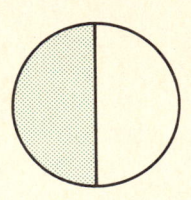 $\dfrac{1}{2}$

3. 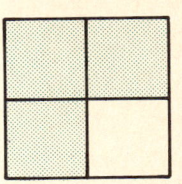 $\dfrac{3}{4}$

◆ Compare the fractions. Write > or < in the box. pages 142–143

4. $\dfrac{4}{7} > \dfrac{3}{7}$

5. $\dfrac{2}{5} < \dfrac{4}{5}$

6. $\dfrac{7}{9} > \dfrac{6}{9}$

◆ Write an equivalent fraction in lowest terms in the box. pages 144–147

7. $\dfrac{9}{12} = \dfrac{9 \div 3}{12 \div 3} = \dfrac{3}{4}$

8. $\dfrac{6}{12} = \dfrac{6 \div 6}{12 \div 6} = \dfrac{1}{2}$

9. $\dfrac{10}{15} = \dfrac{10 \div 5}{15 \div 5} = \dfrac{2}{3}$

◆ Write a mixed number for each picture. pages 148–149

10. 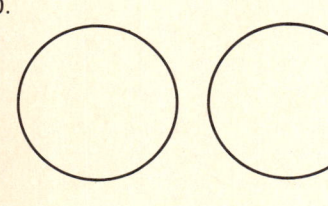 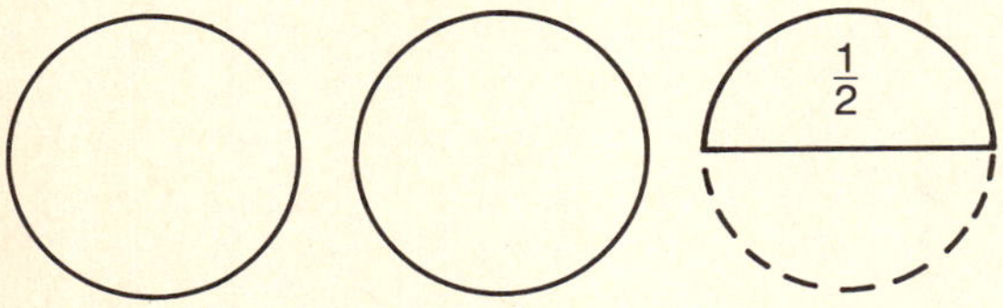 $2\dfrac{1}{2}$

11. 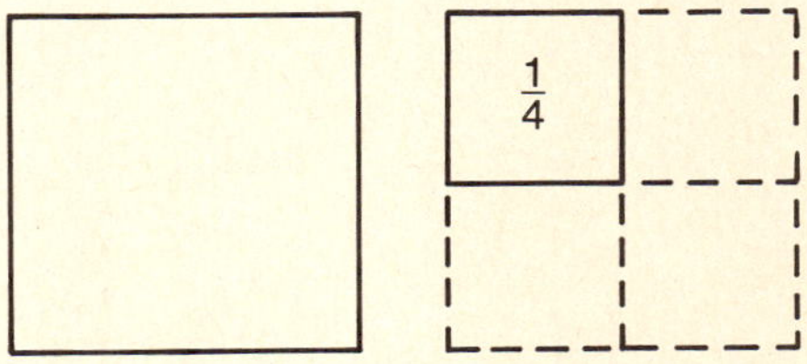 $1\dfrac{1}{4}$

◆ Ring the word that completes each sentence. pages 150-151

12. To measure the length of a house use ___. liters (meters)

13. To weigh a young child use ___. (pounds) quarts

163

CHAPTERS 6–7

◆ Cross out the fact you do not need. Then solve the problem. pages 130–131

1. Mike works out 7 days a week. He runs 4 miles each day. ~~Then he lifts weights for 30 minutes.~~ How many miles does Mike run each week?

$$\begin{array}{r} 7 \\ \times\ 4 \\ \hline 28 \end{array}$$ miles

2. ~~Kelly babysits 4 days a week.~~ She works 3 hours each day. She earns $3 an hour. How much money does Kelly earn babysitting in one day?

$$\begin{array}{r} \$3 \\ \times\ 3 \\ \hline \$9 \end{array}$$ a day

◆ Cross out the fact you do not need. Then solve the problem. pages 152–153

3. ~~There are 276 pages in a book.~~ There are 10 chapters in the book. Leroy read 7 chapters. What fraction of chapters has Leroy read?

$\dfrac{7}{10}$ of the chapters

4. Mr. Andrews has 12 red roses. ~~He has 9 yellow roses.~~ He put 6 red roses in a vase. What fraction of red roses are in the vase?

$\dfrac{6}{12}$ of the red roses

5. Marta has 8 baseball cards. 3 of the baseball cards are autographed. ~~She also has 5 basketball cards that are autographed.~~ What fraction of baseball cards have autographs?

$\dfrac{3}{8}$ of the baseball cards

Extra Practice: This page provides extra practice for the skills in Chapter 1. It is meant to be used after the *Chapter Review* on pages 18–20.

Extra Practice   CHAPTER 1

◆ Complete the expanded form of each number.   pages 2–3

1. 83,678 = 80,000 + __3,000__ + 600 + __70__ + 8

2. 238,412 = 200,000 + __30,000__ + 8,000 + __400__ + 10 + __2__

◆ Write the value of each underlined digit.

3. 7 8 <u>3</u> , 2 0 0   __3,000__

4. <u>6</u> 4 5 , 3 7 0   __600,000__

◆ Add.   pages 4–7

5.	6.	7.	8.
63 +79 ___ 142	165 +497 ___ 662	4,365 +2,367 _____ 6,732	27,406 +19,593 _____ 46,999

◆ Subtract.   pages 8–11

9.	10.	11.	12.
57 −28 ___ 29	629 −288 ___ 341	5,000 −3,496 _____ 1,504	60,000 −25,984 _____ 34,016

◆ Round each number to the nearest ten.   pages 12–13

13. 27 __30__

14. 352 __350__

◆ Round each number to the nearest hundred.

15. 742 __700__

16. 1,695 __1,700__

◆ Ring the unit of measure you would use.   pages 14–15

17. the length of an airplane	18. the length of a whistle
inch (foot)	(inch) foot

165

Extra Practice: This page provides extra practice for the skills in Chapter 2. It is meant to be used after the *Chapter Review* on pages 40–42.

Extra Practice

CHAPTER 2

◆ Multiply.

pages 24–27

1. 46 × 8 = 368
2. 86 × 4 = 344
3. 38 × 20 = 760
4. 82 × 30 = 2,460
5. 17 × 60 = 1,020

pages 28–31

6. 54 × 12 = 648
7. 89 × 19 = 1,691
8. 74 × 18 = 1,332
9. 25 × 34 = 850
10. 36 × 32 = 1,152

pages 32–35

11. 265 × 13 = 3,445
12. 634 × 16 = 10,144
13. 721 × 27 = 19,467
14. 678 × 47 = 31,866
15. 204 × 56 = 11,424

◆ Ring the unit of measure you would use. pages 36–37

16. the length of a toothbrush

    (centimeter)   meter

17. the length of an airplane wing

    centimeter   (meter)

Extra Practice

CHAPTERS 1-2

◆ Round to the nearest hundred.
Estimate to solve. pages 16–17

1. 678 people went to a jazz concert. 420 people stayed until the end of the concert. About how many people left during the concert?

    678 → 700
    − 420 → − 400
    about **300** people

2. There are 327 people sitting in a restaurant. There are 105 empty chairs. About how many seats in all does the restaurant have?

    327 → 300
    + 105 → + 100
    about **400** seats

◆ Round to the nearest hundred.
Estimate to solve. pages 38–39

3. There are 481 nails in one box. Jeff has 5 boxes of nails. About how many nails does Jeff have?

    481 → 500
    × 5 → × 5
    about **2,500** nails

4. There are 163 feet of ribbon on a bolt. There are 8 bolts on a shelf. About how many feet of ribbon are on that shelf?

    163 → 200
    × 8 → × 8
    about **1,600** feet

5. A hotel has 247 rooms. Each room sleeps 4 people. About how many people can sleep in the hotel?

    247 → 200
    × 4 → × 4
    about **800** people

167

Extra Practice: This page provides extra practice for the skills in Chapter 3. It is meant to be used after the *Chapter Review* on pages 62–64.

Extra Practice

CHAPTER 3

◆ Divide.

pages 46–49			
1. 5 R1 3)16	2. 4 R1 7)29	3. 30 R2 3)92	4. 21 2)42

pages 50–53			
5. 24 R1 3)73	6. 15 5)75	7. 52 R1 4)209	8. 76 R4 5)384

pages 54–57			
9. 3 R3 30)93	10. 9 R3 20)183	11. 2 R2 27)56	12. 17 R2 51)869

◆ Mark an X on the containers that equal the first one in the row.   pages 58–59

13.

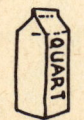

168

Extra Practice: This page provides extra practice for the skills in Chapter 4. It is meant to be used after the *Chapter Review* on pages 88–90.

Extra Practice

CHAPTER 4

◆ Write each decimal. **pages** 72–75

1. 9 tenths = __0.9__

2. 6 hundredths = __0.06__

◆ Compare the decimals. Write > or <. pages 76–77

3. 0.8 __>__ 0.2
4. 1.3 __<__ 1.6
5. 6.87 __<__ 6.89

◆ Add. pages 78–79

6.	7.	8.	9.	10.
5.25	8.62	14.73	27.94	6.39
+4.14	+3.19	+ 2.65	+16.82	+7.44
9.39	11.81	17.38	44.76	13.83

◆ Subtract. pages 80–81

11.	12.	13.	14.	15.
3.86	7.94	16.93	27.49	96.08
−1.72	−3.82	− 6.20	−13.74	−16.07
2.14	4.12	10.73	13.75	80.01

◆ Write the zeros. Then add or subtract. pages 82–83

16.	17.	18.	19.	20.
9.26	26.2	16.8	29.93	6.8
+1.3	+13.48	− 9.25	−13.6	−1.27
10.56	39.68	7.55	16.33	5.53

◆ Ring the unit of measure you would use. pages 84–85

21. gasoline in a truck

   milliliter   (liter)

22. grape juice in a cup

   (milliliter)   liter

Extra Practice

CHAPTERS 3–4

◆ Use two steps to solve.
pages 60–61

	Step 1	Step 2
1. There were 26 people working at a grocery store. At noon, 5 workers went home. Then 13 other people came to work. How many workers were in the store then?	26 − 5 21	21 + 13 34 people
2. The theater has 254 seats on the main floor section and 152 seats in the balcony. 383 people came to see a play. How many empty seats were there during that show?	254 + 152 406	406 − 383 23 empty seats

◆ Use two steps to solve.
pages 86–87

	Step 1	Step 2
3. Dustin had $7.85. He spent $6.00 for a movie ticket. Then his aunt gave him $5.00. How much money did Dustin have then?	$7.85 − $6.00 $1.85	$1.85 + $5.00 $6.85
4. Barb bought a salad for $3.25 and a soda for $1.19. She gave the sales clerk $10.00. How much change did Barb get back?	$3.25 + $1.19 $4.44	$10.00 − $ 4.44 $ 5.56
5. Ms. Ashad paid $34.31 for her softball uniform and $39.95 for a new glove. Then she paid $3.00 for the team dues. How much money in all did Ms. Ashad spend?	$34.31 + $39.95 $74.26	$74.26 + $ 3.00 $77.26

Extra Practice: This page provides extra practice for the skills in Chapter 5. It is meant to be used after the *Chapter Review* on pages 110–112.

Extra Practice   CHAPTER 5

◆ Write each decimal.   pages 94–95

1. 394 thousandths = __0.394__
2. 6 and 45 thousandths = __6.045__
3. 4 and 9 tenths = __4.9__
4. 18 and 27 hundredths = __18.27__

◆ Multiply.

pages 96–99

5. 0.4 × 8 = 3.2
6. 3.25 × 6 = 19.5
7. 8.7 × 0.3 = 2.61
8. 4.7 × 7.8 = 36.66

pages 100–103

9. 3.93 × 4.1 = 16.113
10. 6.42 × 4.6 = 29.532
11. 0.17 × 0.2 = 0.034
12. 0.03 × 2 = 0.06

pages 104–105

13. 10 × 2.8 = __28__
14. 100 × 3.76 = __376__
15. 1,000 × 4.039 = __4,039__
16. 100 × 8.42 = __842__

◆ Ring the word that completes each sentence.   pages 106–107

17. Kathy weighs about 95 ___.   ounces   (**pounds**)
18. A pad of notepaper weighs 7 ___.   (**ounces**)   pounds

171

Extra Practice: This page provides extra practice for the skills in Chapter 6. It is meant to be used after the *Chapter Review* on pages 132–134.

Extra Practice

CHAPTER 6

◆ Divide.

pages 116–119			
1. 9.1 5)4 5.5	2. 4.6 4)1 8.4	3. 6.9 8 3)2 0.9 4	4. 4.3 2 6)2 5.9 2
pages 120–125			
5. 0.5 3 6)3.1 8	6. 1.0 0 5 5)5.0 2 5	7. 0.0 6 8 8)0.5 4 4	8. 1.3 2 5 4)5.3 0 0

◆ Divide. Then check your answer by multiplying. pages 126–127

9. 68 ÷ 100 = __0.68__

100 × __0.68__ = __68__

10. 27.4 ÷ 10 = __2.74__

10 × __2.74__ = __27.4__

11. 106 ÷ 1,000 = __0.106__

1,000 × __0.106__ = __106__

12. 52 ÷ 10 = __5.2__

10 × __5.2__ = __52__

◆ Ring the word that completes each sentence. pages 128–129

13. A radio weighs 1 ___.   gram   (kilogram)

14. Your *Mastering Math* book weighs 280 ___.   (grams)   kilograms

172

Extra Practice: This page provides extra practice for the skills in Chapter 7. It is meant to be used after the *Chapter Review* on pages 154–156.

Extra Practice   CHAPTER 7

◆ Write a fraction in each box to name the green part.   pages 138–141

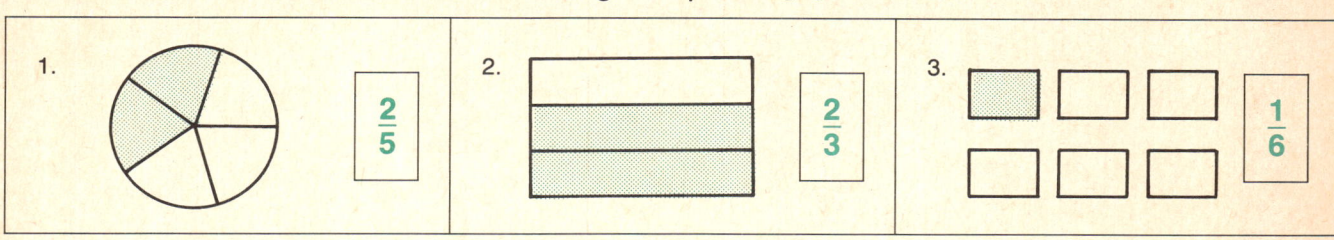

1. $\dfrac{2}{5}$

2. $\dfrac{2}{3}$

3. $\dfrac{1}{6}$

◆ Compare the fractions. Write > or < in the box.   pages 142–143

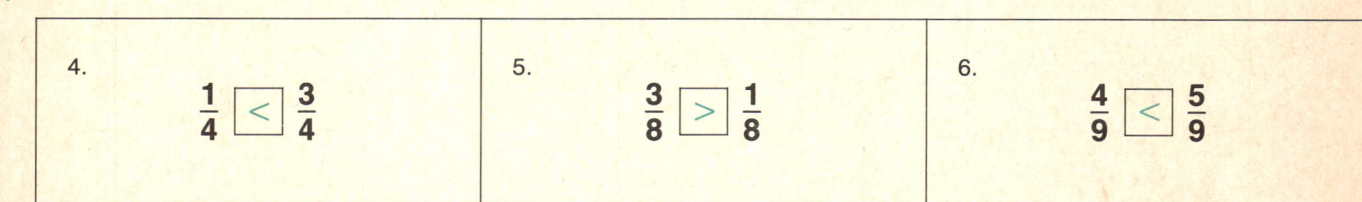

4. $\dfrac{1}{4}\ \boxed{<}\ \dfrac{3}{4}$

5. $\dfrac{3}{8}\ \boxed{>}\ \dfrac{1}{8}$

6. $\dfrac{4}{9}\ \boxed{<}\ \dfrac{5}{9}$

◆ Write an equivalent fraction in lowest terms in the box.   pages 144–147

7. $\dfrac{4}{6} = \dfrac{4 \div 2}{6 \div 2} = \boxed{\dfrac{2}{3}}$

8. $\dfrac{6}{18} = \dfrac{6 \div 6}{18 \div 6} = \boxed{\dfrac{1}{3}}$

9. $\dfrac{9}{12} = \dfrac{9 \div 3}{12 \div 3} = \boxed{\dfrac{3}{4}}$

◆ Write a mixed number for each picture.   pages 148–149

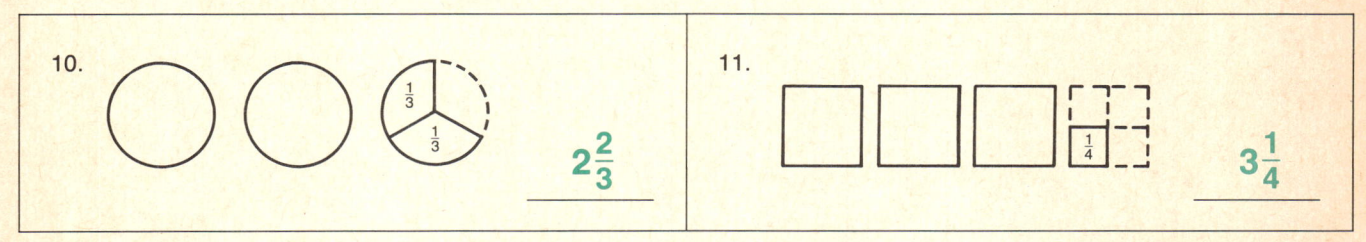

10. $2\dfrac{2}{3}$

11. $3\dfrac{1}{4}$

◆ Ring the word that completes each sentence.   pages 150–151

12. To measure the amount of wood on a truck use ___.

    (kilograms)   liters

13. To measure the amount of water to cook rice use ___.

    inches   (cups)

Extra Practice

CHAPTERS 5–7

◆ Ring the correct problem. pages 108–109

1. There were 126 students going to an art show.
   3 buses were hired to take the students.
   How many students would ride on each bus?

126	126	126	(42 students)
+ 3	− 3	× 3	3)126
129 students	123 students	378 students	

2. Aldo's favorite music tape is 52 minutes long. He listened to the tape 4 times. How many minutes did Aldo listen to the tape?

52	52	(52	13 minutes
+ 4	− 4	× 4)	4)52
56 minutes	48 minutes	208 minutes	

◆ Cross out the fact you do not need. Then solve the problem. pages 130–131

3. Max works 30 hours each week. He works 5 days a week. ~~He plays soccer for 2 hours each week.~~ How many hours a day does Max work?

       6 hours a day
   5)30

◆ Cross out the fact you do not need. Then solve the problem. pages 152–153

4. There are 9 scouts in Mr. Barter's troop. ~~5 scouts are wearing uniforms.~~ 7 scouts came to the meeting. What fraction of all the scouts came to the meeting?

   $\frac{7}{9}$ of the scouts